In the footsteps of St Thomas

Previous books by Serena Fass:

The Magi, their journey and their contemporaries
with a foreword by HM King Simeon II of Bulgaria, 2015

The Cross: meditations and images
with a foreword by HRH The Prince of Wales, 2013

Faces of India: meditations and photographs
on behalf of Mother Teresa of Calcutta, 1974

This edition first published in 2017 by Serena Fass
Published by Chesil Court Publishing,
2 Chesil Court, Chelsea Manor St. London SW3 5QP
in association with Brown Dog Books,
7 Green Park Station, Bath BA1 1JB.
Printed and bound in the UK.
www.acnuk.org/donate. or Tel. 0208642 8668

All rights reserved © Serena Fass 2017

The right of Serena Fass to be identified as the author of this work has been asserted in accordance with Section 77 of the Copyright, Designs and Patents Act 1988.

No part of this publication may be copied, reproduced, stored in a retrieval system, or transmitted, in any form or by any means without the prior permission of the publisher, nor be otherwise circulated in any form of binding or cover other than that in which it is published and without a similar condition being imposed on the subsequent purchaser.

While every effort has been made to trace the owners of copyright material reproduced herein, the publishers would like to apologise for any omissions and will be pleased to incorporate missing acknowledgements in any further editions.

Typeset by Serena Fass

Cover design by Serena Fass

A CIP record for this book is available from the British Library

ISBN 978 - 1 78545 - 185 - 0

In the footsteps of St Thomas:
the Apostle of the East

Serena Fass

Foreword by His Holiness Baselios Marthoma Paulos II

Introduction by historian and TV film-maker Michael Wood

For my godchildren

Candida, Melissa, Alain, Justin, Julian,
Claudia, Johnny, Harriet, Francis and Catriona.

Frangipani, Chennai, India (2013).

The Malankara Orthodox Syrian Church
CATHOLICATE OF THE EAST

BASELIOS MARTHOMA PAULOSE II
CATHOLICOS OF
THE APOSTOLIC THRONE OF
ST. THOMAS
AND MALANKARA METROPOLITAN

CATHOLICATE PALACE
KOTTAYAM-686 038
KERALA, INDIA

The Feast of the Ascension 2017

It is a real pleasure to introduce this delightful book about our beloved patron, Saint Thomas the Apostle, who first brought the Christian Faith to our shores in AD 52. His apostolic ministry is among the earliest Christian traditions and has sustained the Faith through many generations, so that the same vibrant witness, held by millions today, owes everything to his legacy.

Over many years Serena Fass has been following in the footsteps of Saint Thomas from his birth in Galilee, to Taxila in modern-day Pakistan, and also extensively in Kerala and through to his martyrdom in Mylapore, Tamil Nadu. She has beautifully illustrated this volume with her evocative photographs, providing the reader with an unique insight into the journey of the saint and the places where he founded churches.

I pray that all who follow in the footsteps of Saint Thomas will receive peace and joy in the Risen Christ, God's favour and protection and the benediction of the Lord's faithful Apostle. May this book be a blessing to all who read it!

God bless,

Baselios Marthoma Paulos II.

His Eminence Abba Seraphim, Metropolitan of Glastonbury with His Holiness Moran Baselios Marthoma Paulose II, 8th Catholicos of the East, 21st Malankara Metropolitan and 91st Successor of the Throne of St Thomas the Apostle. Photograph taken in Kerala (2010).

Introduction

The story of the early spread of Christianity is full of tales of amazing bravery, endurance and faith. But the most remarkable by far are the legends of St Thomas, who took the Gospel to India, according to traditions which first appear in the late 2nd century AD. In this book Serena Fass tells us this story with a traveller's eye and deep empathy across the roads of ancient Parthia and Gandhara to the palm forests of tropical South India. As a traveller's tale alone it takes some beating. But of course it is much more.

Scholars these days tend to think the goal of Thomas's mission was the court of King Gondophares of Taxila near Rawalpindi in present day Pakistan, but South Indian Christians have always insisted that their church was also founded by Thomas, whose original tomb still stands near Chennai. His landfall is said to have been at a place called Muziris near Cranganore in Kerala, where a gleaming white Christian basilica commemorates him today. What is so intriguing about this tradition is that it pinpoints the very place and the moment when sea voyages linked the Roman world with South India, as we can see in one of the most remarkable texts from the ancient world, the Periplus, or Gazetteer, of the Red Sea. Written in Thomas's lifetime about AD 60, the Periplus lists twenty ports down the west coast of India, just the journey Thomas would have made. And the most important - Pliny calls it 'the first market of India' - was indeed Muziris, where the Greek and Roman colonists even erected a temple to the deified Emperor Augustus.

Here then, of all places, we might imagine the Greek-speaking Thomas to have made his landfall: on a trade route well known to the merchants of the Eastern Mediterranean, who included Jews. Till recently, the site of Muziris had never been discovered in the intricate filigree of lagoons in the Kerala backwaters north of Cochin. But in 2005 archaeologists from Kerala found it four miles inland, by an old bed of the Periyar river. The main mound is 600 metres across, in a shady grove of palms, bananas and jackfruit, festooned with twining pepper vines. Coins of Nero and Tiberius have been found nearby, and excavations have revealed that the mound is stuffed with Roman amphorae, terracottas, Mediterranean glass ornaments, and precious stones. Here then, at last, we may imagine the apostle making his landfall on the outermost edge of the Roman world.

Bough of ripe bananas, Muziris, Kerala, India (2016).

But did he? The earliest Syriac and Greek traditions place him up in the Indo-Greek court at Taxila; but Muziris was a major trading place for the merchants of the eastern Mediterranean in the first two or three centuries AD, and the landing of a Roman Jewish traveller in the Periyar River around the time of the Periplus is plausible in every way. If unverifiable, the tradition *ought to* be true, in a land where oral traditions have had extraordinary tenacity - where among the Tamil Jain communities, for example, entire poems have been handed down from the late Roman world to modern times. So too the tale of Thomas's death is still part of the Tamil Christian tradition at St Thomas's Mount outside Madras (Chennai) from where his remains were translated to Edessa in Syria as recorded by St Ephraim in the 4th century.

It is a literally amazing story; and not content with following Thomas along the Silk Road and down to Chennai, Serena even takes us in a poignant epilogue back to Thomas's final resting place in Ortona on the Adriatic in central Italy. What an adventure!

Michael Wood,
Historian, author and TV film-maker,
Epiphany 2017.

The third c. Armenian-Mesopotamian chalcedony slab from Edessa, Turkey, showing a portrait of St Thomas as a Syrian bishop; the Basilica of St Thomas, Ortona, the Abruzzi, Italy (2016).

Contents

Foreword	9
Introduction	13
Contents	15
Preface	16
My thanks	18
1. Judas Thomas Didymus:	20
The Gospel accounts, Early Christian accounts,	
The Acts of Judas Thomas	
2. The Syrian church:	60
St Addai, St Ephraim the Syrian	
3. The journey by land to Parthia:	78
Syria, Turkey, Iraq, Iran, Afghanistan, Pakistan	
4. The Red Sea:	144
Oman, cotton, silk and spices, The island of Soqotra	
5. Egyptian, Greek and Roman Mediteranean sea routes to India	162
Trade winds, Greek, Ptolemaic and Roman accounts	
6. Kerala:	184
Muziris; The seven and a half "churches" founded by St Thomas	
7. Tamil Nadu:	258
Madurai, Mahabalipuram, Madras (Chennai),	
The arrival of the Portuguese, St Thomas's Mount	
8. Sri Lanka and China	284
9. Martyrdom: Relics, Tombs of St Thomas	292
10. Authors	320
Sources	321
Maps	322
Chronology	324
Aid to the Church in Need	329

Thali lunch, Chennai, India (2014).

Preface

St Thomas has always been my favourite Apostle, largely because of the story of his first doubting the Resurrection and then being convinced, something that probably applies to many of us in our walk with Jesus. And he was the most adventurous traveller of the eleven remaining disciples.

I have been a passionate traveller since childhood and have been fortunate enough to go to many of the places where St Thomas went, although in my case in comfort, by air, ship and car; in his, by boat, perhaps by horse or camel and on foot. I share his love of India. Little did I realise that my first visit in 1969 would lead me back me to India nearly every year, often taking people with me to share its magic. Meeting Mother Teresa in Calcutta in 1971 was a life-changing experience.

When it was suggested that I compile this book, I realised that I had most of the material I needed if I wanted to follow in St Thomas' footsteps: in the Middle East, Afghanistan, Pakistan, India, Sri Lanka and China; with countries like Syria and Iraq sadly being completely unvisitable now. Other places have been destroyed and places that I photographed then are not there to take now.

The many introductions I had during my recent journey in Kerala proved invaluable. Having compiled my book of the Magi and their journey, I was fully immersed in the Roman, Jewish and Parthian world of the first century AD.

Did Jesus' Apostle Judas Thomas take the Gospel to the East in the middle of the first century? Did he only go to King Gondophares in Taxila (Parthia) in what is now Pakistan, but what was then Northern India and die there, as some think, or did he also go by ship to Kerala and evangelise Southern India and continue from there to Sri Lanka and China? There are many compelling early accounts that say he did, as well as statements from Prime Minister Jawaharlal Nehru and Dr Rajendra Prasad, President of India, that the vibrant church of Thomas Christians in South India is a living witness that St Thomas did indeed bring the Good News to India, both North and South. Or did Christianity only reach Kerala with Persian Nestorian merchants in the 3rd and 4th centuries? Or with the Jewish Christian merchant Kanai Thomas, accompanied by 72 Syrian families in AD 345?

Let the reader decide which of these traditions is true and I hope they will enjoy the quest as much as I have.

Serena Fass,
Pentecost 2017.

My thanks

The mosaic portrays Jesus and "doubting Thomas" with Jesus pulling His hand to His crucifixion wound. Commissioned in 1060 by the Crusader King Amalric I and the Byzantine emperor Manuel Comnenus, the mosaics were made with tiles of glass, mother-of-pearl, and local stones, with gold and silver leaf pressed under clear glass. The Basilica of the Nativity, Bethlehem (2016).

My thanks are due to His Holiness, Moran Baselios Mar Thoma Paulose II, 8th Catholicos of the East, 21st Malankara Metropolitan and 91st Successor of the Throne of St Thomas the Apostle, for graciously writing the foreword.

To historian and TV film-maker Michael Wood for his inspired introduction.

To His Eminence Abba Seraphim, Metropolitan of Glastonbury, for suggesting that I write this book; for his invaluable introductions in Kerala; for writing a piece especially for the book; for introducing me to Coptic texts on St Thomas and for checking my Coptic and Syrian entries.

To George Alexander in Cochin, Professor Curian in Muziris, Ravi Menon in Chennai, Fr Abraham Thomas in Kumarakom for all his special help, Dr Kurian Thomas in Niranam, Jeevan Thomas in Cochin, and TransIndus Travel, Cochin and London, for all their help.

Nandy Bull, Kalasanthe Shiva Temple, early 7th c. AD, Kanchipuram, Tamil Nadu India (2013).

To the late Tessa Findlay whose legacy enabled me to trace St Thomas' footsteps to Tamil Nadu and Kerala in India and to the late Richard Hawkins for his generous legacy which enabled me to make a reconnaissance of North-West Iran and of the central portion of the Silk Route from Bukhara in Uzbekistan to Kashgar in China.

To Della Howard for enabling me to return to Bethlehem to photograph the newly uncovered mosaic of Doubting Thomas in the Basilica of the Nativity and to the Italian restoration team in the Basilica, for allowing me to climb up behind the scaffolding to take an image of the mosaic.

To Grazia Marchi Gazzoni for her hospitality in Bologna and for enabling me to reach Ortona to photograph the final resting place of St Thomas in his Basilica.

To Dr Remo di Martino, the Mayor of Ortona, for his help in Ortona, including giving me a copy of his book of his journey from Ortona to Chios, Edessa and Chennai.

To Giancarlo Elia, David A E Hunt, The Rev'd Prebendary Brian Leathard, Rector of Chelsea, and John L F Wright for writing pieces especially for the book.

To Archimandrite Maximus Lavriotes of Peterhouse College Cambridge, for checking all my Greek Orthodox entries.

To Caroline Lees for painting an icon of St Thomas especially for the book and for generously giving it to be auctioned on behalf of Aid to the Church in Need. Also for her help with the map of Indo-Roman trade routes.

To Jennifer, Marchioness of Bute, Caroline Lees, Roland Howard, Claire-Lise Presel, Nicholas Talbot-Rice, Metropolitan Abba Seraphim, Aditya Singh of New Delhi, Jane Taylor and Jim Wheeler for the use of their photographs.

To Douglas Walker and his team at Brown Dog Books of Bath, for their help in the production and publication of this book.

Serena Fass,
Lent 2017.

1. Judas Thomas Didymus:

The gospel accounts
Early Christian accounts
The Acts of Judas Thomas

The Gospel accounts

And it came to pass in those days, that he went out into a mountain to pray, and continued all night in prayer to God.

And when it was day, he called unto him his disciples: and of them he chose twelve, whom also he named apostles; Simon, (whom he also named Peter,) and Andrew his brother, James and John, Philip and Bartholomew, Matthew and Thomas, James the son of Alphaeus, and Simon called Zelotes, and Judas the brother of James, and Judas Iscariot, which also was the traitor.

And he came down with them, and stood in the plain, and the company of his disciples, and a great multitude of people out of all Judaea and Jerusalem, and from the sea coast of Tyre and Sidon, which came to hear him, and to be healed of their diseases.

Luke 6: 12-16.

And he called unto him the twelve, and began to send them forth by two and two; and gave them power over unclean spirits; And commanded them that they should take nothing for their journey, save a staff only; no scrip, no bread, no money in their purse: But be shod with sandals; and not put on two coats.

And he said unto them, in what place soever ye enter into an house, there abide till ye depart from that place. And whosoever shall not receive you, nor hear you, when ye depart thence, shake off the dust under your feet for a testimony against them. Verily I say unto you, it shall be more tolerable for Sodom and Gomorrha in the day of judgment, than for that city.

So they went off and preached repentance.

Mark 6 7-12.

Previous page: The Apostle St Thomas, El Greco, Oil on canvas, 1610-14. Museo El Greco, Toledo, Spain (2014).

Right: The "Jesus boat" 1st c. BC - 1st c. AD, recovered from the seabed of the Lake of Galilee, Israel (2015). It is exactly the type of boat that Jesus' disciples would have used and might even be their very boat: when it was floated after its discovery, a triple rainbow appeared over the lake.

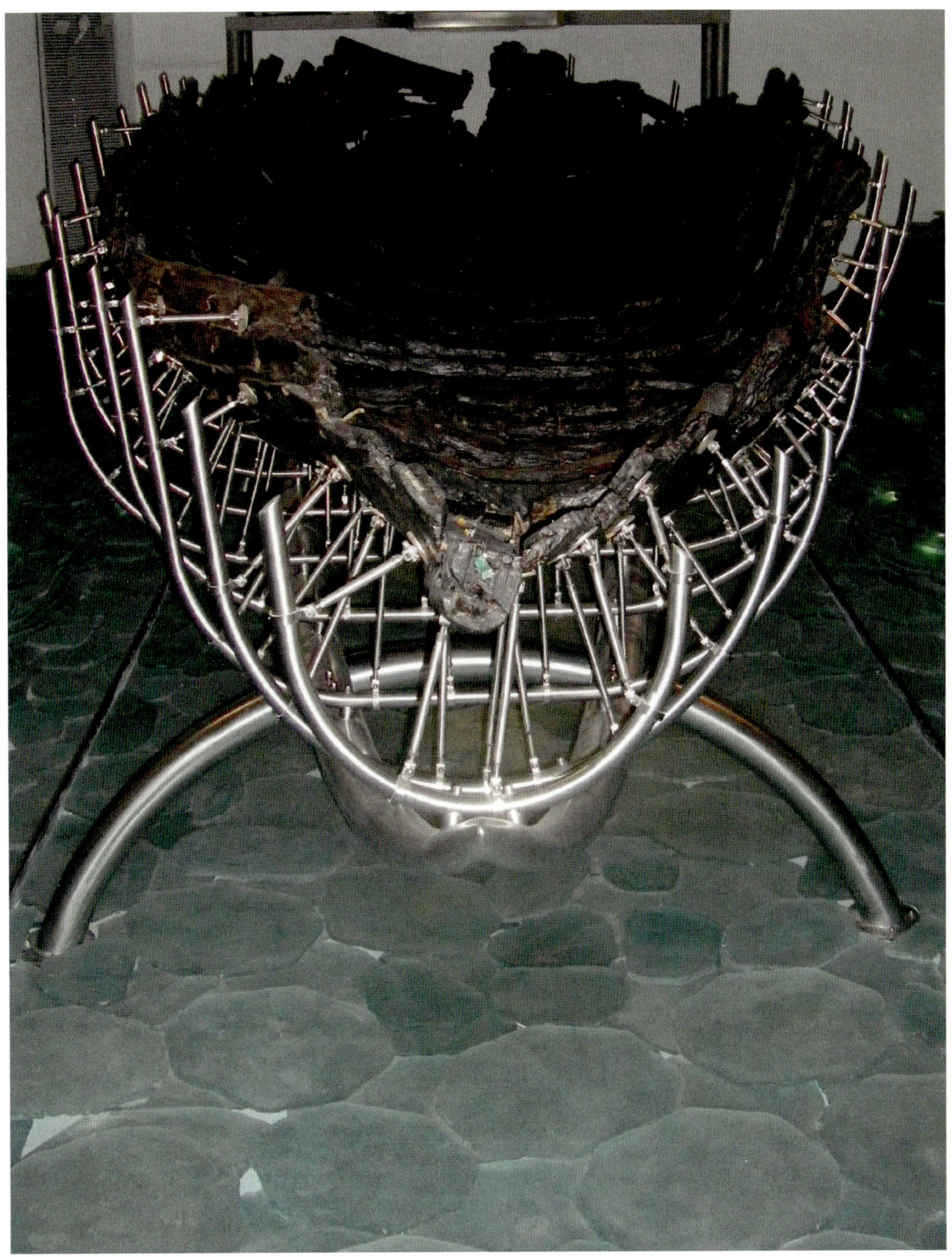

Bethany

The House of Martha and Mary, Bethany, Israel (2014).

Steps leading out of the tomb of Lazarus, Bethany, Israel (2014).

Now a certain man was sick, named Lazarus, of Bethany, the town of Mary and her sister Martha. (It was that Mary which anointed the Lord with ointment, and wiped his feet with her hair, whose brother Lazarus was sick.) Therefore his sisters sent unto him, saying, Lord, behold, he whom thou lovest is sick. When Jesus heard that, he said, This sickness is not unto death, but for the glory of God, that the Son of God might be glorified thereby.

Now Jesus loved Martha, and her sister, and Lazarus. When he had heard therefore that he was sick, he abode two days still in the same place where he was. Then after that saith he to his disciples, Let us go into Judaea again. His disciples say unto him, Master, the Jews of late sought to stone thee; and goest thou thither again? Jesus answered, Are there not twelve hours in the day? If any man walk in the day, he stumbleth not, because he seeth the light of this world. But if a man walk in the night, he stumbleth, because there is no light in him.

These things said he: and after that he saith unto them, Our friend Lazarus sleepeth; but I go, that I may awake him out of sleep. Then said his disciples, Lord, if he sleep, he shall do well. How be it Jesus spake of his death: but they thought that he had spoken of taking of rest in sleep. Then said Jesus unto them plainly, Lazarus is dead. And I am glad for your sakes that I was not there, to the intent ye may believe; nevertheless let us go unto him. Then said Thomas, which is called Didymus, unto his fellow disciples, Let us also go, that we may die with him.

John 11:1-16.

Jerusalem

The western and southern walls of the Temple, Jerusalem, showing the dome of the Aqsa Mosque. To the far left (just out of sight) is the only part of the Western Wall now accessible to Jews (2011).

The platform of Temple Mount, showing where Herod the Great's Temple stood until its destruction by Titus in 70 AD, to be replaced by the Dome of the Rock, completed in AD 691 under the Umayyad Caliph Abd al-Malik; Jerusalem, Israel (2014).

Let not your heart be troubled

Let not your heart be troubled: ye believe in God, believe also in me. In my Father's house are many mansions: if it were not so, I would have told you. I go to prepare a place for you. And if I go and prepare a place for you, I will come again, and receive you unto myself; that where I am, there ye may be also. And whither I go ye know, and the way ye know.

Thomas saith unto him, Lord, we know not whither thou goest; and how can we know the way?

Jesus saith unto him, I am the way, the truth, and the life: no man cometh unto the Father, but by me. If ye had known me, ye should have known my Father also: and from henceforth ye know him, and have seen him.

John 14:1-6.

Duccio di Buoninsegna; c. 1255/60 - c. 1318/19, panel on the reverse of the Maestà, Christ Taking Leave of the Apostles 1308-11; Museo dell'Opera Metropolitana del Duomo, Siena, Italy.

Mary Magdalene Announces the Resurrection to the Apostles

Now when Jesus was risen early on the first day of the week, he appeared first to Mary Magdalene, out of whom he had cast seven devils. And she went and told them that had been with him, as they mourned and wept.

Mark 16:9-10.

Mary Magdalene Announcing the Resurrection to the Apostles, unknown artist, 12th century
St Albans Psalter, St Albans Abbey, England. The Dombibliothek, Hildesheim, Germany.

Mary's authoritative role as 'apostle to the apostles' derives from her witness of Christ's risen body. A column divides the scene into unequal parts, with Mary Magdalene in profile isolated commandingly in her own rectangle while the eleven apostles crowd together under an arch. Mary is telling the disciples that she has seen the risen Lord (John 20:18). The apostles look amazed, clutching books and raising their hands. At this date Mary Magdalene's announcement to the apostles is rare in western art, although it is depicted in Byzantine manuscripts.

My Lord and my God

On the evening of that first day of the week, when the disciples were together, with the doors locked for fear of the Jewish leaders, Jesus came and stood among them and said, "Peace be with you!" After he said this, he showed them his hands and side. The disciples were overjoyed when they saw the Lord.

Again Jesus said, "Peace be with you! As the Father has sent me, I am sending you." And with that he breathed on them and said, "Receive the Holy Spirit. If you forgive anyone's sins, their sins are forgiven; if you do not forgive them, they are not forgiven."

Now Thomas (also known as Didymus), one of the Twelve, was not with the disciples when Jesus came. So the other disciples told him, "We have seen the Lord!"

But he said to them, "Unless I see the nail marks in his hands and put my finger where the nails were, and put my hand into his side, I will not believe."

A week later his disciples were in the house again, and Thomas was with them. Though the doors were locked, Jesus came and stood among them and said, "Peace be with you!" Then he said to Thomas, "Put your finger here; see my hands. Reach out your hand and put it into my side. Stop doubting and believe."

Thomas said to him, "My Lord and my God!"

Then Jesus told him, "Because you have seen me, you have believed; blessed are those who have not seen and yet have believed."

John 20:19-24.

The Incredulity of Saint Thomas, Michelangelo di Caravaggio (1571-1610), oil on canvas, c. 1601–1602.; The Cerasi Chapel, Santa Maria del Popolo, Rome, Italy.

The Appearance of the Lord to Thomas

Doubting Thomas, tempera colours and gold leaf on parchment, medieval illumination. Unknown Northern English artist c. 1190–1200.

On this day is the commemoration of the appearance of the Lord Christ, to Whom is the glory, to Thomas the Apostle on the eighth day from the glorious Resurrection as the Bible said: "And after eight days His disciples were again inside, and Thomas was with them. Jesus came, the doors being shut, and stood in the midst, and said, "Peace to you!" Then He said to Thomas, "Reach your finger here, and look at My hands; and reach your hand here, and put it into My side. Do not be unbelieving, but believing." And Thomas answered and said to Him, "My Lord and my God!" Jesus said to him, "Thomas, because you have seen Me, you have believed. Blessed are those who have not seen and yet have believed." (John 20:26-29). When St Thomas put his hand in the side of the Lord, his hand was about to be burned by the fire of the Divinity, and when he confessed His Divinity his hand was healed from the pain of the burning.

May the prayers of this Apostle be with us. Amen.

The Commemoration of the Appearance of the Lord to Thomas the Apostle after His Resurrection.

The Ethiopian Synaxarium,
(The Coptic Orthodox Calendar for Baramoudah 6:14 April).

The Incredulity of St Thomas

Almighty and eternal God, who, for the firmer foundation of our faith, allowed your holy apostle Thomas to doubt the resurrection of your Son till word and sight convinced him: grant to us, who have not seen, that we also may believe and so confess Christ as our Lord and our God; who is alive and reigns with you, in the unity of the Holy Spirit, one God, now and for ever.

The Anglican collect for St Thomas' day, 3rd July.

The Orthodox church celebrates October 6th as the day of St Thomas' martyrdom, while July 3rd is the day his body arrived in Edessa in the fourth century. The Orthodox church also celebrate St Thomas on the first Sunday after Easter Day and people named Thomas celebrate their name day.

Thomas is listed eighth in the Luke and Mark lists, seventh in Matthew, being promoted a place by swapping with Matthew himself, and sixth in Acts, being promoted ahead of both Bartholomew and Matthew. Interestingly, he appears second, after only Simon Peter, in the list of seven disciples noted at Jesus' post-resurrection appearance at the Sea of Galilee. (John 21).

The image of the Incredulity of St Thomas was formerly in the small chapel of St Blaise, in Westminster Abbey. It survived until the 18th century, when it was bricked up until 1934. Oil on a thin primed ground attributed to Master Walter of Durham, the King's Painter. 1270-1300. Westminster Abbey, London, England. Photograph: Caroline Lees (2016).

St John Chrysostom

What, therefore, did they say to Thomas? We have seen the Lord? Well, he told them, even if you saw Him, I certainly will not believe the rest. Having seen Him, do you preach Him? As for me, unless I behold in hands the mark of the nails, and place my finger in the mark of the nails, and place my hand into His side, I will not believe. For you did not believe until you first saw Him, and thus with me, I will not believe unless I see. Hold on, O Thomas, with this fervor, and hold on well, that you might see me and that I might confirm you in soul. Hold on, and seek Him Who says: 'Seek and ye shall find'. Do not not stand by simply as an observer, if you do not find the treasure Whom you seek. Hold on, and knock at the door of indisputable knowledge, until He opens to you, Who says: 'Knock, and the door will be opened to you.' I embrace these senseless thoughts, that cut away every senselessness; I love the manner by which you wish to learn, which dashes apart every love of strife; and I especially hear you who say many times: "Unless I see in His hands the marks of the nails, I will not believe."

For by your doubting, I am taught to believe; by your forked-tongue that revealed the wound on the divine body that was pierced, I harvest the fruit for myself without pain. [For you said] unless I see with my eyes the wounds in His holy hands, then the impious would question, without accepting our words. Unless I place this my finger into the marks of the nails, then they will not receive our Gospel. Unless I place this my hand into that side, the untrampling witness of the resurrection, they will not believe my words…From now on, people will be preached of the wonders of the teacher: how will they accept these without seeing with their eyes? How will the faithless come to believe, and ultimately follow Him Whom I did? Will I say to the Judeans and Greeks that the Crucified One and my Master is risen, but I did not see Him, but simply heard of Him? And who will not laugh at my voice? Who will not ignore my preaching? It is one thing to hear, and another to see. It is one thing to receive words, and another to see and touch something. Therefore doubt conquered the mind of Thomas, and after eight days again the Master appeared to His disciples who were gathered together. He left Thomas during these days to be preached to by the others, and to fill him with the thirst for the vision of Him, and his soul was greatly inflamed with the desire to see. Therefore, at the proper time, the one who was desiring perceived the One Who is desired.

St John Chrysostom,
347-407.
Excerpt from the Homily on St Thomas on the Second Sunday of Pascha.

Doubting Thomas, portion of a Byzantine wall mosaic, 1060, the Basilica of the Nativity, Bethlehem, the Palestinian Territories (2016).

St Romanos the Melodist

Who protected the hand of the disciple which was not melted
At the time when he approached the fiery side of the Lord ?
Who gave it daring and strength to probe
The flaming bone ?
Certainly the side was examined.
If the side had not furnished abundant power,
How could a right hand of clay have touched
Sufferings which had shaken Heaven and earth ?
It was grace itself which was given to Thomas
To touch and cry out,
"Thou art our Lord and God."

Truly the bramble which endured fire was burned but not consumed.
From the hand of Thomas I have faith in the story of Moses.
For, though his hand was perishable and thorny, it was not burned
When it touched the side which was like burning flame.
Formerly fire came to the bramble bush,
But now, the thorny one hastened to the fire;
And God, Himself, was seen to guard both.
Hence I have faith; and hence I shall praise
God Himself, and man, as I cry,
"Thou art our Lord and God."

For truly the boundary line of faith was subscribed for me
By the hand of Thomas; for when he touched Christ
He became like the pen of a fast-writing scribe
Which writes for the faithful. From it gushes forth faith.
From it, the robber drank and became sober again;
From it the disciples watered their hearts;
From it, Thomas drained the knowledge which he sought,
For he drank first and then offered drink
To many who had a little doubt. He persuaded them to say,
"Thou art our Lord and God."

St Romanos the Melodist,
Sixth century Kontakion on Doubting Thomas 30:1-3 which likens St Thomas's touch of the Risen Christ to Moses at the Burning Bush.

Contemporary statue of St Thomas with the spear that killed him, Paravur, Kerala, India (2016).

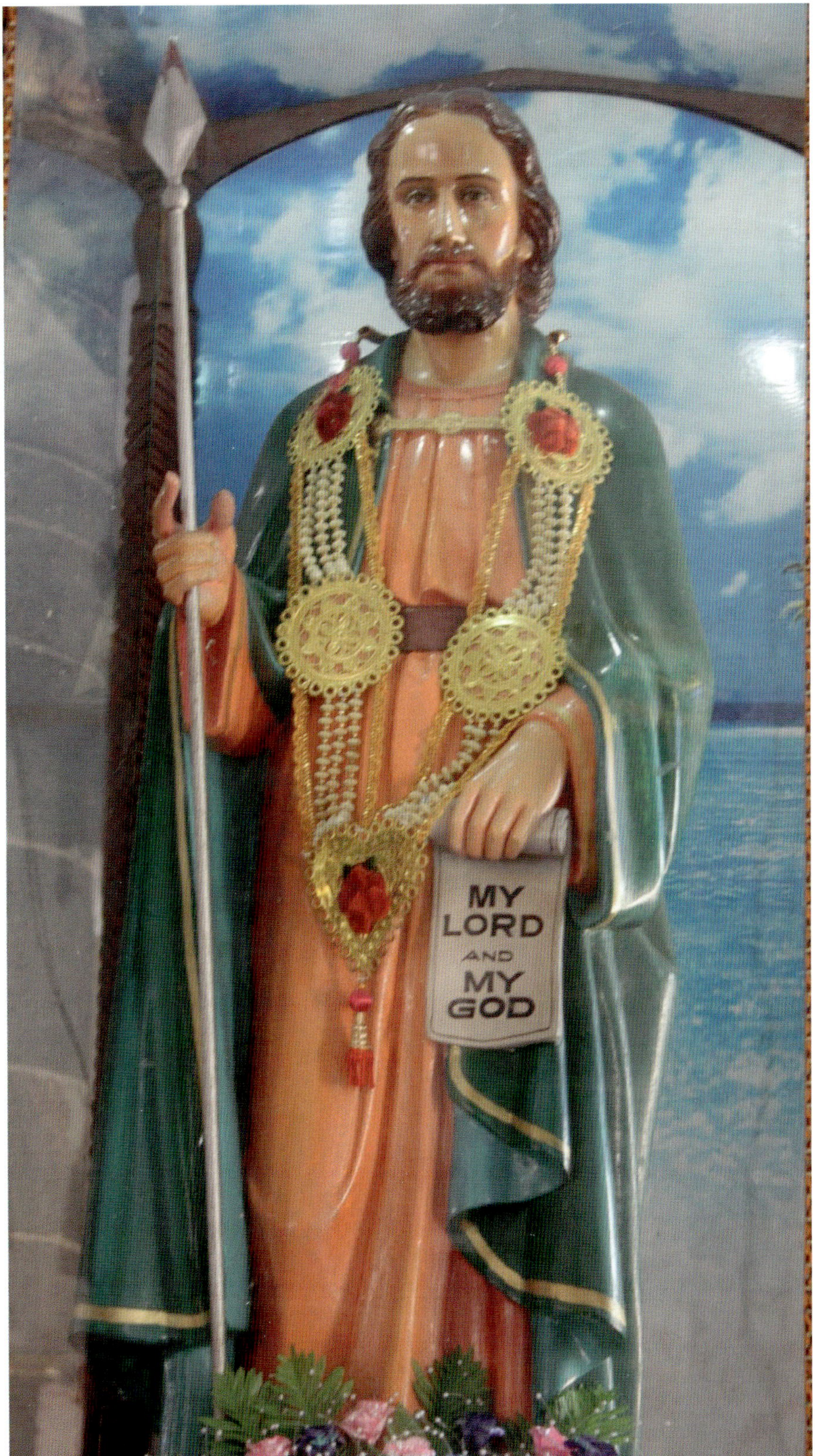
MY
LORD
AND
MY
GOD

Let us go, that we may die with Him

"Let us go, that we may die with Him"
St Thomas spoke, knowing the Jews would stone
And cast him headlong, blood bespattered, prone
As dust in Judea – yet he could not swim
The resurrection tide that breached the rim
Of his credulity – until there came his groan
'My Lord, My God' to sadly now disown

His unbelief and sing an Easter hymn.
How blessed are those, who by report perceive
The Truth of God and joyfully believe;
How blessed are those with faith that never fails
Who have not touched His flesh nor felt his nails;

Who go with Thomas, sure each day to choose
To preach the glorious Gospel's marvelous news.

John L F Wright,
2015.

Icon, St Thomas based on the 12th century St Albans Psalter; Caroline Lees, egg tempera on gesso (specially painted in 2016).

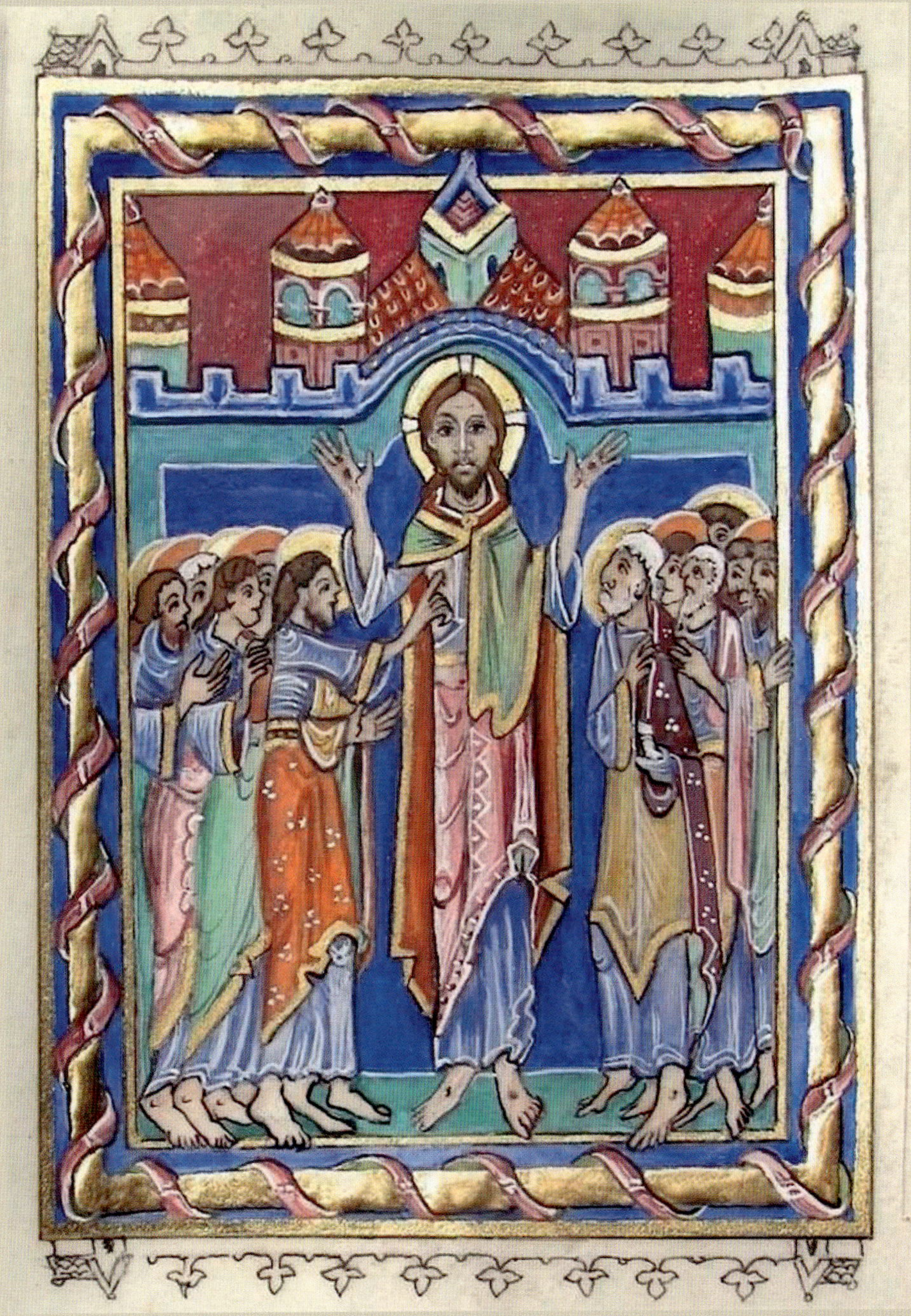

Thomas! Your name for doubting goes before you

Thomas! Your name for doubting goes before you,
Yet you have preached the Gospel near and far,
And many are the unbaptised who saw you
In Persia, Babylon and Malabar.

Espousing India to the One-Begotten,
Dispelling darkness with your brightest dawn,
Many you clad in robes of whitest cotton -
These were your Christians, baptised and twice-born.

"I'll not believe it" once you said, still doubting,
"Until I see the thing with my own eyes.
The laws of Nature were not made for flouting.
You are deluded. Dead men do not rise.

"Except I see the very print of nails,
Except I thrust my hand into His side,
I'll not forgive this greatest of betrayals:
I thought the man immortal – and he died!"

Thomas, your lack of faith was an affliction,
The sceptic's path defiantly you trod –
But then you saw the wounds: these were no fiction!
"My Lord" you uttered, humbled, "and my God!"

So Thomas, we remember you, revere you,
Of sceptics you remain the patron saint,
Your quest is ours, our doubting brings us near you,
With you we seek for proof, our faith is faint.

But Christ said "Blest are those who, without seeing,
Can yet believe". This is our sacred brief -
To pray, with every fibre of our being:
"Lord, I believe: help Thou my unbelief!"

David A E Hunt,
Epiphany 2016.

Marten de Vos (1532–1603) St Thomas Altar, 1574; oil on canvas.
Photograph: the Royal Museum of Fine Arts, Antwerp, the Netherlands.

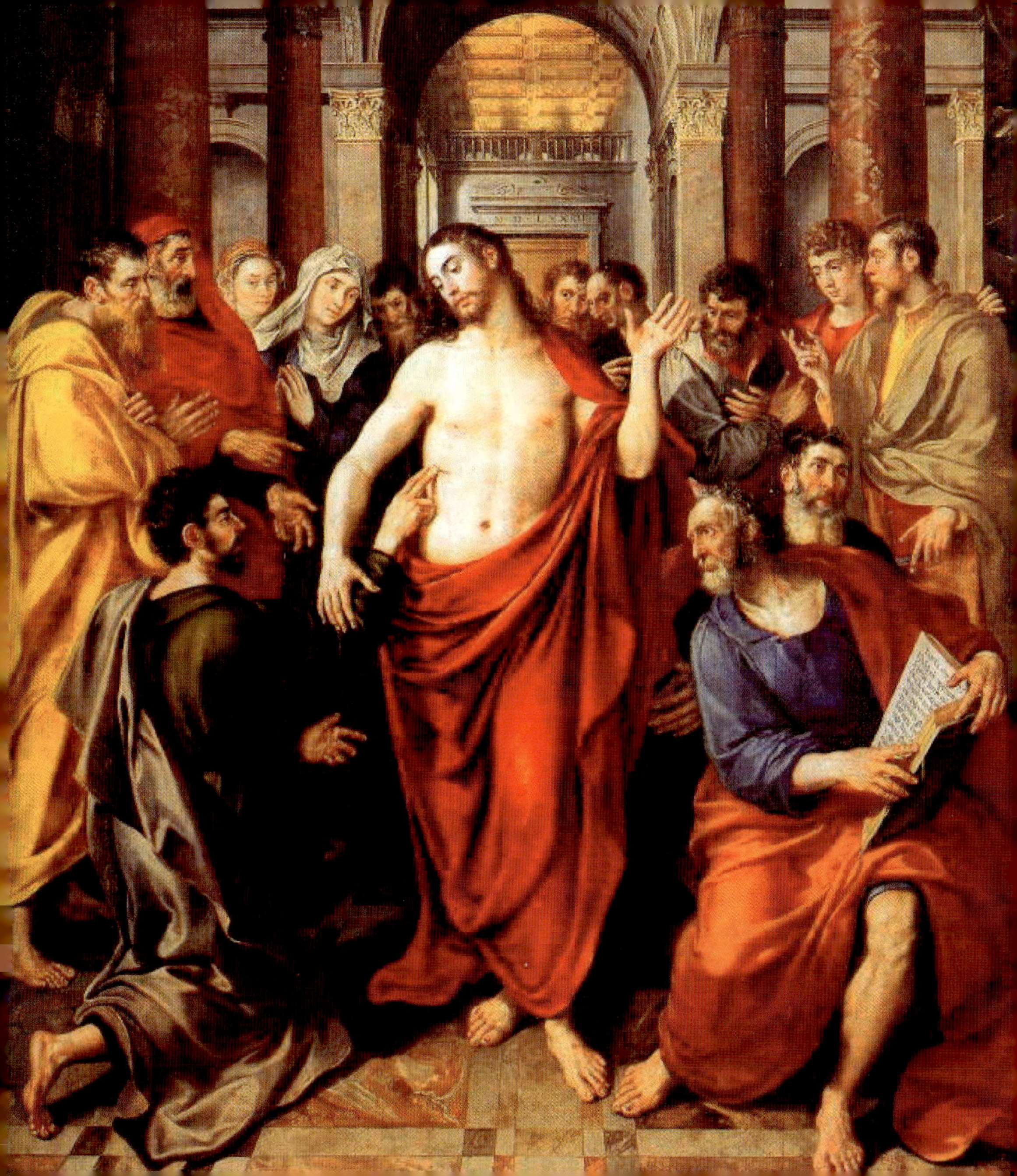

Galilee

The shore at Mensa Christi on the Sea of Galilee where traditionally Jesus appeared to His disciples after the resurrection and cooked them fish for their breakfast (2015).

After these things Jesus shewed himself again to the disciples at the sea of Tiberias; and on this wise shewed he himself. There were together Simon Peter, and Thomas called Didymus, and Nathanael of Cana in Galilee, and the sons of Zebedee, and two other of his disciples. Simon Peter saith unto them, I go a fishing. They say unto him, We also go with thee. They went forth, and entered into a ship immediately; and that night they caught nothing.

But when the morning was now come, Jesus stood on the shore: but the disciples knew not that it was Jesus. Then Jesus saith unto them, Children, have ye any meat? They answered him, No. And he said unto them, Cast the net on the right side of the ship, and ye shall find. They cast therefore, and now they were not able to draw it for the multitude of fishes. Therefore that disciple whom Jesus loved saith unto Peter, It is the Lord. Now when Simon Peter heard that it was the Lord, he girt his fisher's coat unto him, (for he was naked,) and did cast himself into the sea. And the other disciples came in a little ship; (for they were not far from land, but as it were two hundred cubits,) dragging the net with fishes.

As soon then as they were come to land, they saw a fire of coals there, and fish laid thereon, and bread.

Jesus saith unto them, Bring of the fish which ye have now caught. Simon Peter went up, and drew the net to land full of great fishes, an hundred and fifty and three: and for all there were so many, yet was not the net broken.

Jesus saith unto them, Come and dine. And none of the disciples durst ask him, Who art thou? knowing that it was the Lord. Jesus then cometh, and taketh bread, and giveth them, and fish likewise.

This is now the third time that Jesus shewed himself to his disciples, after that he was risen from the dead.

John 21:2-14.

Talipa fish (also known as St Peter's fish) from the Sea of Galilee, Israel (2012).

St Thomas is assigned to Parthia

According to Eusebius' record (263-339), St Thomas and St Bartholomew were assigned to Parthia and India. The Didascalia (dating from the end of the 3rd century) states, "India and all countries bordering it, even to the farthest seas... received the apostolic ordinances from Judas Thomas, who was a guide and ruler in the church which he built." There is a wealth of confirmatory information in the Syriac writings, liturgical books, and calendars of the Church of the East, the writings of the Church Fathers, the calendars, the sacramentaries, and the martyrologies of the Roman, Greek and Ethiopian churches.

The early third-century Syriac work known as the Acts of Thomas connects the apostle's Indian ministry with two kings, one in the north and the other in the south. According to one of the legends in the Acts, Thomas was at first reluctant to accept this mission, but the Lord appeared to him in a night vision and said: "Fear not, Thomas. Go away to India and proclaim the Word, for my grace shall be with you." But the Apostle still demurred, so the Lord overruled the stubborn disciple by ordering circumstances so compelling that he was forced to accompany an "Indian" merchant, Abbanes, as a slave to his native place in northwest 'India', where he found himself in the service of the Indo-Parthian king, Gondophares. According to the Acts of Thomas, the apostle's ministry resulted in many conversions throughout the kingdom, including the king and his brother. Although little is known of the immediate growth of the church, Bar-Daisan (154–223) reports that in his time there were Christian tribes in India which claimed to have been converted by St Thomas and to have books and relics to prove it. But at least by the year of the establishment of the Second Persian Empire (226), there were bishops of the Church of the East in northwest India (Afghanistan and Baluchistan), with laymen and clergy alike engaging in missionary activity.

It is significant that, aside from a small remnant of the Church of the East in Kurdistan, the only other churches to maintain a distinctive identity are the St Thomas Christian congregations along the Malabar Coast (modern-day Kerala) in southwest India. According to the most ancient tradition of this church, St Thomas evangelised this area and then crossed to the Coromandel Coast of southeast India, where, after carrying out a second mission, he died at Mylapore. Throughout the period under review, the church in India was under the jurisdiction of Edessa, which was then under the Mesopotamian patriarchate at Seleucia-Ctesiphon and later at Baghdad and Mosul.

The Ascension of Christ, Andrei Rublev. c. 1408. Paintings for the Assumption Cathedral in Vladimir; Tretyakov Gallery, Moscow, Russia.

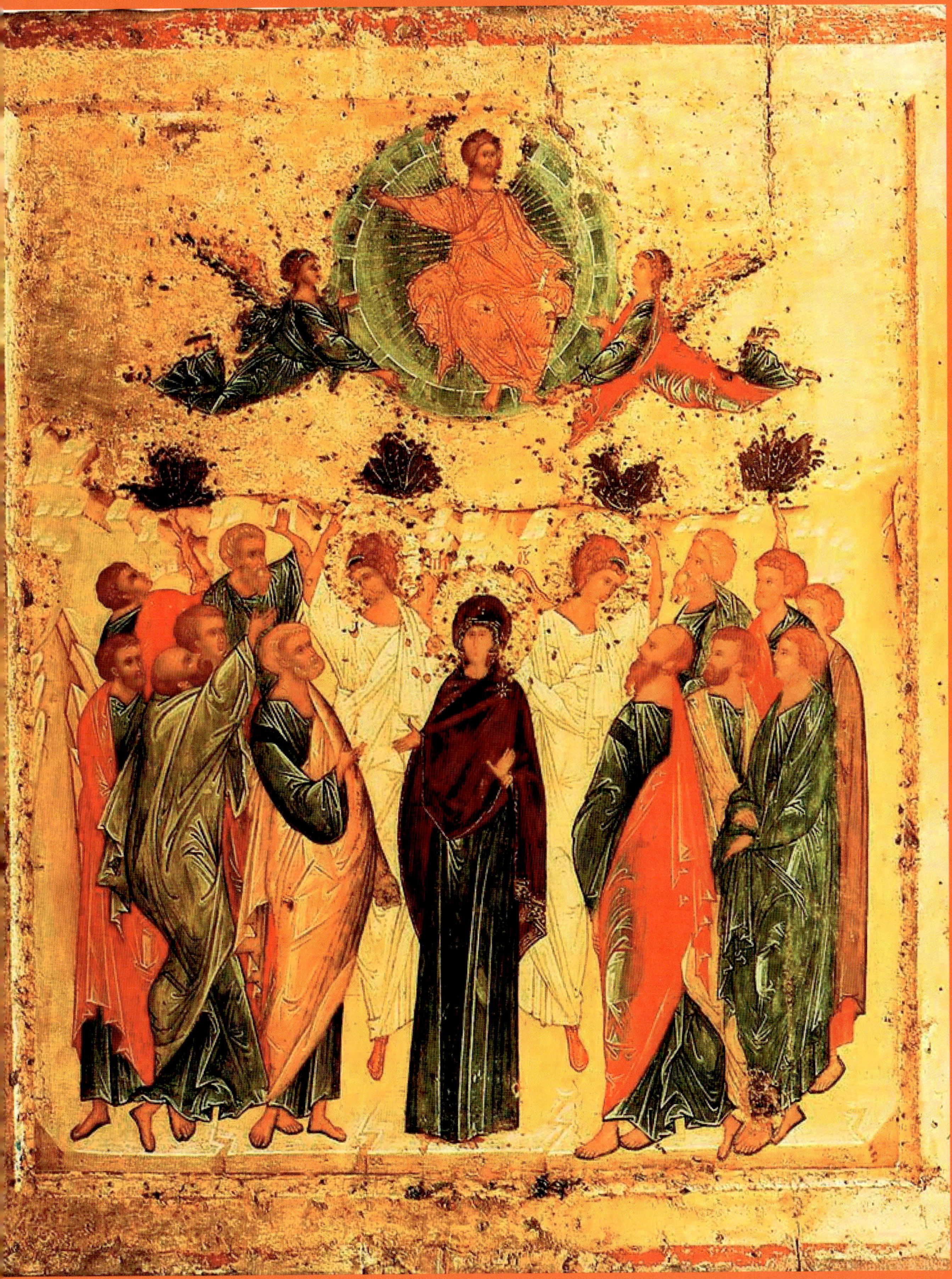

The Parthians

The Parthian empire is the first of the homelands mentioned by the Jewish pilgrims to Jerusalem in the Pentecost account:

Now there were staying in Jerusalem God-fearing Jews from every nation under heaven. When they heard this sound, a crowd came together in bewilderment, because each one heard their own language being spoken. Utterly amazed, they asked: "Aren't all these who are speaking Galileans? Then how is it that each of us hears them in our native language? Parthians, Medes and Elamites; residents of Mesopotamia, Judea and Cappadocia, Pontus and Asia, Phrygia and Pamphylia, Egypt and the parts of Libya near Cyrene; visitors from Rome (both Jews and converts to Judaism); Cretans and Arabs—we hear them declaring the wonders of God in our own tongues!"

Acts 2:5-11.

By this time the Mede and Elamite empires had been replaced or subsumed by the Parthian Empire. Mesopotamia is the area between the Tigris and Euphrates rivers, in southern Turkey and Iraq, with the heartland of Media to the east, and that of Elam lying on the Persian Gulf south of Media. The Parthian Empire lasted from 247 BC to AD 224 and geographically included the modern states of Iran, Iraq, and much of Syria, Afghanistan and even Pakistan.

Left: Parthian warrior, 1st c. AD.
Photograph: Roland Howard (2007).

Right: Small lapis lazuli head of a bearded Achaemenid prince;
Photograph: Jim Wheeler (2007).
Both statues are in the National Museum, Tehran, Iran.

47

Early Christian accounts

A number of early Christian writings from the centuries immediately following the first Ecumenical Council of AD 325 mention St Thomas' mission. It was not until the middle of the 19th century that such evidence was forthcoming.

"What? were not the Apostles strangers amidst the many nations and countries over which they spread themselves? ... Peter indeed may have belonged to Judea; but what had Paul in common with the gentiles, Luke with Achaia, Andrew with Epirus, John with St Ambrose of Milan (337-397) was thoroughly acquainted with the Greek and Latin Classics, and had a good deal of information on India and Indians." He speaks of the Gymnosophists of India, the Indian Ocean, the River Ganges etc., a number of times. He quotes his contemporary St John Chrysostom:

"It was his (Thomas') mission to espouse India to the One-Begotten. The merchant is blessed for having so great a treasure in his charge."

St Gregory of Nazianzus,
329–390.

St Jerome (347 - 420) in *Scti Hieron Epistolae, LIX, ad Marcetla*, written in Bethlehem, speaks of the Divine Word as being everywhere present in His fullness: "*cum Thoma in India, cum Petro Romae, cum Paulo in Illyrico*".

"Parthia receives Matthew, India Thomas, Libya Thaddeus, and Phrygia Philip".

St Paulinus of Nola,
354-431.

St Thomas among the Indians, Andrew and Luke at the city of Patras are found to have closed their careers."

St Gaudentius, Bishop of Brescia,
c. 427.

"India, an immense and thickly populated country, is situated at a great distance from Egypt and is separated from that country by the Ocean. It touches Persia on one side of the land. The most holy Thomas, one of the twelve Apostles, was sent to India to preach the Gospel of salvation."

St John of Damascus,
676-749.

St Jerome and St John of Damascus

The tomb of St Jerome (347-420), Doctor of the Church, where he lived and translated the Bible into the Latin Vulgate in the caves beneath the Basilica of the Nativity, Bethlehem, Palestine (2016).

The monastery of Mar Saba, home to St John of Damascus (676-749), prayer and hymn writer, historian of the Early Church, Palestine. Photograph: Jennifer, Marchioness of Bute (2014).

St Thomas travels through Parthia

St Thomas left Jerusalem after the persecution of Acts 8, and travelled east along the Silk Road to preach in the kingdom of Parthia, where there were well-established Jewish communities, including some who had witnessed the events of Pentecost recounted in Acts 2.

The Parthian Empire and Mesopotamia became centres of the early church in the second and third centuries, so perhaps St Thomas succeeded in establishing churches. At some point he moved on, probably overland following the southern branch of the Silk Road, to end up at Taxila, staying there and in the surrounding kingdoms for some time.

The Parthians had frequent conflicts with the Romans, particularly over the control of Greater Armenia. There was a civil war between rival claimants to the Armenian throne from about AD 38 to 49. A ruling Parthian dynasty was established in Armenia in AD 54, which survived until AD 428.

Parthia is synonymous with Persia, Mesopotamia and the former Mede and Elamite empires of Old Testament days. According to Sophronius, St Thomas not only preached but also established the faith amongst the Medes, Persians, Carmanians, Hyrcanians, Bactrians, and other nations in those parts.

The Medes and Persians lived in what was at that time the Parthian empire. The Bactrians lived to the north-east of the Parthian Empire, north of the Hindu Kush mountains. Bactria extended across part of what is now Afghanistan, Pakistan and Tajikistan. According to Pliny, after the Parthians' defeat of Crassus and his Roman army in 53 BC, 10,000 Roman prisoners were sent by the Parthians to Bactria to act as mercenaries and guard the eastern frontier of their empire. Despite this, and having previously been part of the heavily Greek influenced Indo-Parthian Empire, the Kushans invaded from the east. By the time of St Thomas' ministry, Bactria was subject to influence from the Greeks and Romans from recent history and the Silk Road merchants, from the powerful Parthians to the immediate west, and the ruling Kushans, the most westerly extreme of the Chinese Han Empire, to the east. By AD 30, Kushan control had extended south across the Hindu Kush mountains well into India! The legendary Gandhara is an area of northern Pakistan and southern Afghanistan.

A Mede, the Apadana staircase, sixth c. BC, Persepolis, Iran (2010).

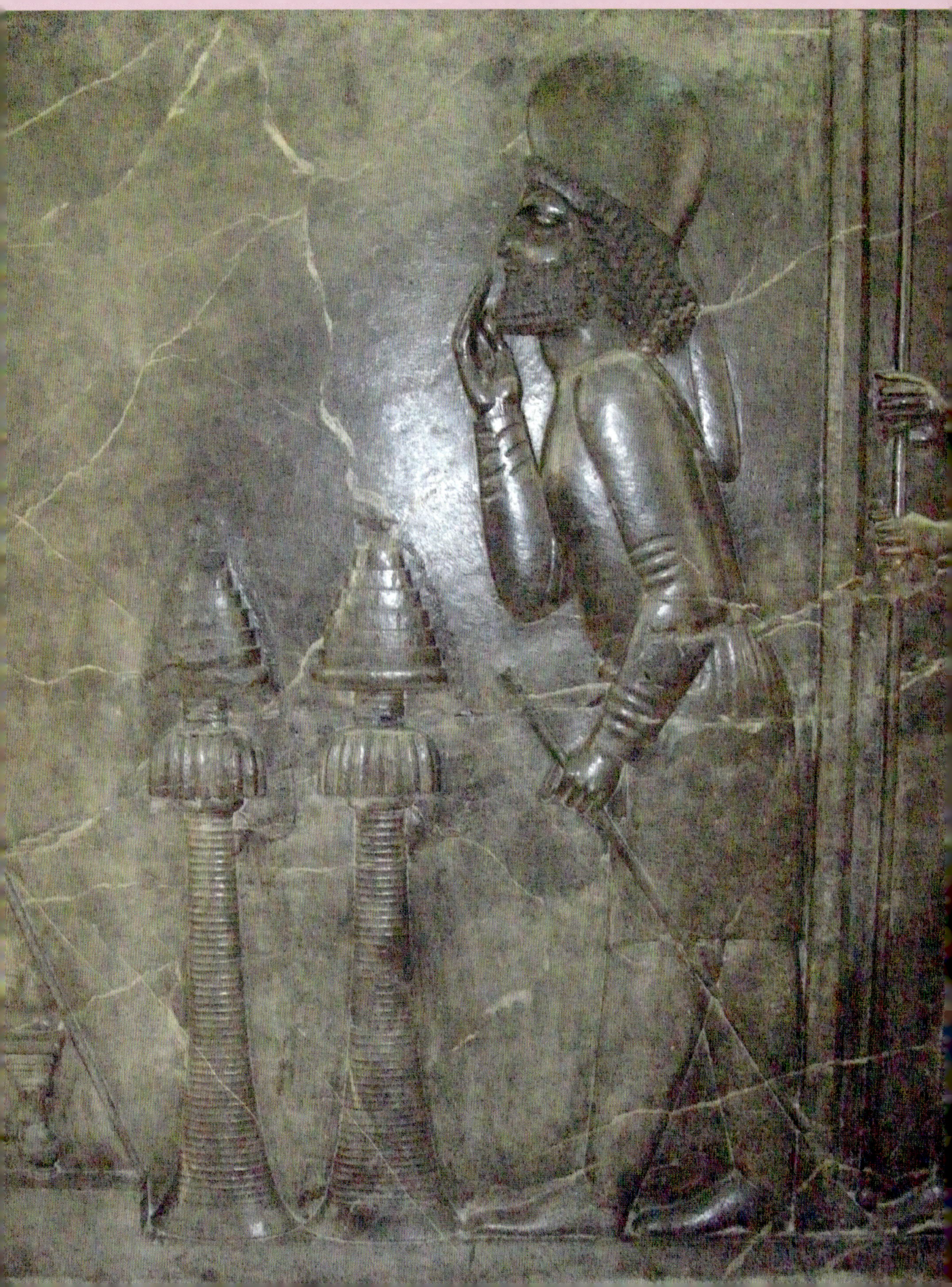

India received Thomas

The merchant Habban receives St Thomas, wall painting, St Mary's Jacobite Cathedral, Angamaly, Kerala.

Jesus gives St Thomas to Habban, wall painting, St Mary's Jacobite Cathedral, Angamaly, Kerala (2016).

India, and all the countries belonging to it and round about it, even to the farthest sea, received the apostolic ordination... from Judas Thomas, who was the guide and ruler in the church he had built there, in which he also ministered.

The Teaching of The Twelve Apostles, (an ancient Syriac document) Roberts & Donaldson, *The Writings of the Fathers Down to 325 AD*, vol. 8, 671-672)

A host of similar examples may be cited, from both western and eastern traditions. Despite these early witnesses, it seems that no ancient Christian community has survived in what is now this part of Pakistan (the Kingdom of Indo-Parthia at the time of St Thomas). Any that did survive the Buddhist domination of the early centuries AD would have been swept away by the arrival of Islam in the early eighth century.

Today's Indian and Pakistani Christians, both Roman Catholic and Protestant, trace their roots to the servants of the British Raj in the 19th century.

The Mar Thoma Christians of Southern India are a different matter, however, having been discovered by the Portuguese in 1498 living in an extensive area along the south-west coast of Southern India. They are quite clear and unambiguous: they very definitely trace their origins directly back to St Thomas. They currently number about two and a half million in 1500 parishes in the Kerala region, and they still use the ancient language, Syriac, as part of their liturgy. Syriac is a very close relative of the Aramaic spoken by Jesus and the Disciples, and is the liturgical language of the family of Syrian Orthodox churches. The supposed tomb of St Thomas is in Mylapore, just south of Chennai on the Bay of Bengal.

St Thomas, wall painting, St Mary's Jacobite Cathedral, Angamaly, Kerala, India (2016).

The Virgin Mary's girdle

The Virgin Mary throws her girdle to St Thomas as she ascends into Heaven (he was on his way home from India when she died). Modern Orthodox icon courtesy of Abba Seraphim (2016).

On this day, Our Lady, the all pure, Virgin St Mary, the Mother of God, departed. As she was always praying in the holy sepulchre, the Holy Spirit informed her that she was about to depart from this temporal world. When the time of her departure arrived, the virgins of the Mount of Olives came to her, with the apostles, who were still alive, and they surrounded her bed.

The Lord Jesus Christ, to Whom is the glory, with a host of thousands and thousands of angels came to her and comforted her and told her about the eternal joy that was prepared for her, and she rejoiced.

The apostles and the virgins asked her to bless them. She stretched her hand and blessed them all, and she gave up her pure spirit into the hands of her Son and God, and He took her spirit to the heavenly mansions.

The apostles prepared the body in a fitting manner and carried it to Gethsemane.

Some of the Jews blocked their way to prevent them from burying the body. One of the Jews seized the coffin with his hands, which were separated instantly from his body and they remained attached to the coffin.

He regretted his evil deed and wept bitterly. Through the supplications of the saintly apostles, his hands were reattached to his body, and he believed in the Lord Christ.

When they placed the body in the tomb, the Lord hid it from them.

St Thomas the Apostle was not present at the time of St Mary's departure. He wanted to go to Jerusalem and a cloud carried him there.

On his way, he saw the pure body of St Mary carried by the angels and ascended to heaven with it. One of the angels told him, "Make haste and kiss the pure body of St Mary," and he did.

When St Thomas arrived where the disciples were, they told him about St Mary's departure and he said to them, "You know how I conducted myself at the resurrection of the Lord Christ, and I will not believe unless I see her body."

They went with him to the tomb, and uncovered the place of the body, but they did not find it, and everyone was perplexed and surprised. St Thomas told them how he saw the holy body and the angels that were ascending with it.

Her intercession and blessings be with us. Amen.

The Coptic Synaxarium,
(The Coptic Orthodox Calendar for the 21st Day of Tubah: 29 January).

The Assumption of the Virgin Mary

Details of the Dormition (Orthodox) or Assumption (Catholic) of the Virgin Mary, adjudged heretical by Pope Gelasius I in 494, stated that Thomas was the only witness of the Assumption of the Virgin Mary into Heaven on his way back from India, from where he witnessed her bodily assumption into Heaven and as she ascended, she dropped her girdle to St Thomas.

The Orthodox church maintains an unbroken tradition that the Virgin Mary had a vision and knew that in three days' time she would die; the other Apostles had been summoned and were gathered around her deathbed in Jerusalem to bid farewell, receive a blessing and to witness her death. She is reported to have said: "I give my soul to my son Jesus and my body to the earth." She was fully dead and the Apostles buried her according to Jewish customs, her body packed with flowers and precious spices.

When St Thomas returned to Jerusalem a week after her burial, he was taken to her tomb in a cave in the Kidron Valley near the Garden of Gethsemane. The apostles removed the slab that covered the tomb and were amazed that nothing remained except the flowers and precious spices that had surrounded her body and her robe: her body was not there.

In an inversion of the story of St Thomas' doubts, the other Apostles were sceptical of St Thomas' story until they saw the empty tomb and the girdle in his hands. St Thomas' receipt of the girdle is commonly depicted in medieval and pre-Tridentine Renaissance art.

The old ecclesiastical records of Glastonbury, confirmed by many other ancient writers, state that the Virgin Mary departed this life in the year AD 48.

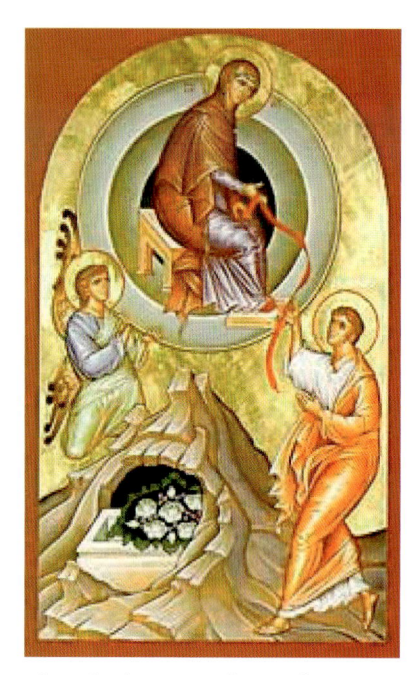

The Virgin Mary throws her girdle to St Thomas, modern Greek icon.
Image: Abba Seraphim (2016).

Modern statue of the Virgin Mary, the Catholic church of the Assumption, Mount Zion, Jerusalem, Israel (2016).

The tomb of the Virgin Mary, the Orthodox cave church of the Dormition, the Kidron Valley, Jerusalem, Israel (2016).

The Falling Asleep of the Holy Mother of God

From the earliest Christian traditions surrounding the Assumption, the answer to the question of whether the Blessed Virgin died like all men do has been "yes". The Feast of the Assumption was first celebrated in the sixth century in the Christian East, where it was known in both Eastern and Western traditions as the Dormition of the Most Holy Theotokos (the Mother of God).

To this day, among Eastern Christians, both Catholic and Orthodox, the traditions surrounding the Dormition are based on a fourth-century document: *The Account of St John the Theologian of the Falling Asleep of the Holy Mother of God.* This document, written in the voice of St John the Evangelist (to whom Christ, on the Cross, had entrusted the care of His mother), recounts how the Archangel Gabriel came to Mary as she prayed at the Holy Sepulchre (the tomb in which Christ had been laid on Good Friday, and from which He rose on Easter Sunday). Gabriel told the Blessed Virgin that her earthly life had reached its end, and she decided to return to Bethlehem to meet her death.

All of the apostles, having been caught up in clouds by the Holy Spirit, were transported to Bethlehem to be with Mary in her final days. Together, they carried her bed (again, with the aid of the Holy Spirit) to her home in Jerusalem, where, on the following Sunday, Christ appeared to her and told her not to fear. While Peter sang a hymn, the face of the mother of the Lord shone brighter than the light, and she rose up and blessed each of the apostles with her own hand, and all gave glory to God; and the Lord stretched forth His undefiled hands, and received her holy and blameless soul. . . . And Peter, and I John, and Paul, and Thomas, ran and wrapped up her precious feet for the consecration; and the twelve apostles put her precious and holy body upon a couch, and carried it. The apostles took the couch bearing Mary's body to the Garden of Gethsemane, where they placed her body in a new tomb.

And, behold, a perfume of sweet savour came forth out of the holy sepulchre of our Lady the mother of God; and for three days the voices of invisible angels were heard glorifying Christ our God, who had been born of her. And when the third day was ended, the voices were no longer heard; and from that time forth all knew that her spotless and precious body had been transferred to paradise.

"The Falling Asleep of the Holy Mother of God" is the earliest extant written document describing the end of Mary's life, and as we can see, it clearly indicates that Mary died before her body was assumed into Heaven. The earliest Latin versions of the story of the Assumption, written a couple of centuries later, differ in certain details but agree that Mary died, and Christ received her soul; that the apostles entombed her body; and that Mary's body was taken up into Heaven from the tomb.

The fourth-century Greek Apokryphon on St John the Evangelist.

The Dormition of the Virgin Mary with the apostles and leaders of the Jerusalem Church gathered round her deathbed. Jesus is seen receiving her soul; mosaic, 1315-1321, the Greek Orthodox church of St Saviour in Chora (Kariye Camii), Istanbul, Turkey (2013).

2.
The Syrian church:

St Addai
St Ephraim the Syrian

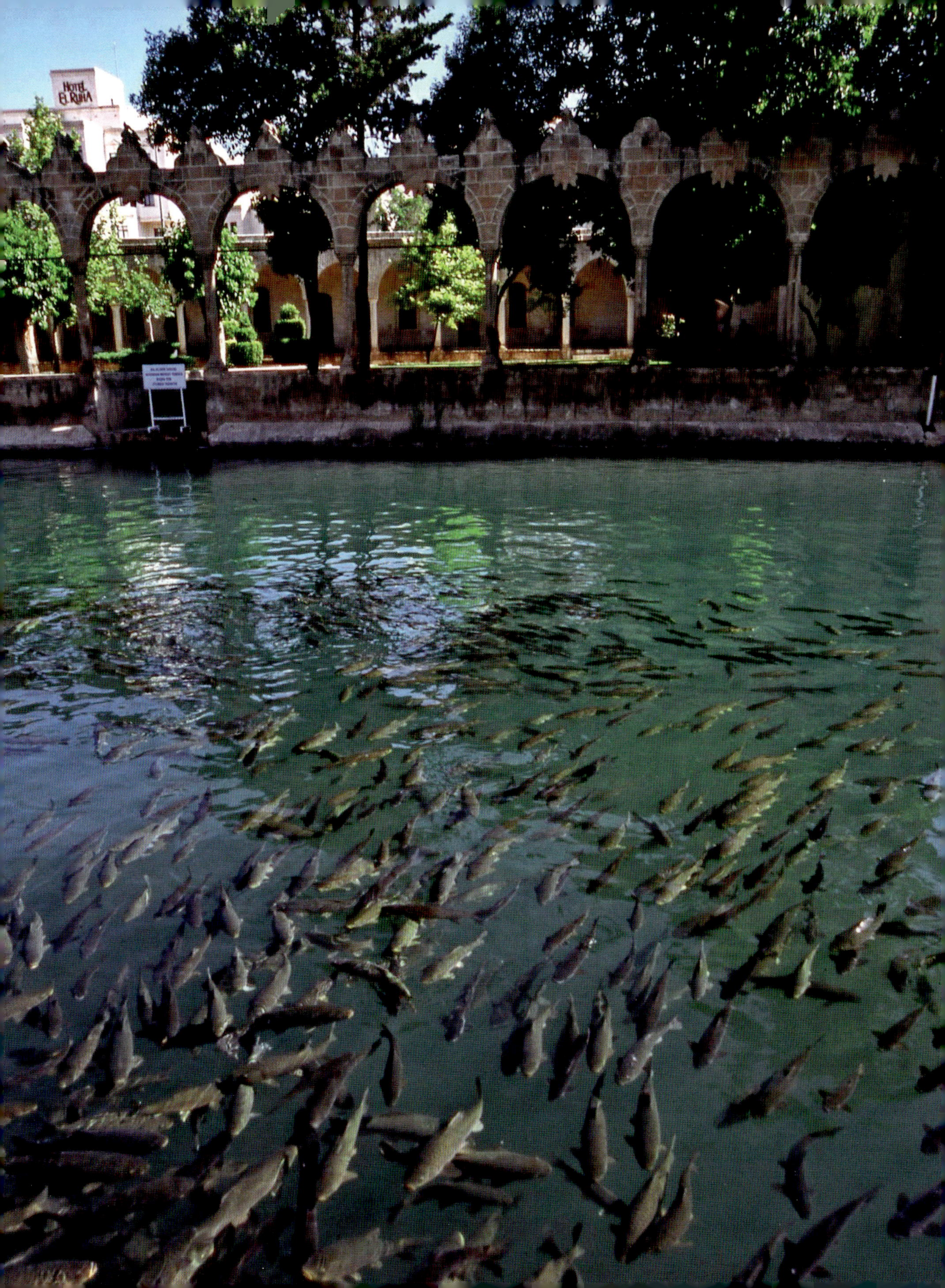
HOTEL
EL RUHA

St Thomas is sent to Parthia

Origen (185–254) who taught with great acclaim in Alexandria and then in Caesarea, is the first known writer to record the casting of lots by the Apostles. Origen's original work has been lost, but his statement about Parthia falling to Thomas has been preserved by Eusebius (263-339): *"When the holy Apostles and disciples of our Saviour were scattered over all the world, Thomas, so the tradition has it, obtained as his portion Parthia...Judas, who is also called Thomas"* has a role in the legend of King Abgar of Edessa (Urfa), for having sent Thaddaeus to preach in Edessa after the Ascension.

St Ephraim the Syrian (c. 306-373) also recounts this legend. He also bears witness to the Edessan Church's strong conviction concerning St Thomas's Indian Apostolate. There the devil speaks of St Thomas as "the Apostle I slew in India":

> "The bones the merchant hath brought
> In his several journeyings to India
> And thence on his return
> All riches which there he found
> Dirt in his eyes he did repute
> when to thy sacred bones compared".

In another stanza the devil cries:

> "Into what land shall I fly from the just?
> I stirred up Death the Apostles to slay,
> that by their death I might escape their blows.
> But harder still am I now stricken:
> the Apostle I slew in India has overtaken me in Edessa;
> here and there he is all himself.
> There went I, and there was he:
> here and there to my grief I find him".

In another hymn St Ephraim speaks of the mission of St Thomas:

"The earth darkened with sacrifices' fumes to illuminate, a land of people dark fell to thy lot, a tainted land Thomas has purified, India's dark night was flooded with light by Thomas".

Overleaf: The Fishponds of Abraham, Edessa, Turkey. Photograph: Jane Taylor (2006).

Right: Brahmin priest, Tamil Nadu, India (2010).

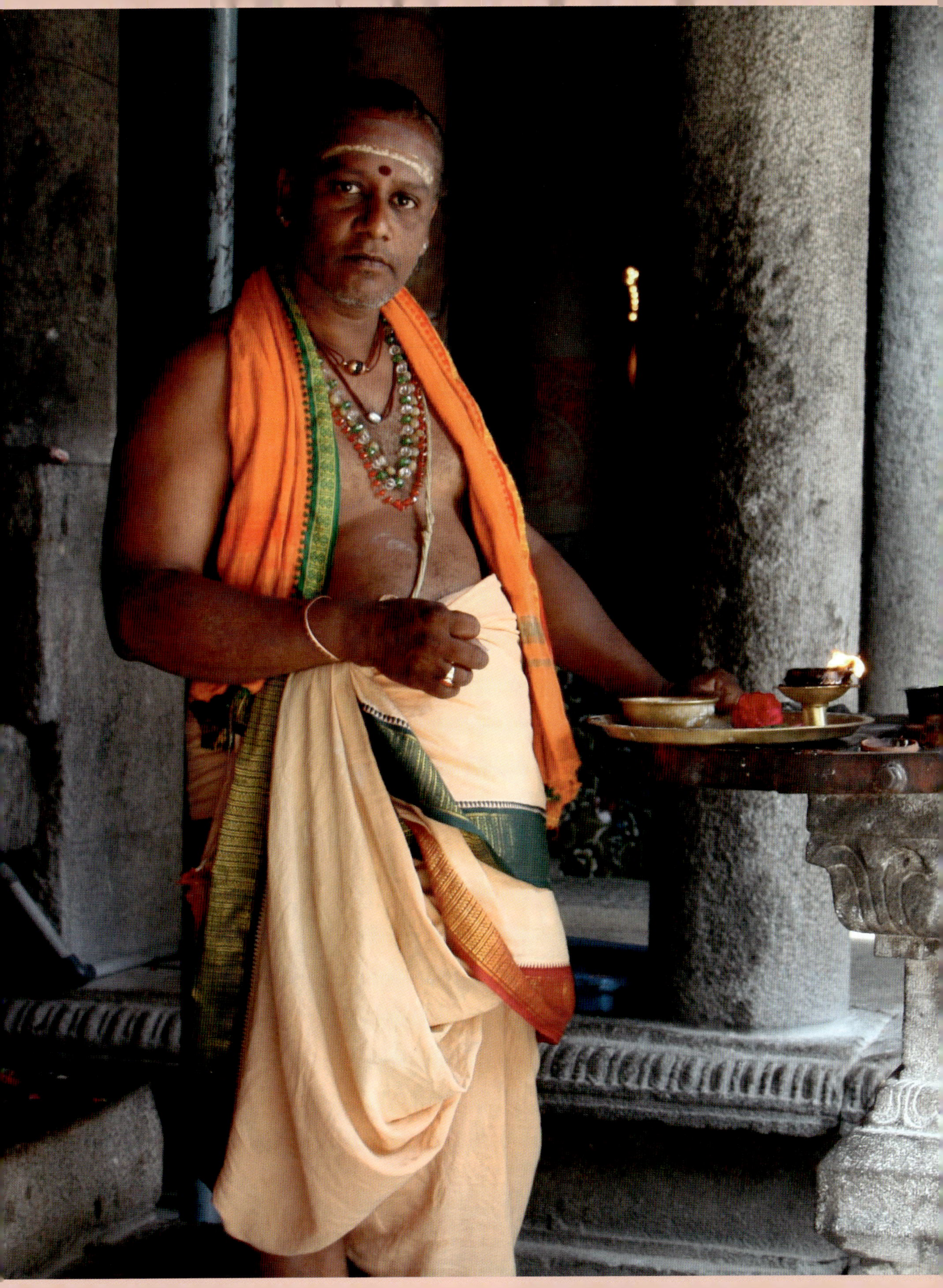

The Doctrine of St Addai

And after the death of the apostles there were Guides and Rulers in the churches, and whatsoever the apostles had committed to them, and they had received from them, they taught to the multitudes all the time of their lives. They, again, at their deaths also committed and delivered to their disciples after them everything which they had received from the apostles; also what James had written from Jerusalem, and Simon from the city of Rome, and John from Ephesus, and Mark from the great Alexandria, and Andrew from Phrygia, and Luke from Macedonia, and Judas Thomas from India: that the epistles of an apostle might be received and read in the churches that were in every place, like those Triumphs of their Acts, which Luke wrote, are read; that by this the apostles might be known, and the prophets, and the Old Testament and the New; that one truth was preached by them all, that one Spirit spoke in them all from one God, whom they had all worshipped and had all preached. And the various countries received their teaching.

The Doctrine of St Addai,
friend and disciple of St Thomas,
Edessa, 1st century AD.

According to Eastern Christian traditions, Thaddeus (Syriac-Aramaic Addai or Aday), was one of the seventy disciples of Christ, possibly identical with Thaddeus (Jude the Apostle) one of the Twelve Apostles.

There is no consensus about the life and death of St Thaddeus of Edessa (Mar Addai or Mor Aday). Some historians and researchers dispute that St Thaddeus of Edessa and Addai are the same individual. Based on various Eastern Christian traditions, St Thaddaeus was a Jew born in Edessa, at the time a Syrian city (now in Turkey).

St Addai, encaustic icon. Sinai.

King Abgar with the Mandylion, Orthodox encaustic icon.
Both: Monastery of St Catherine, Mount Sinai, Egypt.

The Liturgy of St Addai and St Mari is a Divine Liturgy of the East Syrian Rite, which originated around the year AD 200 in Edessa (now Urfa, Turkey) and is in regular use, even if in different versions, by the Assyrian Church of the East and the Chaldean Catholic Church who claim a connection to the saint and also by the Chaldean Syrian Church and Syro-Malabar Catholic Church in India founded by St Thomas the Apostle.

This liturgy is traditionally attributed to St Addai (the disciple of St Thomas the Apostle) and St Mari (a disciple of St Addai). One of the oldest manuscripts of the High Middle Ages, this *anaphora* does not include the Words of Institution, a matter that raised ecumenical concerns.

The *anaphora* or Eucharistic Prayer that is part of this liturgy is of particular interest, being one of the oldest in Christianity, possibly dating back to 3rd-century Edessa, even if the outline of the current form can be traced as far back only as the time of the Patriarch Mar Isho-Yab III in the 7th century.

Hymns by St Ephraim (composed in Edessa) and others are often sung during the communion. A piece of dough from the eucharistic bread is saved from week to week, not as reserve sacrament but as leaven for the next week's bread. Authors from Theodore of Mopsuestia (c. 400) to Mar Eshai Shimun XXIII in the mid-20th century and Mar Aprem Mooken of India in the early 21st century have identified the *Epiclesis*, beginning with the words *Neethi Mar Rukhakha Qaddisha…* (May the Holy Spirit come…) as the high point of the Holy Qurbana.

In the Syro-Malabar Catholic Church this liturgy has three forms: a simplified form, a standard form for Sunday use, and a highly solemn form, known as the "Raza", used only on solemnities. A reform of the Raza in order to return to the original form was issued in 1985, and another in 2007, making uniform the many different uses of each parish and removing additions introduced over the centuries in imitation of the Roman Rite. The main changes were: a return to the ancient arrangement of the interior of churches, restoration of the preparation of the bread and wine before the beginning of the service and removal of the Filioque from the Creed.

The St Thomas Christians still use the two earliest Christian liturgies in existence: the Mass of Addai and Mari, and the Liturgy of St James, once used by the early Church of Jerusalem. More remarkable still, these ancient services are still partly sung in Aramaic, the language spoken by Jesus and St Thomas.

The letters of St Thomas to St Addai

Modern Greek Orthodox icon.

This would be the second of his letters sent from India to the Church of Edessa, according to the statement of the Syriac Didascalia.

Edessa, modern Urfa in south-eastern Turkey, is mentioned in various Greek, Latin, Syriac and Arabic sources. These describe the city as a Hellenistic stronghold, the first Christian kingdom and the cradle of Syriac literature. The historical position made the city an important station on the Silk Route - like Nisibis and Singara to the east and as such it linked India and China with the Mediterranean world.

The Edessenes believed that their Church stood in peculiarly close relations with the Apostle Thomas, that he was, in the fullest sense, the friend of the Church of Edessa. This deeply rooted feeling comes out clearly in the extraordinary belief that it was Thomas who sent Addai to them. From the same feeling, that Thomas was their Apostle, came the exploit in which a few Edessenes moved or stole the relics of the Apostle and brought them to Edessa.

There would be great excitement in the church at Edessa, when the Apostle's letter arrived and was read at the service on Sunday; and from that day those Christian men and women would feel very closely bound to the daring leader who had carried the message of the Cross into the very heart of Asia. The letter would be frequently read or referred to in the church services; and the whole community would feel that Judas Thomas was their Apostle, although he had never visited their city. Every Edessene Christian knew that the land of Thomas's apostolate was India.

If Thomas actually wrote a letter to the Church in Edessa, how did it not become known throughout the Christian world? Why is it not found in the New Testament? The reason is that it was a news-letter rather than a letter of spiritual edification. Therefore, other Christian centres would be less likely to desire to possess copies of it for reading in their churches.

But for the Church of Edessa it had the most supreme interest, first, because it was a real apostolic letter; secondly, because it was addressed to the Church in Edessa; thirdly, because it was written in Aramaic; and lastly, because of the bonds which bound their own beloved leader Tobias to Habban and the Apostle.

As soon as the first church building was erected in Edessa, the letter would be kept, along with the other apostolic documents (gospels or epistles) which they possessed, in the Church itself; and this Church (the earliest church building of which we have any record) was destroyed by a flood of the River Daisan in AD 201 and all the precious manuscripts perished in the disaster. As the author of The Acts of Judas Thomas was able to copy out the historical details contained in the letter, we may safely conclude that his original work must be dated before AD 201.
St Addai heard the preaching of John the Baptist. After being baptised by John in the Jordan River, he remained in Palestine. He later met and became a follower of Jesus; he was chosen to be one of the seventy disciples, whom Jesus sent in pairs to preach in the cities and places.

The legend of the correspondence between King Abgarus V of Edessa and Jesus was first recounted in the fouth century by the church historian Eusebius of Caesarea. In the origin of the legend, Eusebius had been shown documents said to contain the official correspondence that passed between Abgar and Jesus, and he was well enough convinced by their authenticity to quote them extensively in his Ecclesiastical History.

"Thomas, one of the twelve apostles, under divine impulse sent Thaddeus, who was also numbered among the seventy disciples of Christ, to Edessa, as a preacher and evangelist of the teaching of Christ."

Eusebius,
Historia Ecclesiastica, I, xiii
263 - 339 AD, Palestine.

The story of the healing and Thaddeus' evangelising efforts resulted in the growth of Christian communities in northern Mesopotamia and in Syria east of Antioch. Thaddeus' story is embodied in the Syriac document, *Doctrine of Addai,* which recounts the role of Addai and makes him one of the 70 Apostles sent out to spread the Christian faith. By the time the legend had returned to Syria, the purported site of the miraculous image, it had been embroidered into a tissue of miraculous happenings: the story was retold in elaborated form by St Ephraim the Syrian (c. 306-373).

Eusebius of Caesarea

Among the rejected writings must be reckoned also the Acts of Paul, and the so-called Shepherd, and the Apocalypse of Peter, and in addition to these the extant epistle of Barnabas, and the so-called *Teachings of the Apostles*; and besides, as I said, the Apocalypse of John, if it seems proper, which some, as I said, reject, but which others class with the accepted books. And among these some have placed also the Gospel according to the Hebrews, with which those of the Hebrews that have accepted Christ are especially delighted. And all these may be reckoned among the disputed books.

But we have nevertheless felt compelled to give a catalogue of these also, distinguishing those works which according to ecclesiastical tradition are true and genuine and commonly accepted, from those others which, although not canonical but disputed, are yet at the same time known to most ecclesiastical writers— we have felt compelled to give this catalogue in order that we might be able to know both these works and those that are cited by the heretics under the name of the apostles, including, for instance, such books as the Gospels of Peter, of Thomas, of Matthias, or of any others besides them, and the Acts of Andrew and John and the other apostles, which no one belonging to the succession of ecclesiastical writers has deemed worthy of mention in his writings.

And further, the character of the style is at variance with apostolic usage, and both the thoughts and the purpose of the things that are related in them are so completely out of accord with true orthodoxy that they clearly show themselves to be the fictions of heretics. Wherefore they are not to be placed even among the rejected writings, but are all of them to be cast aside as absurd and impious.

Eusebius of Caesarea, *Church History* Book 3: 1. AD 263-339.

Eusebius is the only source who says that the body of St Thomas was brought back from India to Edessa. "India" was a large area that also encompassed Afghanistan, Sri Lanka and Burma.

The Codex Zacynthius, which dates to the sixth or seventh century, has been held in Cambridge University Library since 1984.

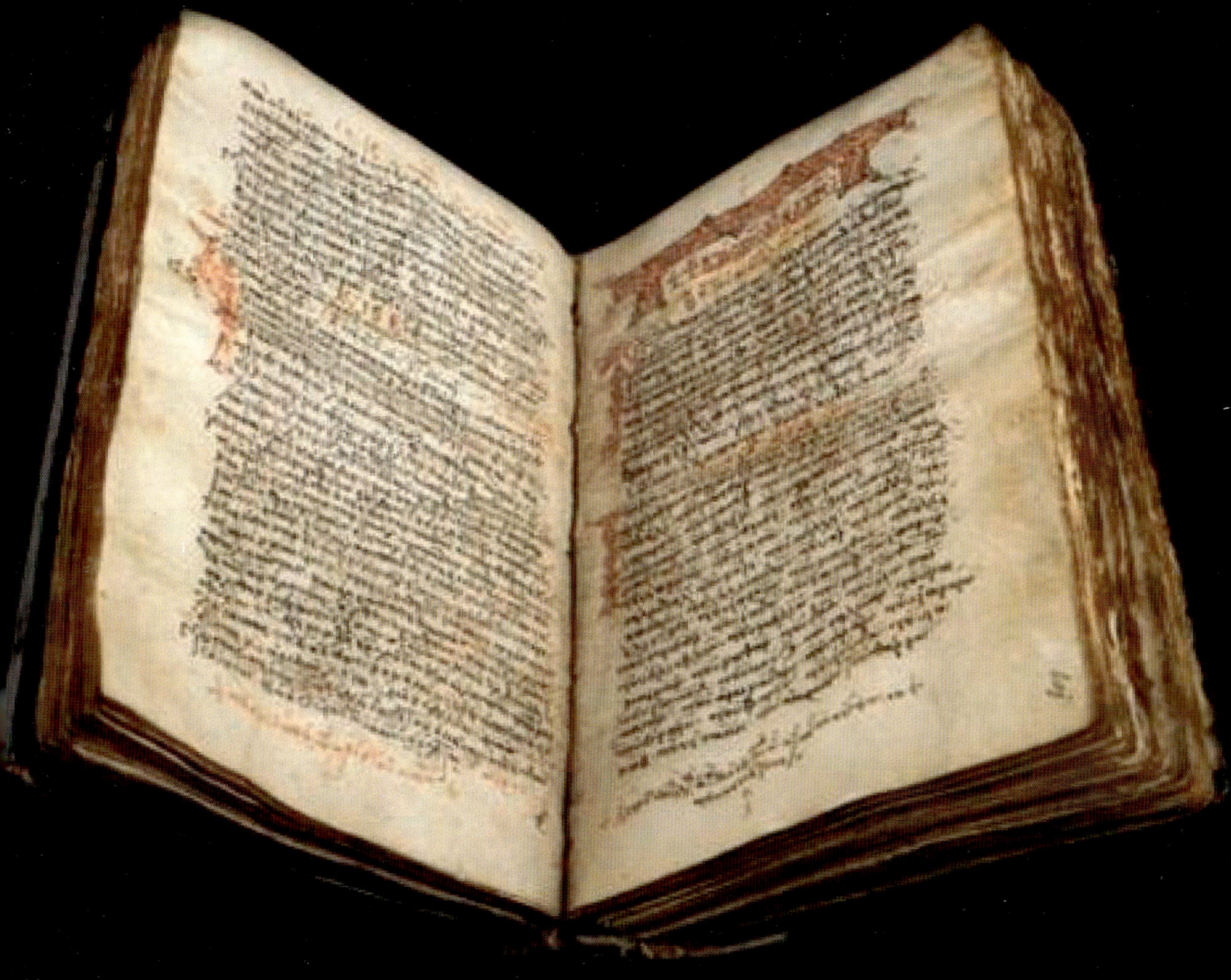

The letters of St Thomas to Edessa

The Citadel, Edessa, Turkey.
Photograph: Nicholas Talbot-Rice (2013).

There is one very definite statement in early Syriac literature to the effect that he sent letters from India; and there is abundance of indirect evidence that such a letter as we have described lay in Edessa until the close of the second century at least.

In all references to Thomas in literature arising from Edessa, the Apostle is called Judas Thomas; and it seems clear that the double name comes from the Apostle's letter. In writing the letter he would inevitably use his own name, and would naturally add to it the word for "twin," which had been so universally used instead of his real name.

There are two possibilities of Thomas the Apostle writing to the Church in Edessa from Taxila and from Malabar.
As soon as he was settled in Muziris, he would wish to communicate, if possible, with Habban. If Gudnaphar had a Trade Agent (panyadyaksha) in the port of Muzeris as seems probable, he would arrange to forward Thomas's letter at the first opportunity. Otherwise, Thomas would get one of his commercial friends to send the letter by the first ship sailing to the Indus. If St Thomas had sent a letter from Taxila to Edessa with the news of his arrival in Gudnaphar's capital he would be most eager to write again to the Church, to tell them about his new field.

Trade between the Persian Gulf and India began at very early dates and plays a large part in Indian commerce to-day. In the first century, we hear of ships sailing from Charax Spasini, Apologus, and the other ports of the Gulf to Barygaza and other Indian markets. Thus, when a ship arrived in Muziris from Charax, it would be possible, on its return voyage, to send by it a letter, which, delivered to an agent in Charax, would be sent by road to Edessa.

A little to the south-west of the pool complex was the Church of St John and St Addai, one of the most highly revered in Edessa because, as universally believed in the first millennium, it had been Addai, as one of Jesus' seventy 'outer circle' of disciples, who had brought Christianity to Edessa only very shortly after Jesus' crucifixion, healing Edessa's king of the time, Abgar, and converting him to Christianity.

At the end of the 5th century both Addai's remains, and those of Abgar, were reverently exhumed from their tombs outside Edessa's walls and reburied in a special silver shrine within this church, a church later embellished by the Crusaders.

Because to the early Edessans Addai was essentially their exact equivalent of St Peter for Rome, many of the city's bishops and other leading lights chose to be buried in this church, as close as possible to their founding predecessor. Further south still, here by a stream fed from Edessa's long-renowned spring, stood the Basilica of St Thomas, so named because that was universally supposed to be where the body of the apostle himself was laid after its having been brought from India in the fourth century AD. An abbess of that time, Egeria (or Etheria), travelled all the way from Spain to pray at this shrine as part of her 'Grand Tour', and she wrote a travel diary which not only describes her visit, but also provides our best description of Edessa as it looked in this early period. One feature that Egeria particularly remarked on then, and which you can still see today, is the *baliklar* or fish pool, brimming with carp too sacred for anyone to catch.

The Fishpond of Abraham, Edessa, Turkey. The church in Edessa, destroyed in 201 after a flood, was the oldest known Christian edifice. Photograph: Nicholas Talbot-Rice (2013).

Just across the stream from this pool here stood the earlier mentioned Monophysite or Jacobite church of the Mother of God. Just a short walk eastwards, but demanding a climb up onto the city's citadel was the Monophysites' Church of St Theodore, a location in which, according to one Edessan story, the Image of Edessa alias the Shroud was kept for a while in a subterranean chapel between this and the Mary, Mother of God Church.

Bardesanes of Edessa and St Pantaenus

Tomb portrait of an Egyptian priest, 2nd c. AD, The Benaki Museum, Athens, Greece (2010).

Bardesanes of Edessa (154-223), was a Syrian poet, astrologist, and philosopher born of wealthy Persian or Parthian parents. Though he started as a Gnostic he became a strong Christian. He is said to have visited Kerala and met the Gnostic Manicaen in Ranny. He is probably the poet who wrote "*The Acts of Thomas*". He reports that in his time there were Christian tribes in North India which claimed to have been converted by St Thomas and to have books and relics to prove it. But at least by the time of the establishment of the Second Persian Empire (AD 226), there were bishops of the Church of the East in north-west India, Afghanistan and Baluchisten, with laymen and clergy alike engaging in missionary activity.

St Pantaenus (180–216) was a Christian theologian who founded the Catechetical School of Alexandria c. 190. This school was the earliest catechetical school, and became influential in the development of Christian theology. Pantaenus was a Stoic philosopher teaching in Alexandria. He converted to the Christian faith, and sought to reconcile his new faith with Greek philosophy. Pantaenus initiated the study of Christian theology, on the interpretation of the Bible, the Trinity, and Christology. Being familiar with the Gnostic movement, he was the main supporter of Serapion of Antioch in acting against the influence of Gnosticism. A deputation from India reached Alexandria some time in AD 179 or 189. In 189 Pantaenus himself went on a missionary tour to India, and Eusebius says that he brought home with him the Gospel of Matthew, in Hebrew, that had been carried to India by St Bartholomew. (St Bartholomew's mission was in Kalyan near Bombay.) Some believe that the name Bartholomew is a corruption of Mar Thoma.

St Pantaenus brought the gospel back with him to Alexandria, where he returned after several years instructing the Indians in the faith. St Pantaenus continued to teach in private till c. 216.
His most famous student, Clement (AD 150 - 215), was his successor as head of the Catechetical School.

(Eusebius, *Church History V.10*).

The Tur Abdin

The hills of the Tur Abdin near Mardin, Eastern Turkey (2013).

St Thomas reputedly passed through the mountainous plateau of the Tur Abdin region of Eastern Turkey (the Mountain of the Servants of God in Syriac), the eastern half of the province of Mardin, and the province of Şırnak, west of the Tigris between the cities of Mardin (to the west), Nusaybin (to the south), Hasankeyf (to the north) and Cizre (to the east).

Since the fourth century it has been, and remains, the heartland of Syriac Christianity: its name is tied to the many monasteries that sprang up in the region in early Christian history. One of them, the Monastery of Mor Gabriel, is the oldest functioning Christian monastery in the world. The litany in the churches and monasteries of the Tur Abdin area is still in Aramaic, the language of both Jesus and St Thomas.

The plateau dominates and looks down on the wide plains of Syria and was a stronghold of Zoroastrianism in the period of St Thomas' visit.

Blessed art thou, Thomas

Blessed art thou, Thomas, the Twin, in thy deeds !
twin is thy spiritual power ; nor one thy power, nor one thy name:
But many and signal are they ; renowned is thy name among the Apostles.
From my lowly state thee I haste to sing.
Blessed art thou, O Light, like the lamp, the sun amidst darkness hath placed;
the earth darkened with sacrifices' fumes to illuminate. A land of people dark fell to
thy lot that these in white robes thou shouldest clothe   and cleanse by baptism: a
tainted land Thomas has purified the solar ray from
the great orb; thy grateful dawn India's painful darkness doth dispel.
Thou the great lamp, one among the Twelve, with oil from the Cross replenished,
India's dark night floodest with light.

Blessed art thou whom the Great King hath sent,
that India to his One-Begotten thou shouldest espouse;
above snow and linen white, thou the dark bride didst make fair.
Blessed art thou, who the unkempt hast adorned, that having become
beautiful and radiant, to her Spouse she might advance.
Blessed art thou, who hast faith in the bride,
whom from heathenism, from demons' errors,
and from enslavement to sacrifices thou didst rescue.
Her with saving bath thou cleansest, the sunburnt thou hast made fair,
the Cross of Light her darkened shades effacing.

Blessed art thou, O merchant, a treasure who broughtest where
so greatly it was needed; thou the wise man, who to secure
the great pearl, of thy riches all else thou givest;
The finder it enriches and ennobles:
indeed thou art the merchant who the world endowest!
Blessed art thou, O Thrice-Blessed City! that hast acquired this pearl,
none greater doth India yield;
Blessed art thou, worthy to possess the priceless gem! Praise to thee,
Son, Who thus Thy adorers dost enrich!

St Ephraim the Syrian,
c. 306-373

This hymn is in regular use, even if in different versions.

Young Tamil girl with Vishnavite markings in tumeric paste, Tamil Nafu, India (2015).

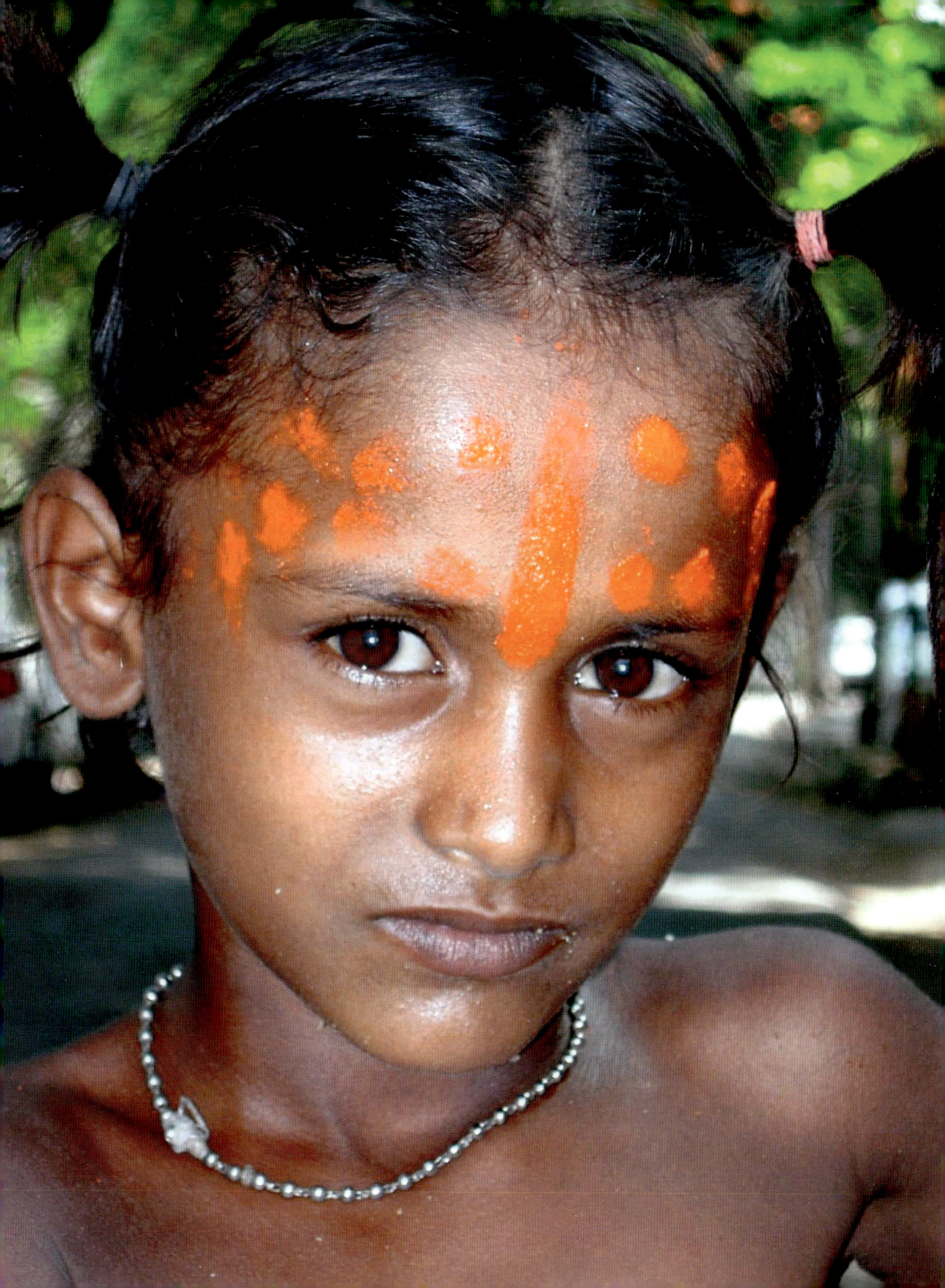

French and Spanish accounts

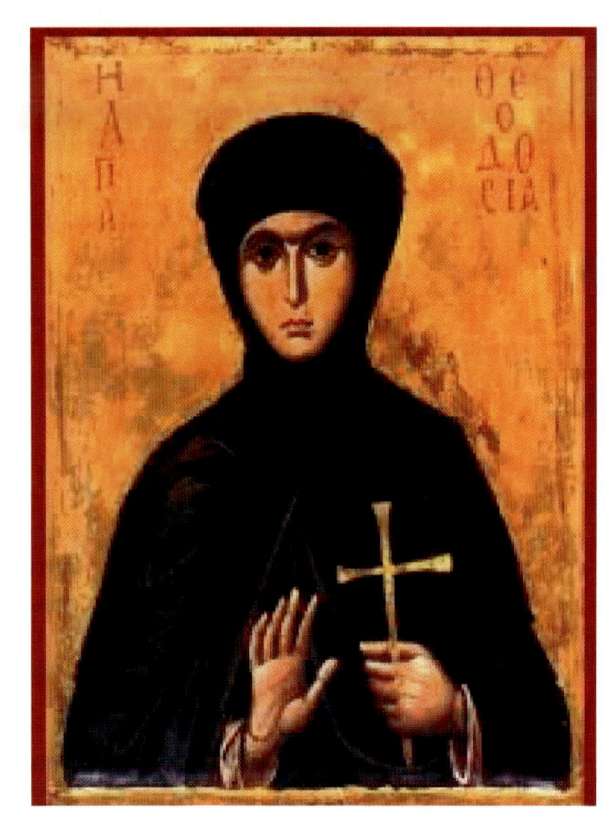

Greek Orthodox icon of St Theodosia, tempera and gold on panel, early 13th c. Constantinople, the Holy Monastery of St Catherine, Sinai, Egypt.

Egeria the Abbess, describing her visit to the Holy Land and the other Holy Places in a letter of 381-384: *Itinerario Egeriae* that she sent to her community of nuns at home:

"We arrived at Edessa in the Name of Christ our God, and, on our arrival, we straightway repaired to the church and memorial of saint Thomas. There, according to custom, prayers were made and the other things that were customary in the holy places were done; we read also some things concerning saint Thomas himself. The church there is very great, very beautiful and of new construction, well worthy to be the house of God, and as there was much that I desired to see, it was necessary for me to make a three days' stay there."

"Thomas the Apostle, according to the narrative of his martyrdom is stated to have suffered in India. His holy remains (corpus), after a long interval of time, were removed to the city of Edessa in Syria and there interred. In that part of India where they first rested, stand a monastery and a church of striking dimensions, elaborately adorned and designed. This Theodore, who had been to the place, narrated to us."

St Gregory of Tours,
538-594.

"This Thomas preached the Gospel of Christ to the Parthians, the Medes, the Persians, the Hyrcanians and the Bactrians, and to the Indians of the Oriental region and penetrating the innermost regions and sealing his preaching by his passion, he died transfixed with a lance at Calamina (present-day Mylapore), a city of India, and there was buried with honour."

St Isidore of Seville,
560-630.

English accounts

"Peter receives Rome, Andrew Achaia; James Spain; Thomas India; John Asia.

St Bede the Venerable,
 c. 673-735.

"In the year 883, Alfred, King of England, hearing that there existed a Christian church in the Indies, dedicated to the memory of St Thomas and St Bartholomew, dispatched one Sighelm, or Sithelm, a favourite ecclesiastic of his court, to carry his royal alms to that distant shrine. Sighelm successfully executed the honourable commission with which he had been entrusted, and returned in safety into England."

William of Malmesbury,
1080-1143.
De Gestis Regum Anglorum.

According to the Anglo Saxon Chronicle, King Alfred of Wessex (reigned 871-899) - he of the burned cakes - sent Bishop Sighelm of Sherborne "to St Thomas in India"; years later, the bishop returned (883-884) carrying with him "precious stones and the odiferous essences of that country" referring to the gifts sent by King Alfred to "St Thomas in India".

What seems stranger still, he sent an embassy all the way to India, with alms for the Christians there, called the Christians of St Thomas and St Bartholomew.

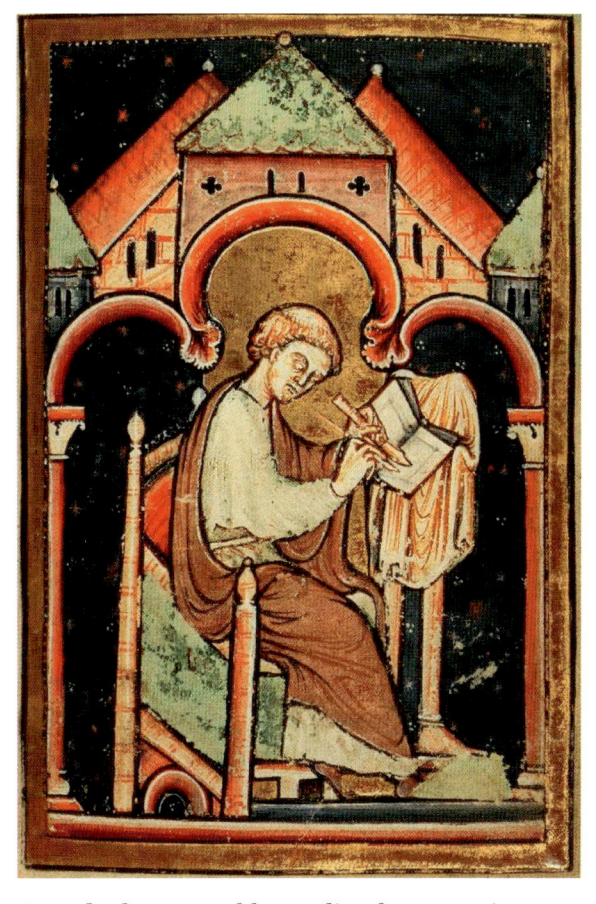

St Bede the Venerable, medieval manuscript.

Asser, Bishop of Sherborne, died, and was succeeded (as bishop) by Swethelm, who carried King Alfred's Alms to St Thomas in India and returned thence in safety.

On one occasion to the Indian Christians at Meliapur (Mylapore) Alfred also sent gifts. Swithelm, the bearer of the royal alms, brought back to the king several oriental pearls, and aromatic liquors.

3.
The journey by land to Parthia:

Syria
Turkey
Iraq
Iran
Afghanistan
Pakistan

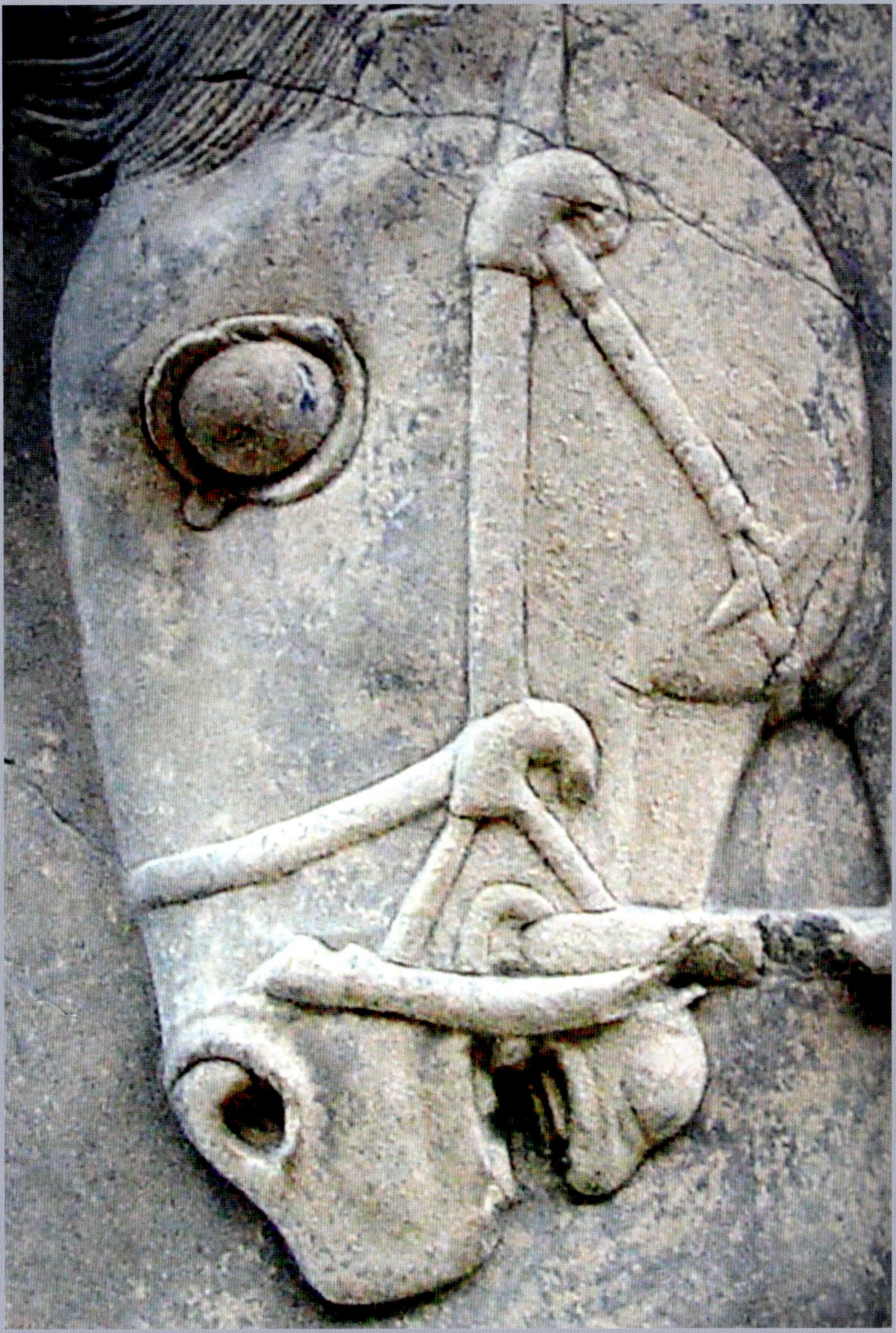

Antioch

Roman sarcophagus showing a fire altar, 1st c. AD. The Archaeological Museum, Antioch, Turkey. Photograph: Claire-Lise Presel (2007).

As the capital of the Roman Province of Syria, it is likely that St Thomas went to Antioch where St Peter was preaching and where he might have met St Paul with St Barnabas.

Then Barnabas went to Tarsus to look for Saul, and when he found him, he brought him to Antioch. So for a whole year Barnabas and Saul met with the church and taught great numbers of people. The disciples were called Christians first at Antioch.

Acts 11:25, 26

The Church traces its origins to the Christian community founded in Antioch by people known as "Followers of the Way," and was later recognised by the Apostle St Peter. St Paul was one of its leading members. It later became one of the five major patriarchates of the state church of the Roman Empire. According to Acts 11:19-26, the Christian community at Antioch began when Christians who were scattered from Jerusalem because of persecution fled to Antioch. Tradition holds that the first Gentile church was founded here, where it is recorded that the disciples of Jesus Christ were first called Christians.

After the dispersion of the original Church at Jerusalem, following the stoning of Stephen, certain Cypriote and Cyrenaic Jews, who had been brought up in Greek communities and who had different perspectives on the world than the Palestinian Jews, came to Antioch. There they made the "innovation" of addressing not merely Jews but also Greeks. The words used imply successful preaching and the admission of Greeks to the Christian congregation, and that such an innovation took place by slow degrees, and began in the synagogue, where Greek proselytes heard the word.

Antioch is intimately connected with the early history of the gospel and St Matthew's gospel is thought to have been written here. It was the great central point from where missionaries to the Gentiles were sent out, so it is likely that St Thomas, at the very least, passed through Antioch on his way east.

Overleaf: Marble relief, Persepolis, fifth c. BC Iran (2007).

Now in the church at Antioch there were prophets and teachers: Barnabas, Simeon called Niger, Lucius of Cyrene, Manaen (who had been brought up with Herod the Tetrarch) and Saul (Acts 11:26). The cave church where St Peter preached and where Christians were first called Christians. Photograph: Claire-Lise Presel (2007).

The Nestorians: the Church of the East

Nestorian cross with *flora sinensis* at the bottom, Sri Lanka (2016).

In AD 431 cataclysmic events were afoot in Constantinople. As the Byzantine emperor frantically prepared for a cosmic confrontation with the Sassanian Persians to the East, the Church found itself in a threatening predicament of its own. The third ecumenical council had convened for over a month in the Aegean port of Ephesus, where 150 of the Christian World's most prominent theologians and ecclesiastical dignitaries had been feuding over pressing issues of church and doctrine. The Archbishop of Constantinople, Nestorius, was the main topic of discussion here. Nestorius had daringly argued in his sermons that Christ's human and divine natures were distinct - a doctrine known as dyophysitism, literally "two natures"; as opposed to mono, or miaphysitism, "one nature". As a result, Nestorius declared that the Virgin Mary must be referred to by the Greek title *Christokos* "Christ-bearer," in place of the suggestively monophysite *Theotokos*, or "God-bearer". After a series of tempestuous deliberations, the synod made its decision: Nestorius was officially condemned in five separate canons produced at the council, declared a heretic, excommunicated from Christianity, and exiled from the realm. The deposed Patriarch gathered his followers and embarked on an exodus to the East, all the time insisting his ideals were in fact "orthodox". But Nestorius was not alone – the Council's findings were rejected by many of the attendees from the fringes of the Byzantine Empire, including the Syriacs, the Egyptians, the Ethiopians and the Armenians, all of whom thereafter became alienated from Western Christendom.

These dramatic events in the fifth century AD amounted to the "Nestorian Schism", which gave birth to the Persian Church (the Church of the East) and resulted in the dissemination of Nestorius' creed from Egypt in the west to China in the east.

Within a short period, the Nestorians would reach the T'ang court at Chang'an (Xi'an), and would enjoy evangelical success among Mongol tribesmen, Sogdian merchants, Chinese sailors, and South Indian farmers.

Lotus flower, Sri Lanka, the base of all Mar Thoma crosses (2014).

Miaphysites and Nestorian Christians of the Church of the East

The ruins of Nisibis, Eastern Turkey (2013).

The difference between Miaphysites and Nestorian Christians of the Church of the East is that the Miaphysites are following St Cyril of Alexandria's Christology but they disagree with the terminology the Fourth Ecumenical Council (AD 451) has employed to express St Cyril's teaching. So they use very much the term *Mia Physis* without alternating it with the term *Mia Hypostasis* as Cyril did.

The Church of the East are following faithfully Nestorius' teaching on *Dyo Physis* (two natures) in Christ without accepting the doctrine on *Dyo Physeis* introduced by the Fourth Ecumenical Council. So both Churches remain Anti-Chalcedonian Churches to this day.

Archimandrite Maximus Lavriotes,
Peterhouse College Cambridge.

Nestorianism

Nestorianism is a Christological doctrine that emphasises the disunion between the human and divine natures of Jesus. It was advanced by Nestorius (386–450), Patriarch of Constantinople from 428 to 431, influenced by Nestorius' studies under Theodore of Mopsuestia at the School of Antioch. Nestorius' teachings brought him into conflict with other prominent church leaders, most notably Cyril of Alexandria, who criticised his rejection of the title Theotokos (Bringer forth of God) for the Virgin Mary. Monophysitism survived and developed into the Miaphysitism of the modern Oriental Orthodox churches. Following the exodus to Persia, scholars expanded on the teachings of Nestorius and his mentors, particularly after the relocation of the School of Edessa to the Persian city of Nisibis in 489 (where it became known as the School of Nisibis). Nestorius and his teachings were eventually condemned as heretical at the First Council of Ephesus in 431 and the Council of Chalcedon in 451, leading to the Nestorian Schism, in which churches supporting Nestorius broke with the rest of the Christian Church. Following that, many of Nestorius's supporters relocated to the Sasanian Empire, where they affiliated with the local Christian community, known as the Church of the East. Over the next decades the Church of the East became increasingly Nestorian in doctrine, leading to it becoming known alternately as the Nestorian Church. Nestorianism never again became prominent in the Roman Empire or later in Europe, though the diffusion of the Church of the East in and after the seventh century spread it widely across Asia. But not all churches affiliated with the Church of the East appear to have followed Nestorian Christology; indeed, the modern Assyrian Church of the East, which reveres Nestorius, does not follow all historically Nestorian doctrine. Nestorianism is a form of dyophysitism, and can be seen as the antithesis to monophysitism, which emerged in reaction to Nestorianism. Where Nestorianism holds that Christ had two loosely united natures, divine and human: monophysitism holds that he had but a single nature, his human nature being absorbed into his divinity.

Nestorian Christology can be given as: "Jesus Christ, who is not identical with the Son but personally united with the Person of the Son, who lives within him the human, is one hypostasis and one nature."

Despite this initial Eastern expansion, the Nestorians' missionary success was eventually deterred. By the end of the fourteenth century, however, the Nestorian and other churches - which at one time had dotted the landscape of all of Central and parts of East Asia were all but wiped out. Isolated pockets of Christianity survived only in India. The religious victors on the vast Central Asian mission field of the Nestorians were Islam and Buddhism.

Mosul

Iraq's Eastern Aramaic-speaking Assyrian communities are believed to be among the oldest in the world.

Christianity was brought to Iraq in the first century AD by Thomas the Apostle and Mar Addai (Thaddeus of Edessa) and his pupils Aggai and Mari.

Mosul stands on the west bank of the River Tigris, opposite the ancient Assyrian city of Nineveh on the east bank, but the metropolitan area has now grown to encompass substantial areas on both banks. Until 2014 the city was a historic centre of Assyrian Nestorian Christianity, containing the tombs of several Old Testament prophets including Jonah. The name of the city is first mentioned by Xenophon in 401 BC.

Mosul succeeded Nineveh as the Tigris bridgehead of the road that linked Syria and Anatolia with the Median Empire. Cyrus the Great, together with the alliance of Nabopolassar king of Babylon and the Sagartians, conquered Nineveh in 612 BC. It became part of the Seleucid Empire after Alexander's conquests in 332 BC. While little is known of the city from the Hellenistic period, Mosul belonged to the Seleucid satrapy of Mesopotamia, which was conquered by the Parthian Empire in a series of wars that ended in 129 BC with the victory of Phraates II over the Seleucid king Antiochus VII.

St Thomas made Mosul his headquarters when the Assyrians converted to Christianity during the first and second centuries. St Thomas made many converts in Mosul, a city which had a large Jewish population in the first century AD.

The city changed hands once again with the rise of Sassanid Persia in AD 225. Christianity was present among the indigenous Assyrian people in Mosul as early as the 2nd century.

Mosul became an episcopal seat of the Nestorian faith in the 6th century. In 637 during the period of the Caliph Umar ibn al-Khattab, the city was annexed to the Rashidun Caliphate.

A community of Assyrian Christians also had a presence in the villages around Mosul; the majority followed the Catholic, the Syriac Catholic and the Syriac Orthodox Church, and a minority followed the Assyrian Church of the East. There were also a number of Arab Christians belonging to the Greek Orthodox Church, the Roman Catholic Church, the Chaldean Catholic Church, the Syriac Orthodox Church, and a number of Protestant churches. Long before the Muslim conquest of the seventh century, the old city of Nineveh also became a Christian city.

Syrian Orthodox Bishop Sakar in the doorway of St Thomas' church, Mosul. Iraq.

Photograph: Jane Taylor (1991).

شيد بلس عبد

قداسة الحبر الأعظم		غبطة مار اغناطيوس
مار اغناطيوس	✠	يعقوب الثالث بطريرك
يعقوب الثالث بطريرك		انطاكية وسائر المشرق
انطاكية وسائر المشرق		
١٩٦٥ سنة		

Hatra

The Great Temple of Hatra, one of thirteen temples that are a part of the Shrine of Hatra, Iraq. Photograph: Jane Taylor (2001).

The city of Hatra on an important trade route south of Mosul and 180 miles northwest of Baghdad in the ancient Persian province of Khvarvaran was probably built in the 3rd or 2nd century BC by the Seleucid Empire. Between 161 and 140 BC, as Mithradates I conquered the entire Iranian plateau, Parthia began to extend westward, threatening the Seleucids. The struggle over Mesopotamia intensified, and by 126 BC, Mesopotamia was in Parthian hands. After its capture it flourished during the 1st and 2nd centuries AD as a religious and trading centre, famed for its fusion of Greek, Mesopotamian, Canaanite, Aramean and Arabian pantheons.

Except for a brief period of Roman rule under Emperor Trajan, c. AD 117, during the lengthy wars between Rome and Parthia, Hatra was an important fortified frontier city which withstood repeated attacks by the Roman Empire and played an important role in the Second Parthian War. It repulsed the sieges of both Trajan (116-117) and Septimius Severus (198-199).

It is almost certain that St Thomas would have spent some time in both Hatra and Babylon, then in Parthian hands.

Babylon

By the time Parthian rule was secure, Babylon was a virtual ruin, but the Parthians restored the city; traces of a large building with a pillared hall have been found near the temple of Marduk, and the theatre was rebuilt.

St Thomas would have seen and passed under the Ishtar Gate as he entered the city whose large Jewish community thrived as a centre of Jewish learning. The Jews had a Babylonian as their high priest, which indicates the importance enjoyed by the Jews here. In religious matters the Babylonians, as indeed the whole diaspora, were in many regards dependent upon Judea and went on pilgrimages to Jerusalem for the festivals.

A few cuneiform texts were still produced during this time by the very last generation to use this writing system, mainly mathematical and astronomical documents, with the latest known dated text from Babylon about AD 75. After that, and some 5000 years of continuous existence, cuneiform as a form of communication was abandoned forever.

Glazed tiles of a bull from the Ishtar Gate, Babylon, Iraq. The Archaeological Museum, Istanbul, Turkey (2013).

Lake Orumieh

Orumieh, in north-west Iran, is the largest lake in the Middle East and the third-largest salt lake on earth: it dates from the period of the Flood and has more than 100 rocky islands. Like the Dead Sea, Lake Orumieh is full of minerals and salts which are used to cure various ailments such as rheumatism. The lake is one of the environmental wonders of the world; however, it has shrunk by 60% and could disappear entirely within a few years.

St Thomas passed this way along the Royal Road from Babylon to Persepolis and founded a church dedicated to the Virgin Mary in Orumiyeh, built over a Zoroastrian temple where the Three Magi are said to have built a shrine, having returned from Palestine. Dating to the Sassanian period, it was destroyed in 1918.

Orurmia's Christians are Armenian, Assyrian, Chaldean and Nestorian. Today their population is small, but the number of stone built churches in the city constructed mainly between the fourth and seventh centuries AD is a testimony to their historical roots.

Further west down the Royal Road taken by all travellers is Mount Behistun (along whose hillside is carved the famous rock relief of Darius); it is the branch of the Aryan trade roads that linked Babylon with Ecbatana - Hamadan and Kermanshah.

Early Armenian church, Lake Orumieh, North-West Iran (2016).

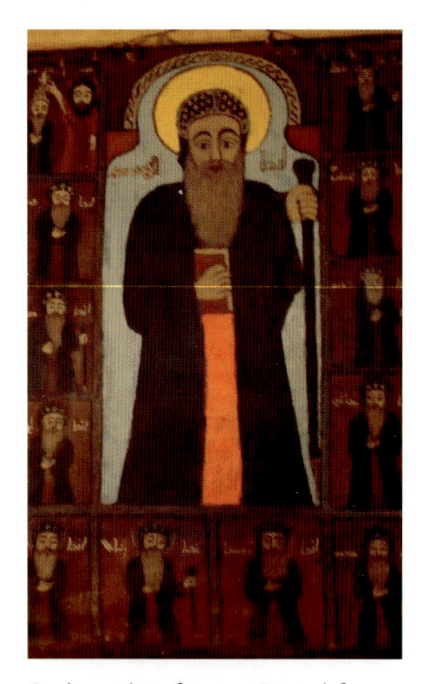

Syriac saint, fresco, Orumieh, North-West Iran (2016).

The Parthian Prince Balash wearing a typical tunic and baggy trousers pouring incense onto a fire altar to celebrate the victory of Gotarzes II over his enemy Mehrdad, AD 50, Bisitun, Kermanshah province, Iran (2016).

Bisitun

Takht-e-Soleyman

The World Heritage fortified archaeological site of Takht-e-Soleyman, also known as "the Fire of the Warrior Kings", is built on a volcano crater rim. It lies midway between Urmia and Hamadan in North-West Iran. The citadel includes the remains of a Zoroastrian fire temple built during the Sassanid period on a previous Parthian site, which was partially rebuilt during the Ilkhanid period. (The site got this Semitic name after the Arab conquest.) Its temple housed one of the three "Great Fires" or "Royal Fires" before which the Sassanid rulers humbled themselves in order to ascend the throne. The fire at Takht-e-Soleyman was called *ādur Wishnāsp* and was dedicated to the warrior class of the Sassanids.

Archaeological excavations have revealed traces of 5th-century BC occupation during the Achaemenid period, as well as later Parthian settlements in the citadel. Coins belonging to the reign of Sassanid kings, and that of the Byzantine Emperor Theodosius II (408-450), have also been discovered there.

St Thomas would almost certainly have come to this, the holiest site in Zoroastrianism, as he travelled through Parthia.

Left: The volcanic crater at Takht-e-Soleyman, filled with constantly flowing spring water, has many water channels flowing from it which water the surrounding area (2016).
Below: The remains of the "Great Fire" in the Fire Temple, Takht-e-Soleyman, North-West Iran (2016).

Ecbatana - Hamadan

In 324 BC Alexander the Great set up this stone lion in memory of his dear friend Hephaestion - one part of the 'Lions Gate' which sits on a hill where a Parthian era cemetery was said to be located; the Lion of Hamadan as evidence for Hephaestion's remains being in Ecbatana. Aelian, who in his story of gold and silver being melted together with the corpse on Hephaestion's pyre, speaks of Alexander's having demolished the walls of the acropolis of Ecbatana and gives no hint that the pyre was supposed to have been in Babylon. Hamadan, Iran (2016).

Hamadan is believed to be among the oldest Iranian cities and one of the oldest in the world. It is possible that it was occupied by the Assyrians in 1100 BC; the Greek historian, Herodotus, states that it was the capital of the Medes, around 700 BC. Hamadan is mentioned in the biblical book of Ezra as the place where a scroll was found giving the Jews permission from King Darius to rebuild the Temple in Jerusalem. (Ezra 6:2). Its ancient name of Ecbatana is used in the Ezra text. Because it was a mile above sea level, it was a good place to preserve leather documents.

During the Parthian era (247 BC to AD 224), Ctesiphon was the capital of the country, and Hamadan the summer capital and residence of the Parthian rulers. It is almost certain that St Thomas would have visited Hamadan on his journey through Parthia; it still had a large Jewish population who would initially have made him welcome. The supposed tomb of Queen Esther and her uncle, Mordechai, was venerated here; today it is the most important pilgrimage site for Jews in Iran.

According to the biblical book named after her, Esther was a beautiful young Jewish woman who caught the eye of the Persian King Xerxes, became Queen, and with the assistance of her uncle, Mordechai, saved all the Jews throughout the Persian Empire from annihilation. Every year in March, on the holiday of Purim, Jews around the world celebrate this miraculous salvation by reading the Book of Esther, dressing in costumes, and eating delicacies.

Mount Alvand, which overlooks the city, housed the summer residence of the Persian royalty of the Achaemenid Empire (the period when the Purim story is believed to have happened). Tradition has it that Esther and Mordechai - after spending their final years at the royal court - were buried in the city, next to one another, with a shrine constructed over their graves. While the date of the original shrine is unknown, its date of destruction at the hands of Mongol invaders occurred in the 14th century. Historian Ernst Herzfeld contends that the current structure of 1602 may actually belong to Shushan Dokht, the Jewish queen of King Yazdegerd I (c. 399-420 AD), who is credited with securing permission for Jews to live in Hamadan.

Hebrew verse on the wall; the tomb of Esther and Mordechai, Hamadan, Iran (2016).

Greater Armenia

The sixth c. Armenian church of the Mother of God on the River Arax-Gihon, one of the four rivers of Paradise, marking the border with Azerbaijan. Julfa, North-West Iran (2016).

Greater Armenia is the name given to the state of Armenia that emerged on the Armenian Highlands during the reign of King Artaxias I at the turn of the second century BC. The term was used to refer to Armenian kingdoms throughout the classical, late antique, and medieval periods by contemporary Armenian and non-Armenian authors alike. Though its borders were in a constant state of flux, Greater Armenia roughly encompassed the area stretching from the Euphrates River in the west, the region of Artsakh and parts of contemporary Iranian Azerbaijan to the east, parts of the modern state of Georgia to the north, with its southern boundary abutting the northern tip of Mesopotamia.

The Kingdom of Armenia existed from 321 BC to 428 AD. Its history is divided into successive reigns by three royal dynasties: Orontid (321–200 BC), Artaxiad (189 BC to AD 12) and Arsacid (AD 52–428). The root of the kingdom lies in one of the satrapies of the Achaemenid Empire of Persia which was formed from the territory of the Kingdom of Ararat (860–590 BC) after it was conquered by the Median Empire in 590 BC. The satrapy of Armenia became a kingdom in 321 BC during the reign of the Orontid dynasty after the conquest of Persia by Alexander the Great, which was then incorporated as one of the Hellenistic kingdoms of the Seleucid Empire.

Under the Seleucid Empire (312-63 BC), the Armenian throne was divided in two – Armenia Maior and Sophene – both of which passed to members of the Artaxiad dynasty in 189 BC. During the Roman Republic's eastern expansion, the Kingdom of Armenia, under Tigranes the Great, reached its peak, from 83 to 69 BC, after it reincorporated Sophene and conquered the remaining territories of the falling Seleucid Empire, effectively ending its existence and raising Armenia into an empire for a brief period, until it was itself conquered by Rome in 69 BC. The remaining Artaxiad kings ruled as clients of Rome until they were overthrown in AD 12 due to their possible allegiance to Rome's main rival, Parthia.

St Thaddeus

During the Roman-Parthian Wars, the Arsacid dynasty of Armenia was founded when Tiridates I, a member of the Parthian Arsacid dynasty, was proclaimed King of Armenia in AD 52. Throughout most of its history during this period, Armenia was heavily contested between Rome and Parthia. From 114 to 118, Armenia briefly became a province of the Roman Empire under Emperor Trajan. The Kingdom of Armenia often served as a client state or vassal at the frontier of the two large empires and their successors, the Byzantine and Sassanid empires. In 301, Tiridates III proclaimed Christianity as the state religion of Armenia, making the Armenian Kingdom the first state officially to embrace Christianity.

St Thomas would have passed this way and it is believed that his friend St Thaddeus of Edessa, one of the Seventy Disciples of Jesus, was martyred here sometime around the year AD 65. According to tradition, the first church was built on the site around AD 68, a few years after Thaddeus' death. Over the centuries this was replaced by a series of larger churches, including one from the 10th century and one from the 14th century.

The monastery church of St Thaddeus, Julfa, North-West Iran. Photograph: Jane Taylor (2015).

The Province of Fars

"And how hear we every man in our own tongue, wherein we were born? Parthians, and Medes, and Elamites, and the dwellers in Mesopotamia . . ."

The Parthian Empire is the first of the homelands mentioned by the Jewish pilgrims to Jerusalem in the account of Pentecost in Acts 2.

The Mede and Elamite empires had been replaced or subsumed by the Parthian Empire. Mesopotamia is the area between the Tigris and Euphrates rivers, in southern Turkey and Iraq, with the heartland of Media to the east, and that of Elam lying on the Persian Gulf south of Media. The Parthian Empire lasted from 247 BC to AD 224 and geographically included the modern states of Iran, Iraq, and much of Syria, Afghanistan and even Pakistan.

Between 40 and 37 BC, they even occupied Jerusalem, in the form of their Jewish puppet king Antigonus. This will have left a lasting impact on the Jews of Jesus' time, because Antigonus fought against the Greeks and Romans and their influence.

In 53 BC, the Parthians defeated the Roman army led by Crassus, the general and politician, who was the richest man in Roman history (and who put down the Spartacus revolt).

Hippolytus, who died a martyr during the reign of the Roman Emperor Sirrus (225-235), recorded that "the apostle Thomas after having preached the gospel to the Parthians, Medes, Persians suffered martyrdom at Codamina, a town of India".

Edessa in Syria and Fars in Iran are two places that can be associated with St Thomas with confidence.

There is a long-standing Syriac legend that St Thomas met the biblical Magi in Iran on his way to India. The Syriac martyrologist Rabban Sliba of Hah (the Tur Abdin, Turkey) who died in 1340 dedicated a special day to both the Indian king, his family, and St Thomas.

It is generally accepted that St Thomas established a church in the Province of Fars (southern Iran, from which province the Zoroastrian Parsees also came) and from where many Christian refugees came to Malabar when they were expelled from Iran in the eighth and ninth centuries.

The oldest plane tree in Iran: Fars Province, Iran (2007).

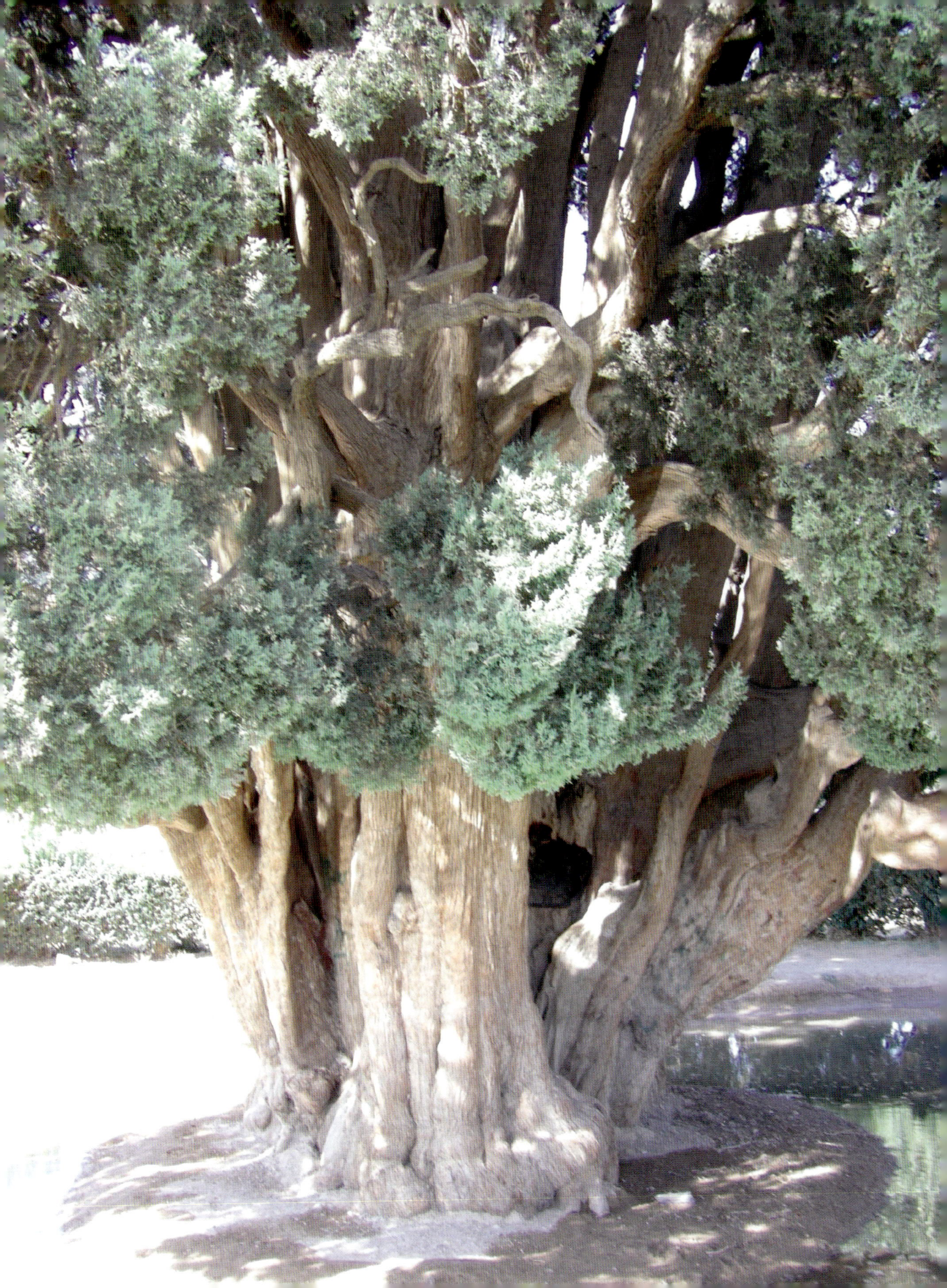

Ahura Mazda

Ahura Mazda, marble column, sixth c. BC, Persepolis, Iran (2007).

Zoroastrianism is one of the world's oldest monotheistic religions. It was founded by the Prophet Zoroaster (or Zarathustra) in ancient Iran approximately 3500 years ago. For a thousand years Zoroastrianism was one of the most powerful religions in the world. It was the official religion of Persia (Iran) from 600 BC to AD and was the religion of the Parthian Empire at the time of St Thomas in the first century AD.

Zoroastrians believe there is one God called Ahura Mazda (Wise Lord) and He created the world. They are not fire-worshippers, but believe that the elements are pure and that fire represents God's light or wisdom and they worship communally in a Fire Temple or *Agiary*. Zoroastrians traditionally pray several times a day.

The Zoroastrian book of Holy Scriptures, The Avesta, can be split roughly into two main sections: The Avesta is the oldest and core part of the scriptures, which contains the Gathas. The Gathas are seventeen hymns thought to be composed by Zoroaster himself. The Younger Avesta is a commentary to the older Avesta, written in later years. It also contains myths, stories and details of ritual observances.

The Towers of Silence

Until forty years ago, corpses could still be found on top of the Towers of Silence in Yazd, Iran, slowly disintegrating or being picked apart by desert vultures.

In the Zoroastrian tradition, once a body ceases to live, it can immediately be contaminated by demons and made impure. To prevent this infiltration, Zoroastrians purified the dead body by exposing it to the elements and local fowl on top of flat-topped towers in the desert called *dakhmas*.

According to a tradition dating back over 3,000 years, bodies were arranged on the towers in three concentric circles. Men were placed in the outer circle, women in the middle, and children in the inner most ring. Bodies were then left until their bones were bleached by the elements and stripped by the vultures.

After the process of purification, bones were placed in ossuaries near, or inside of the towers. Ossuaries from these rituals have been discovered from the fourth and fifth centuries BC.

A similar *dakhma* must have existed in Taxila at the time of King Gondophares.

Dakhma (Tower of Silence), where the Zoroastrian dead are laid out to be devoured by birds, having been washed in one of the small temples below. Yazd, Iran.
Photograph: Jim Wheeler (2007).

The high mountains of the Pamirs

The Pamirs, Tajikistan.
Photograph: Joan Miller (2010).

In the Acts of Thomas, the original key text to identify St Thomas with India (which all other India references follow), historians agree that the term India refers to Parthia (Persia) and Gandhara. The city of Andrapolis named in the Acts, where Judas Thomas and Abbanes landed in India, has been identified as Sandaruk (one of the ancient Alexandrias) in Baluchistan.

"This admitted of the Apostles being sent without delay according to the saying of our Lord Jesus... Even those Kingdoms which were shut out by rugged mountains became accessible to them, as India to Thomas, Persia to Matthew..."

"He (Christ) dwelt in all places: with Thomas in India, Peter at Rome, with Paul in Illyricum."

St Jerome,
(342–420).

Kyrgyzstan

The Silk Roads were not actually called that until 1868 when the German explorer Ferdinand von Richthofen coined the phrase. Beginning during the Han dynasty in 206 BC–AD 220, trade and ideas - and that included religion: Buddhism, Zoroastrianism, Judaism and (from the first century AD), Christianity - began to flow along some 4,000 miles, on a network of roads from China to the Mediterranean, through mountains and deserts and towns that grew up along the way. Merchants, pilgrims, monks, soldiers, nomads, and urban dwellers from China and India, took to the road, principally to satisfy the demands of Rome. The Central Asian sections of the trade routes were expanded around 114 BC by the Han dynasty, largely through the missions and explorations of Chinese imperial envoy, Zhang Qian. The Chinese took great interest in the safety of their trade products and extended the Great Wall of China to ensure the protection of the trade routes.

From its earliest days, Jewish merchants lived and traded in all the major cities and St Thomas would always have found a synagogue and a Jewish audience to welcome him. Aramaic was the *lingua franca* of the route from Parthian India all the way to the Mediterranean, so St Thomas would have had no trouble communicating with everyone he met as he travelled from Jerusalem to Taxila in AD 46.

Mountains along the Silk Road in Kyrgyzstan (2015).

Nestorians on the Silk Roads

Followers of Nestorius moved to Edessa (in Turkey) where they established a theological college. However, this was closed down by Rome and the Nestorians moved further East to Persia. Whilst many settled, the Nestorians were focussed on spreading the Christian Gospel far wider and many became missionaries.

Christianity, like Buddhism and Islam, travelled along the trade routes of the Silk Road, moving ever Eastwards. The Nestorians encouraged not only monks but also lay people to become missionaries. As such, Nestorian traders were able to combine their work and the spreading of their faith, without the need for religious hostelries and church funds, which often hampered monks and other ecclesiastical orders.

The Nestorians were also keen to serve the peoples they met with good works and set up training schools where monks and laypeople would learn about medical work and how to teach literacy.

As a result of their literacy campaigns, the Nestorians taught the White Huns, the Uighars and other Turkic groups to read their own languages. Whilst Nestorians experienced persecution in the West and also amongst some of the Zoroastrian population of Persia, they were also accepted into the courts of many a ruler in Central Asia, valued for their scholarship, hard work and honesty. In some cases this led to the conversion of the King, as was the case in Merv (Turkmenistan) in 644, and there were reputedly many Christian Turkic groups in the lands around the Oxus River. By the eighth century Christianity was well entrenched in Bukhara and the region around the River Oxus. Crosses and other Christian imagery appear on the coinage of that region.

The Arab invasion of Central Asia led to many, including some Christians to convert to Islam. However, once the Caliphate was established, Christians were allowed to practise their faith but not to proselytise, build new churches or display the cross on buildings. They also had to pay the tax that all non-Muslims paid to the Caliph.

Despite these constraints, Nestorians were respected and valued by the Arabs for their scholarship and many Nestorians held important positions in the Arab Caliphate. Most of the Caliphs appointed Nestorians as their personal physicians.

Uighar gentleman, Bokhara, Uzbekistan (2015).

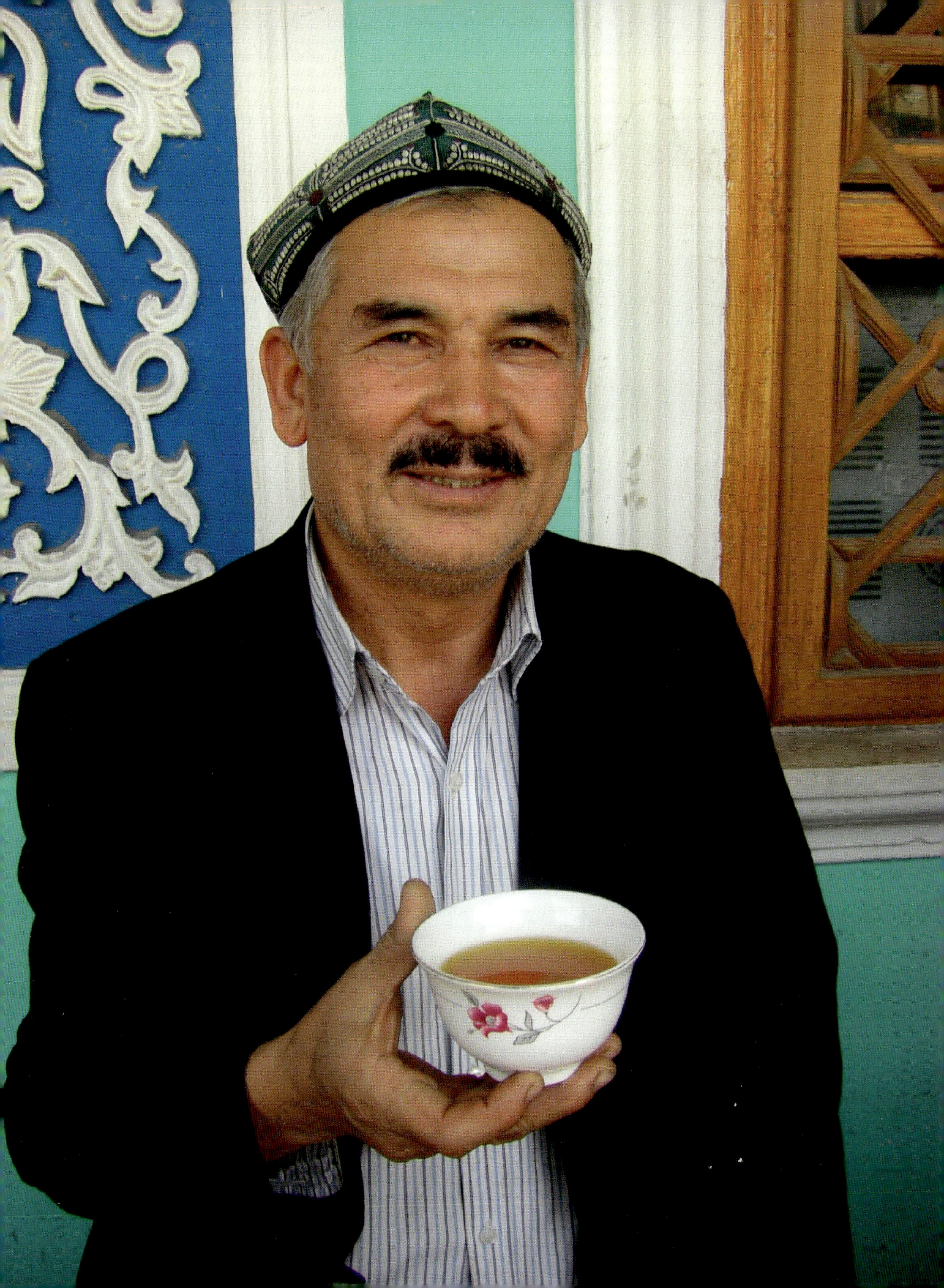

Bukhara

The Magok-i Attari Mosque (now the Museum of Carpets), Bukhara, Uzbekistan, originally a Zoroastrian temple, then a Nestorian church visited by Marco Polo c. 1272 (2015).

The territory of present-day Uzbekistan was at the centre of ancient civilisations from before 1,000 BC. The great trading cities of Samarkand, Bukhara and Khiva grew up at the crossroads of the great caravan routes linking the area with Turkey, the Caucasus, western China, Iran, Afghanistan and India in one large cultural and economic zone. The ancient city of Bukhara was a prominent stop on the Silk Roads between the East and the West, and it is highly likely that St Thomas would have passed through Bukhara on his way east.

The oldest mosque in Bukhara, the Magoki Attari, "the mosque in the pit", is in the centre of the city and was built on a former Zoroastrian fire temple which in turn became a Nestorian church. Before the Arabian conquest, the market for spice and herb sellers (the attars) was established at the site of the mosque. Bukhara became a major medieval centre for Islamic theology and culture as well as trade.

Two-humped camel in front of the Ark, Bukhara, Uzbekistan (2015).

The monastery of Tash Rabat on the Silk Road

The monastery of Tash Rabat, At-Bashy, Kyrgyzstan (2015).

Set at an altitude of 11,500 feet, Tash Rabat was on one of the two routes of the Silk Road that went around Lake Chatyr-Kol and is hidden in a small valley protected from the elements east of the main north-south highway between the Torugart Pass and Koshoy Korgon, a ruined fortress of uncertain date, Tash Rabat is a recently restored 15th century stone caravanserai in the At-Bashy district of Naryn Province, in the remote mountains of Kyrgyzstan and is one of the most intriguing caravanserais in Central Asia.

This was once an important area of Zoroastrian, Buddhist and Nestorian activity. As early as in 1888, a Russian doctor and traveller Nicolai Lovich Zeland, suggested that Tash Rabat was originally a Nestorian or Buddhist monastery. Research undertaken in the late 1970's and early 1980's by the Institute of History of the Kyrgyz Academy of Sciences concluded that it was originally built as a Nestorian monastery in the 10th century, although no Christian artifacts were found during excavations.

The structure consists of 31 rooms including cavities in the central hall. Inside, the dark corridors are lit only by small openings in the roofs and include a well, a dungeon and a mosque. Tash Rabat is completely built of crushed stone on clay.

Trade on the Silk Roads was a significant factor in the development of the civilisations of China, the Indian subcontinent, Persia, Europe, the Horn of Africa and Arabia, opening long-distance, political and economic relations between the civilisations. Though silk was certainly the major trade item from China, many other goods were traded, and religions, syncretic philosophies, and various technologies, as well as diseases, also travelled along this network of routes. In addition to economic trade, the Silk Roads served as a means of carrying out the cultural exchanges of ideas among the diverse civilisations along the way.

Today, we picture the caravans travelling along the Silk Roads from China to the Middle East in a romantic light. This portrayal conceals the real dangers that the journey included, because the Silk Roads crossed some of the most inhospitable regions imaginable, and many travellers died en route. Unlike its name suggests, the Silk Road was not a single route, but a connection of several established tracks, each with its own fair share of threats.

The main traders during antiquity were the Chinese, Persians, Somalis, Greeks, Syrians, Jews, Romans, Armenians, Indians, and Bactrians.

The roads in Kyrgyzstan (2015).

Afghanistan

According to Eusebius' record, the apostles Thomas and Bartholomew were assigned to Parthia (which included north-western Afghanistan), and India. Legend based on the apocryphal Gospel of Thomas and other ancient documents suggests that St Thomas preached in Bactria, which is today northern Afghanistan. The early third-century Syriac work known as the Acts of Thomas connects the apostle's ministry with two kings, one in the north and the other in the south.

It is very likely that St Thomas passed through Bamyan on his way to Taxila.

Bardaisan of Edessa, writing in about 196, speaks of Christians throughout Media, Parthia and Bactria and, according to Tertullian (c.160–230), there were already a number of bishoprics within the Persian Empire by 220. By the time of the establishment of the Second Persian Empire (AD 226), there were bishops of the Church of the East in northwest India, Afghanistan and Baluchistan, with laymen and clergy alike engaging in missionary activity.

In 409, the Church of the East (also sometimes called the Nestorian Church) received state recognition from King Yazdegerd I (reigned 399–409) of the Iranian Sassanid Empire which ruled what is now Afghanistan from 224 to 579.

In 424, Bishop Afrid of Sakastan, an area which covered southern Afghanistan including Zaranj and Kandahar, attended the Synod of Dadyeshu. This synod was one of the most important councils of the Church of the East and determined that there would be no appeal of their disciplinary or theological problems to any other power, especially not to any church council in the Roman Empire. The year 424 also marks the establishment of a bishop in Herat.

Jewish refugees from both the Assyrian and Babylonian captivity in the northwest of India, after fleeing from slavery in Media and Mesopotamia (described in the Bible as the "lost people"), reached the mountainous recesses of Afghanistan, prospecting for blue sapphire in the Bamiyan Valley and plying the caravan trade along the Northern Trade Route and China. These merchants are known to have reached as far as Tamralipti (Calcutta) in India in the east and as deep south as Pondicherry in Tamil Nadu and Muziris (Kodungallur) in Kerala in order to link up with the merchant ships from Rome which used to visit the Malabar coast for spices and sandalwood.

The Bamiyan Buddhas: two monumental statues carved into the side of a cliff in AD 544, a major post on the Silk Road in the Bamiyan valley, the Hazarajat region of central Afghanistan, destroyed by the Taliban in 2001. (1976).

Bamiyan

Jesus, St Thomas and Habban

And our Lord saw him walking in the street, and said to him: "Thou wishest to buy a carpenter?" He saith to him, "Yes." Our Lord saith to him: "I have a slave, a carpenter, whom I will sell to thee." And he showed him Thomas at a distance, and bargained with him for twenty (pieces) of silver (as) his price, and wrote a bill of sale thus: "I, Jesus, the son of Joseph the carpenter, from the village of Bethlehem, which is in Judea, acknowledge, that I have sold my slave Judas Thomas to Habban, the merchant of king Gudnaphar." And when they had completed his bill of sale, Jesus took Judas, and went to Habbān the merchant. And Habbān saw him, and said to him: "Is this thy master?" Judas saith to him: "Yes, he is my master." Habbān the merchant saith to him: "He has sold thee to me outright." And Judas was silent.

And in the morning he arose and prayed, and entreated of his Lord, and said to Him: "Lo, our Lord, as Thou wilt, let Thy will be (done)." And he went to Habbān the merchant, without carrying anything with him except that price of his, for our Lord had given it to him. And Judas went and found Habban the merchant carrying his goods on board the ship, and he began to carry (them) on board with him. And when they had gone on board and sat down, Habban the merchant saith to Judas: "What is thy art which thou art skilled in practising?" Judas saith to him: "Carpentering and architecture - the business of the carpenter." Habban the merchant saith to him: "What dost thou know to make in wood, and what in hewn stone?" Judas saith to him: "In wood I have learned to make ploughs and yokes and ox goads, and oars for ferry-boats, and masts for ships; and in stone, tombstones and monuments, and temples, and palaces for kings." Habban the merchant saith to him: "And I was seeking just such an artificer." And they began to sail, because the breeze was steady; and they were sailing along gently, until they put in at the town of Sandaruk.

The Acts of Judas Thomas,
Edessa,
154.

After a short sea journey, St Thomas and his master Habban landed at Andropolis, a royal city somewhere to the east of Jerusalem. Andropolis has been identified as Sandaruck in Baluchistan, (neighbouring Iran). It is also thought to be the Kingdom of Taxila in what is now Pakistan.

Jesus gives Thomas into the care of the merchant Habban; 12th c. stained glass window, Chartres Cathedral, France.

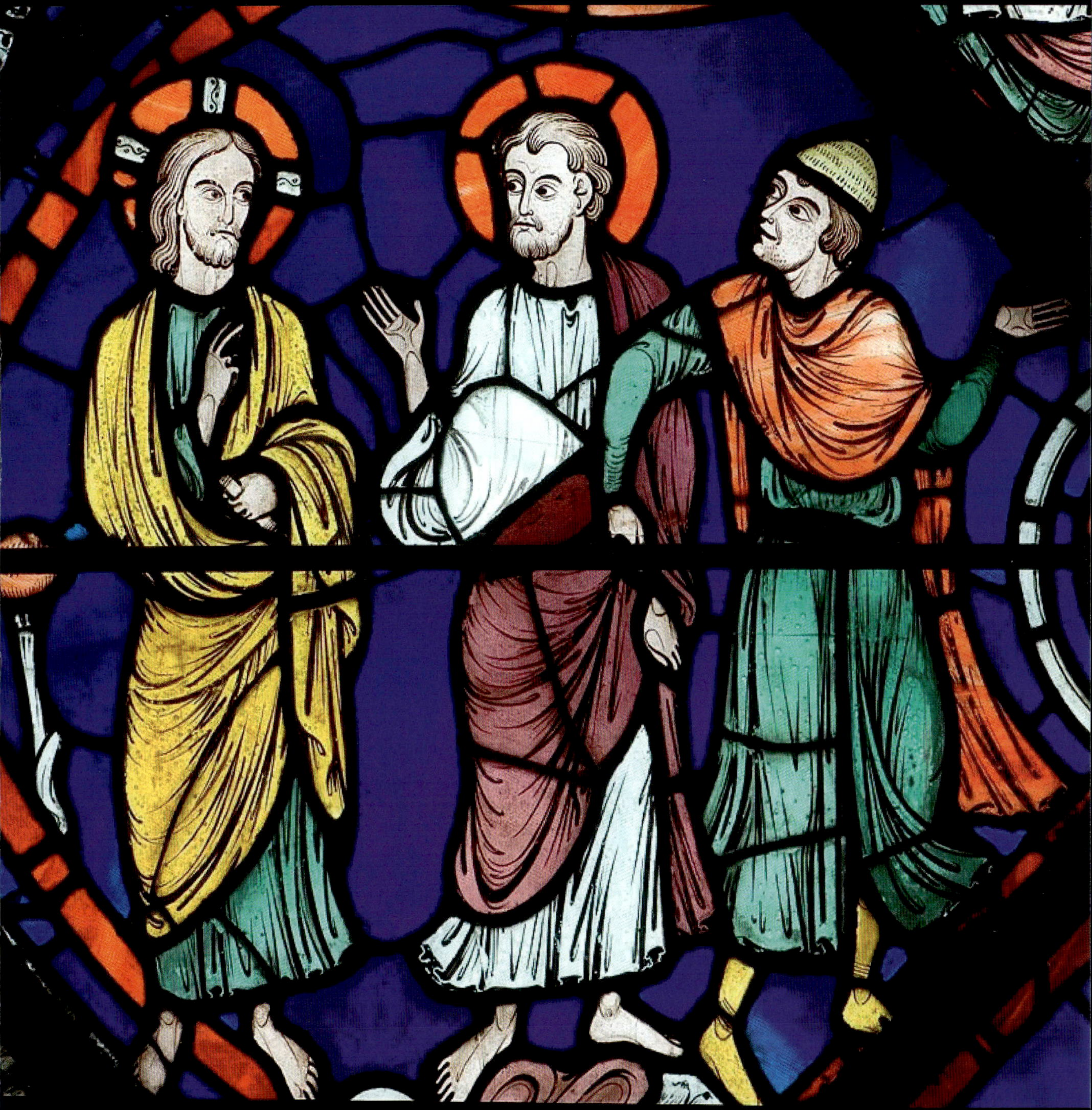

The kingdom of Gandhara

Terracotta head of a nobleman (note the long ear lobes) Gandhara, The Prince of Wales Museum, Mumbai, India (2013).

The Kingdom of Gandhara began in the Vedic period (c. 1500-500 BC).

The district of Gandhara is not mentioned by Alexander's historians, but it is correctly described by Strabo, under the name of Gandharitis, as lying along the River Kophes, between the Choaspes and the Indus.

Ptolemy places the Gandharas in the same position, whose country included both banks of the Kophes immediately above its junction with the Indus. This is the Kien-to-lo, or Gandhara of all the Chinese pilgrims, who are unanimous in placing it to the west of the Indus.

Gandharan art is the result of the fusion of Buddhist and Hellenistic art forms. It is also the ancient term for the city, and old kingdom of Peshawar, which included the Swat valley, and the Potohar Plateau regions of Pakistan, as well as the Jalalabad district of modern-day Afghanistan.

During the Hellenistic period, its capital city was Charsadda. The capital city was moved to Peshawar by the Kushan emperor Kanishka the Great in about AD 127.

It is mentioned in the Zend Avesta as the sixth most beautiful place on earth created by Ahura Mazda. It was known in Sanskrit as Purushapura, meaning "city of men" and as the "crown jewel" of Bactria. It also held sway over Takaśilā (modern Taxila). As a centre of Greco-Buddhism, Bactrian Zoroastrianism and Animism, Gandhara attained its height from the first to the fifth c. AD under the Kushan Kings. It also held sway over Taksasila (modern Taxila).

The Persian term Shahi refers to the ruling dynasty that took over from the Kabul Shahi and ruled the region during the period prior to the Muslim conquests of the 10th and 11th centuries. After it was conquered by Mahmud of Ghazni in AD 1001, the name Gandhara disappeared.

Right: Terracotta head of a nobleman, Gandhara, first c. AD, The Prince of Wales Museum, Mumbai, India (2013).

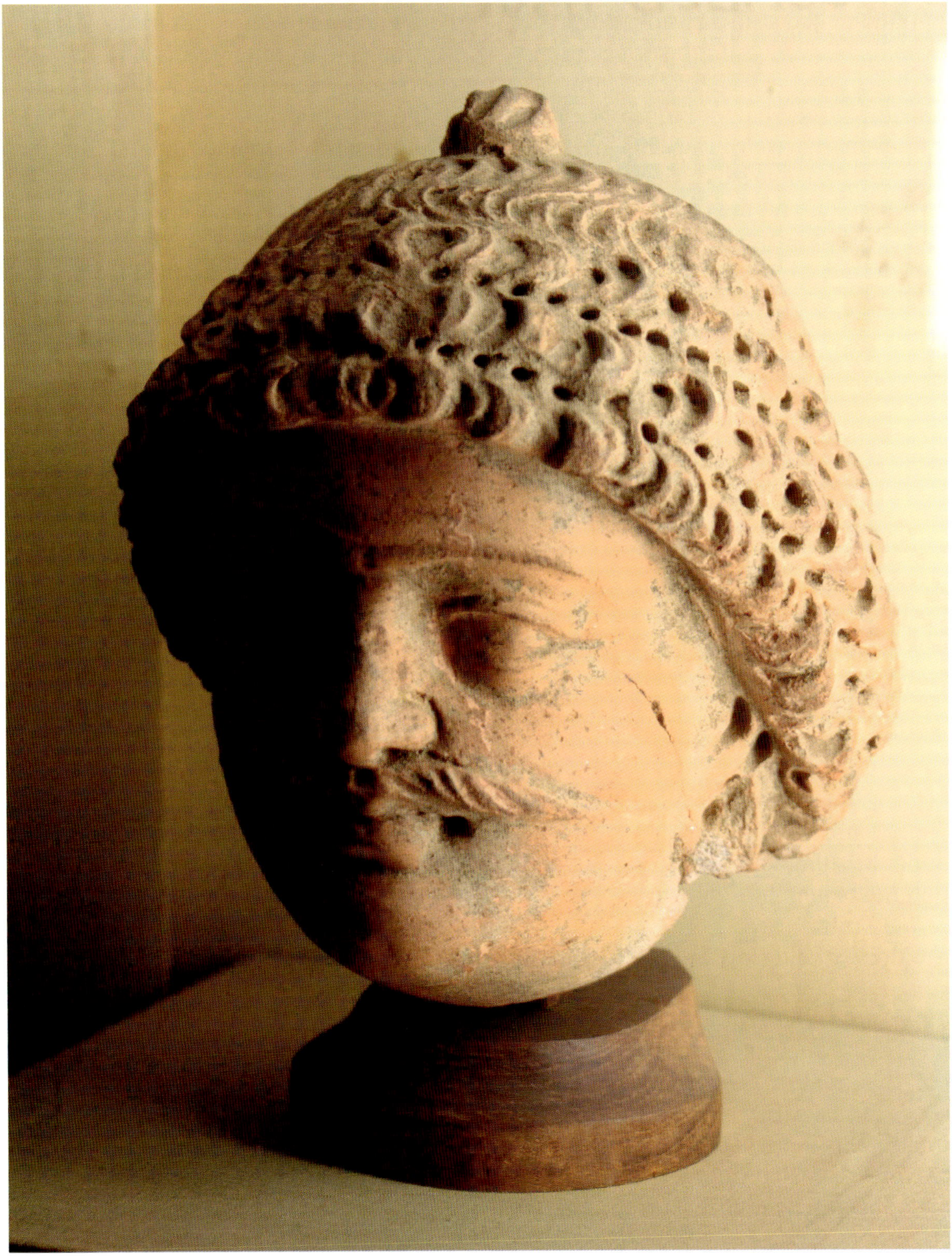

Buddhism

Buddhism had seen a steady growth from its beginnings in the 6th century BC to its endorsement as the state religion of the Maurya Empire under Ashoka in the 3rd century BC. It continued to flourish during the final centuries BC and the first centuries AD, and spread beyond the Indian subcontinent to Central Asia and beyond to China. But a steady decline of Buddhism in India set in during the later Gupta era and under the Pala Empire.

Gautama preached his first sermon at Sarnath, about 5 miles north of the sacred Hindu city of Varanasi around 424 BC. In this sermon, still a definitive text for all Buddhists, he proposes a path to enlightenment very different from the elaborate ceremonies and colourful myths attached to the Hindu deities. Gautama's message is plain to the point of bluntness, at any rate when reduced to a simple list - as it usually is in primers on Buddhism. He states that enlightenment can be achieved by understanding Four Noble Truths; and that the pain of life, with which the Noble Truths are concerned, can be avoided by following an Eightfold Path.

The Four Noble Truths are that pain is inextricably part of mankind's everyday life; that our cravings of all kinds are the cause of this pain; that the way off this treadmill is to free oneself of these cravings; and that this can be achieved by following the Eightfold Path. The Path encourages the Buddhist to live a virtuous life by following the 'right' course of action in eight contexts. Many of these are moral evils to be avoided (as in the Jewish Commandments). But the eighth step, 'Right Concentration', goes to the heart of the Buddhist ideal.

Right Concentration is described in Buddhist scripture as concentrating on a single object, so as to induce a special state of consciousness through deep meditation. In this way the Buddhist hopes to achieve complete purity of thought, leading ideally to nirvana. Nirvana means 'blowing out', as of a flame. It is common to Hinduism and Jainism as well as Buddhism. But in the two older religions it leads to *moksha*, release from the cycle of rebirth, total extinction. In Buddhism it is a blissful transcendent state which can be achieved either in life or after death - and which is achieved by anyone who becomes Buddha.

By the time of his death, at about the age of eighty, the Buddha's followers were established as communities of monks in northern India. Wandering through villages and towns with their begging bowls, eager to describe the path to the truth, they were familiar figures. But so are many other such groups, including the Jains.

Right: Buddhist monks walking beside the remains of the Great Stupa, Sarnath, India (2012).

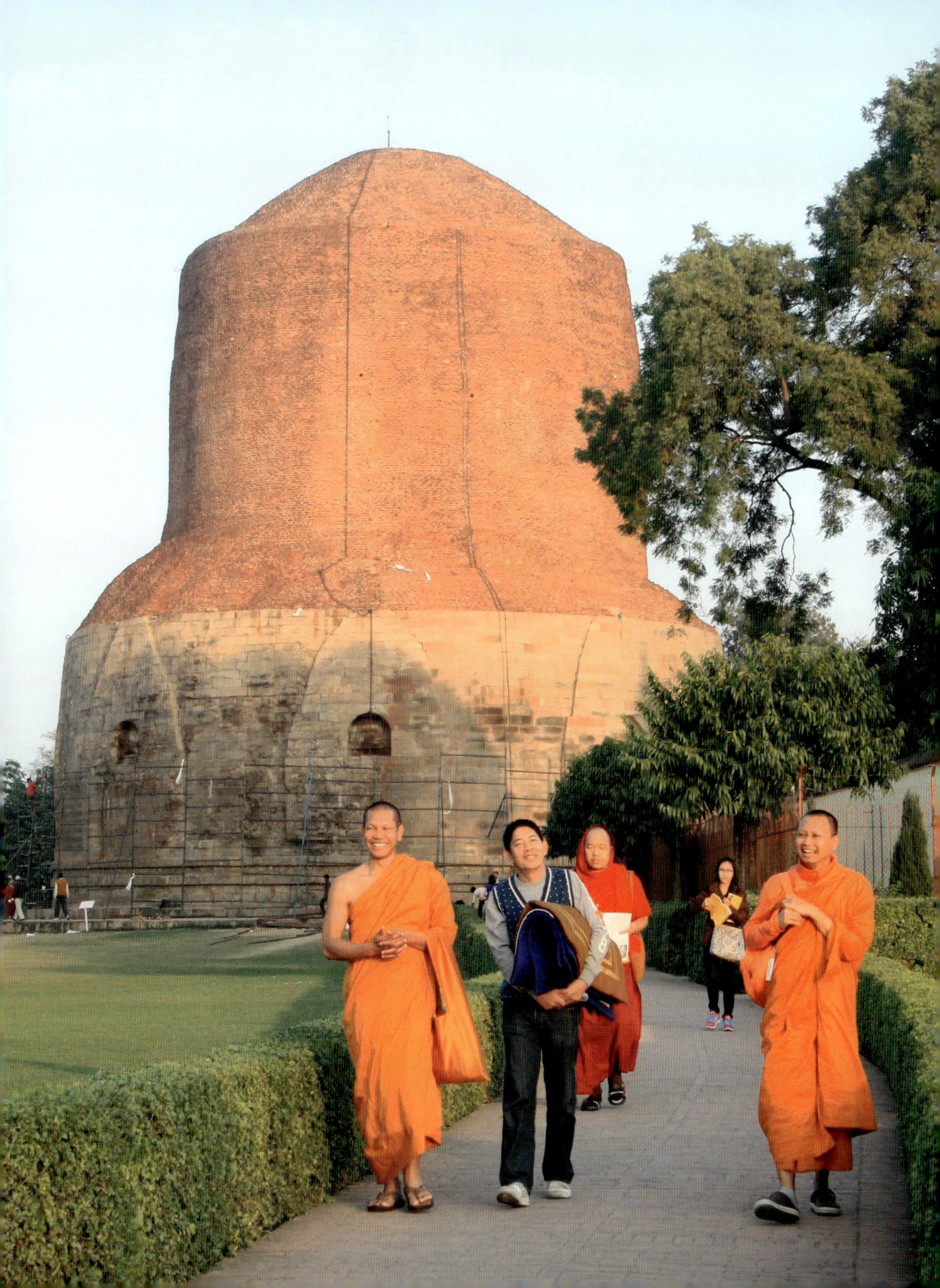

Emperor Ashoka

The advance of Buddhism beyond was largely due to the enthusiastic support of the Emperor Ashoka who ruled over much of the Indian subcontinent in the 3rd century BC. His inscriptions, carved on pillars and rocks throughout his realm, bear witness both to the spread of Buddhism and to his own benevolent support of the Buddha's principles. During Ashoka's reign, and with his encouragement, Buddhism spreads to South India and into Sri Lanka. The latter has remained a stronghold of the earliest form of Buddhism, known as Theravada (meaning the 'school of elders'). By the time of Ashoka there was already a rival tendency within Buddhism, involving an elaboration of the Buddha's essentially simple message of personal salvation. The difference is similar to that between Protestants and Catholics at the time of the Reformation in Christianity. Compared to the puritan standards of Theravada Buddhism, the other sect - which later becomes known as Mahayana - introduces a catholic profusion of Buddhist saints.

Mahayana means the Great Vehicle. Its adherents argue that this form of Buddhism can carry a greater number of people towards the truth than Theravada Buddhism, which they dismiss as Hinayana - the little vehicle. The main distinction is that in Theravada, the Buddha is a historical figure who by his example shows the way towards nirvana; the cult is essentially a human system of self-discipline, with no trace of a god. In the younger but larger sect there is still no god, but there are a great many supernatural beings. In Mahayana, the historical Buddha, Gautama, becomes the latest in a long line of past Buddhas. They exist in some place beyond this world, from which they can offer support. Also in that place are the Bodhisattvas, who have yet to begin the final human life in which they will attain enlightenment as Buddha. They too, can help mortals who show them devotion.

In Theravada, the nearest approach to worship is the veneration of relics of the historical Buddha, whose hair or tooth is made the central feature of a temple. In Mahayana, with its many semi-divine figures, there is opportunity for more varied, more popular and more superstitious forms of worship. It is well suited to become what it claims to be - the greater vehicle.

Buddhism is the first of the world religions to expand from its place of origin. It did so by two distinct routes: Theravada Buddhism was carried eastwards into southeast Asia, in an upsurge of Indian trade from the 1st century AD. The merchants and sailors were either Buddhist or Hindu, and missionaries took advantage of the new opportunities for travel. As a result the kingdoms of southeast Asia, much influenced by the more advanced civilisation of India, variously adopted Buddhist and Hindu religious practices. Which of the two prevails is often the result of the preference of a ruling dynasty. In India, Buddhism flourished alongside Hinduism for many years.

The Rock Edict of Ashoka, 273 BC, Kalinga, Orissa, India (2016).

Buddhist Taxila

The Dharmarajika stupa at Bhir Mound where some of the ashes of the Buddha are believed to be buried, Taxila, Pakistan.

Taxila lies 20 miles north-west of Rawalpindi on the Grand Trunk Road. It is one of the most important archaeological sites in Asia. Situated strategically on a branch of the Silk Road that linked China to the West, the city flourished both economically and culturally. Taxila reached its apogee between the 1st and 5th centuries AD and is mentioned in several languages: in Sanskrit, the city was called Takshaçila (Prince of the Serpent Tribe); in Pâli it was known as Takkasilâ; the Greeks knew the town as Taxila, which the Romans rendered as Taxilla; the Chinese called it Chu-ch'a-shi-lo.

Taxila is known as the cradle of Buddhist civilisation, where numerous Buddhist sites and Buddhist monuments were erected throughout the Taxila valley. It was transformed into a religious heartland and a destination for pilgrims from as far afield as Central Asia and China. The Great Stupa is one of the largest and most impressive in Pakistan, located just to the east of Bhir Mound and Sirkap. It housed some of the ashes of the Buddha. The chapels and chambers around the Great Stupa were built at various times from the 1st century BC to the post-Kushan period. These structures display a wide range of designs and were probably donated by pilgrims, possibly representing various schools of Buddhism. Stone walls, house foundations and winding streets represent the earliest forms of urbanisation on the subcontinent.

According to Philostratus, Taxila was "not unlike the ancient Ninus and was walled in the manner of other Greek towns". For Ninjas, or Nineveh we must read Babylon, as we have no description of the great Assyrian city, which was destroyed nearly two centuries before the time of Herodotus. Strabo also declares it to be a large city, and adds, that the neighbouring country was "crowded with inhabitants, and very fertile". Pliny calls it "a famous city, situated on a low but level plain, in a district called Amanda. These accounts agree exactly with the position and size of the ancient city near Shah-dheri, the ruins of which are spread over several square miles.

In 126 BC Taxila was wrested from the Greeks by the Indo-Scythian Sus or Jars, with whom it remained for about three-quarters of a century, when it was conquered by the later Indo-Scythians under the great Kanishka. During this period Parshawar would appear to have been the capital of the Indo-Scythian dominions, while Taxila was governed by satraps. In the 1st century AD Taxila became part of the Kushan Empire, until it was conquered by the Kidarites at the end of the 4th century AD.

The main road of Sirkap was a straight line, dividing the nearly one mile long town into two halves. The private houses were constructed of rubble masonry covered with lime or mud plaster. Usually, they had a small court, a second floor and a flat roof.

Buddhist stupas in the Taxila Museum, Pakistan.

Indo-Scythian Taxila

Gold coin of King Sothoros Menandros, Taxila, Pakistan.

The city of Taxila was rebuilt by King Sothoros Menandros (165–130 BC). Several coins and inscriptions of these local governors have been found at Shah-dheri and Manikyala. Of these the most interesting is the copper plate containing the name of Takhasila, the Pali form of Tahnhasila, from which the Greeks obtained their name Taxila.

Just before the end of the third century BC, the descendants of the Mauryan kings came into contact with the Bactrian Greeks under Demetrius, the son of Enthydemus, and in the early part of the following century Taxila formed part of the Indian dominions of Eilkratides.

Arrian describes it as "a large and wealthy city, and the most populous between the Indus and Hydaspes. Pliny 23 states that Taxila was only 60 Roman (or 55 English), miles from Peucola'itis, or Hashtnagar, on the River Haro, to the west of Hasan Abdal, or just two days' march from the Indus. The itineraries of Chinese pilgrims agree in placing Taxila at three days' journey to the east of the Indus or in the immediate neighbourhood of Kala-ka-sarai and which is still the third stage from the Indus, both for troops and baggage.

After the earthquake that marks the break between the Indo-Scythian and Indo-Parthian periods, many houses were rebuilt with stronger walls and deeper foundations.

A Greek visitor, whose description of Taxila was included in the *Life of Apollonius* by Philostratus, says that the houses gave the impression of having one storey, but in fact had basement rooms. This visitor may indeed have been the neo-pythagorean visited the Punjab, and much of the information appears to be correct. That the palace of Taxila and a temple in front of the walls were as small as those of Athens.

During the reign of the Parthian King Bardanes (AD 42 -45) Apollonius of Tyana and his companion, the Assyrian Damis visited Taxila and in the narrative of the journey, Philostratus professes to have followed in his *Life of Apollonius*. His account is exaggerated in many particulars regarding the acts and sayings of the philosopher, but the descriptions of places seem to be generally truthful. If they were not found in the narrative of Damis, they must have been taken from the journals of some of Alexander's followers; and in either case they are valuable, as they supply many little points of information that are wanting in the regular histories.

Taxila is known as the cradle of Buddhist civilisation, with numerous Buddhist sites, but in the heart of the great Buddhist civilisation stands a Zoroastrian temple known as the Jandial Temple, which would have been known to St Thomas, Habban and his patron, King Gondophares.

The ruins of Taxila in its mountain setting, as laid out by Alexander the Great in 326 BC, Pakistan. Photograph: Jane Taylor (2012).

Hellenistic Taxila

The temple of the Double-Headed Eagle, second c. BC - second c. AD, Taxila, Pakistan.

Along the main street of Sirkap, the ancient city, sits the temple of the Double-Headed Eagle. Its original name is lost, but it is thus referred to because of the bird bas-relief that adorns the arch. Of Scythian origin, the double-headed bird motif is common in Eurasia, appearing in Byzantine and European armour crests as well. The shrine reflects Bactrian Greek influences brought to the area by Alexander's army, who unwittingly left a Hellenic cultural imprint. The columns decorating the sides of the shrine are clearly Corinthian and the pediment is classically Greek. This is not to say that the shrine is entirely Greek – far from it: Indian influences can be seen in the various ornamented Indian architectural styles.

Taxila must have reminded the Greeks of Babylon by its symmetry as Philostratus goes on to say that the city was "divided into narrow streets with great regularity". He also mentions a temple of the sun, which stood outside the walls, and a palace in which the usurper was besieged. He speaks also of a garden, one stadium in length, with a tank in the midst, which was filled by "cool and refreshing streams", attests to the early influence of Central Asian architectural forms on those of the subcontinent.

Classical writers are unanimous in their accounts of the size and wealth of Taxila.

Zoroastrian Taxila

The Zoroastrian Jandial temple built in the Scytho-Parthian period in the first century BC stands on an artificial mound, north of Sirkap City. It is believed to be the temple described by Philostratus in his Life of Apollonius of Tyana. Only fragments of columns and pilasters made with massive blocks of sandstone built in front of the walls of the temple remain. Stairs leading up to the Jandial temple are pure Greek in their style of architecture. The resemblance of this temple to classical Greek temples is striking. The structure is in limestone and kanjur with plaster on the façade, patches of which are still intact. Kanjur is a porous form of sedimentary stone, used in Gandhara.

This Zoroastrian temple dates from the sixth phase of building in Taxila and its reconstruction by the Parthian King Gondophares (in a style sometimes called "Indo-Parthian") in the years between 30 BC and AD 80, would have been familiar to St Thomas when he lived and worked here for about three years in the court of King Gondophares.

The excavated area is large: nearly a mile long and half a mile wide. The wall that surrounded the city, built in the fifth phase, appears to have had a height of 6-10 metres, was 5-7 metres wide, and almost 4,800 metres long. The walls are made from coursed rubble masonry, which is characteristic of the Greek and Saca periods. The city was rebuilt by King Menander. Different courts, palaces and temples were added to the building infrastructure of the city.

Finally, the city was under the control of Zoroastrian emperors. During this time, the people of the three different religions and cultures lived and flourished together peacefully.

Marble frieze of Magi playing instruments, Taxila, Pakistan.

Gondophares

Copper coin of Gondophares I, who reigned from AD 21 - c. 47 with his capital at Taxila, (now Pakistan).

The name Gondophares was translated into Armenian as "Gastaphar", and then into Western languages as "Gaspard". He may be the "Gaspard, or Caspar, King of Persia", who, according to apocryphal texts and the eastern Christian tradition, was one of the three Biblical Magi who worshipped the infant Jesus. Gondophares purportedly received a letter from St Thomas.

The apocryphal Acts of Thomas mentions a king: Gudnaphar. This king has been associated with Gondophares I by many scholars.

It has been established that there were several kings with the same name. This ruler has been identified with a king called Caspar in the Christian tradition of the Apostle St Thomas. The king who best fits these references was Gondophares-Sases, the fourth king using the title Gondophares. There is historical evidence "that about the year 46 AD a king was reigning over that part of Asia south of Himalayas now represented by Afghanistan, Baluchistan, the Punjab, and Sind, who bore the name Gondophernes or Guduphara."

B N Puri (of the Department of Ancient Indian History and Archaeology at the University of Lucknow, India) also identified Gondophares with the ruler said to have been converted by St Thomas the Apostle. The same goes for the reference to an Indo-Parthian king in the accounts of the life of Apollonius of Tyana. Puri says that the dates given by Philostratus in his Life of Apollonius of Tyana for Apollonius' visit to Taxila in AD 43–44, are within the period of the reign of Gondophares I, who also went by the Parthian name, Phraotes. "St Thomas was brought before King Gundaphar (Gondophares) at his capital, Taxila."

Taxila is the Greek form of the contemporary Pali name for the city, "Takkasila", from the Sanskrit "Taksha-sila". The name of the city was transformed in subsequent legends concerning St Thomas:
In the third India is the kingdom of Tharsis, which at that time was ruled over by King Caspar, who offered incense to our Lord. The famous island Eyrisoulla (or Egrocilla) lies in this land: it is there that the holy apostle St Thomas is buried.

John of Hildesheim,
1364–1375,
Historia Trium Regum.

The Adoration of the Magi, fifth c. mosaic; Sta Maria Maggiore, Rome, Italy (2013).

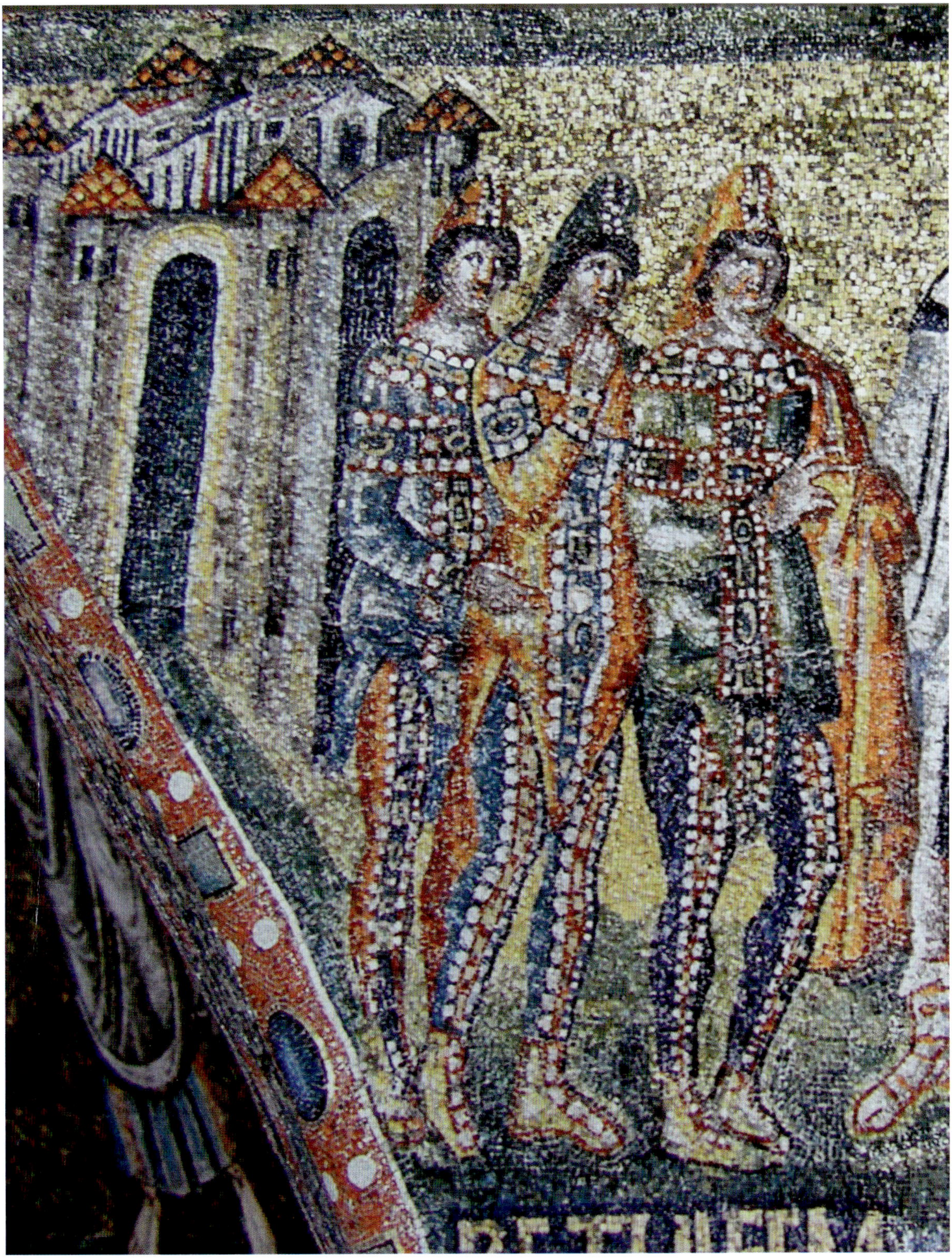

The Wedding Banquet

And on this day also took place the miracle which Thomas the apostle wrought when he went to preach the Gospel in the country of India. Now he was afraid, and he said, "How can I go to India, the country of which I know not?"

Then our Lord Jesus Christ appeared unto him and said unto him, "Fear thou not, for My grace is with thee." And whilst he was with our Lord there came a merchant from India. And our Lord said unto him, "What dost thou want?"

And the merchant said, "I want a carpenter"; and he sold him for three letra of silver. And he wrote a paper which testified, saying, "I have sold my servant, the son of Joseph the carpenter, to "Abenes, a merchant of Gona"; and Thomas's (new) master took him to the city of the king. When they drew nigh unto the city they heard the sound of organs and pipes, and they said, "What is this?" And the people said unto them, "The king has made a marriage-feast for his daughter, and he has ordered that whosoever doth not come to the wedding shall be punished." And Abenes and Thomas went into the room of the feast, and while the guests ate and drank Thomas the apostle ate nothing at all. And there he found a Hebrew singing maiden who was singing songs in the Hebrew language.

And whilst the apostle was praying in the Hebrew language one of those who were at the feast struck him; and the apostle said, "I see a hand with the dogs tearing at it"; and the singing woman alone heard him because he spoke in the Hebrew Language. And the man who smote Thomas went down to the lake (or well) to draw water, and a lion sprang out and slew him and left him lying in pieces. And a dog seized the right hand and carried it in among the people at the feast, and one said unto Thomas, "Who is dead?" And he said unto them, "This is the hand of him who struck one who serveth." When the singing maiden heard this, she cast away her tambourine and went and sat at the feet of the apostle, and she said, "I heard thee say unto him, 'The gods shall tear the hand which smote me.'"

When the people heard this some believed and some did not. When the king heard this he said unto Thomas, "Come and pray over my daughter, for this day have I given her in marriage." And when the apostle had entered the marriage-chamber he prayed to the Lord in the form of Thomas, on behalf of the bride and bridegroom, and admonished them with the words of faith, and they believed the words of the apostle, and abandoned their marriage.

Synaxarium, The Book of the Saints of The Ethiopian Orthodox Tewahedo Church, (Meskerem 18: September 28)

St Thomas and his master Habban at the wedding feast; stained glass window made between 1205 and 1235. Chartres Cathedral, Chartres, France.

129

St Thomas the builder

Remains of some of St Thomas' buildings, influenced by Greek architecture, indicate that he was a great builder. According to the legend, St Thomas was a skilled carpenter and was bidden to build a palace for King Gondophares. However, the Apostle decided to teach the king a lesson by devoting the royal grant to acts of charity and thereby laying up treasure for the heavenly abode.

Although little is known of the immediate growth of the church, Bar-Daisan (154–223) reports that in his time there were Christian tribes in India which claimed to have been converted by St Thomas and to have books and relics to prove it. But at least by the year of the establishment of the Second Persian Empire (226), there were bishops of the Church of the East in northwest India (Afghanistan and Baluchistan), with laymen and clergy alike engaging in missionary activity.

It is most significant that, aside from a small remnant of the Church of the East in Kurdistan, the only other church denomination to maintain a distinctive identity are the St Thomas Christian congregations along the Malabar Coast (modern-day Kerala) in southwest India. According to the most ancient tradition of this church, St Thomas evangelised this area and then crossed to the Coromandel Coast of southeast India, where, after carrying out a second mission, he died near Madras.

Throughout the period under review, the church in India was under the jurisdiction of Edessa, which was then under the Mesopotamian patriarchate at Seleucia-Ctesiphon and later at Baghdad and Mosul. It must be admitted that a personal visit of the Apostle Thomas to South India was easily feasible in the traditional belief that he came by way of Socotra, where an ancient Christian settlement undoubtedly existed. I am now satisfied that the Christian church of South India is extremely ancient...

Vincent A Smith,
The Early History of India,
1908.

St Thomas with his set square, marble statue, Bernini, 16th c. St Peter's Basilica, Rome, Italy.

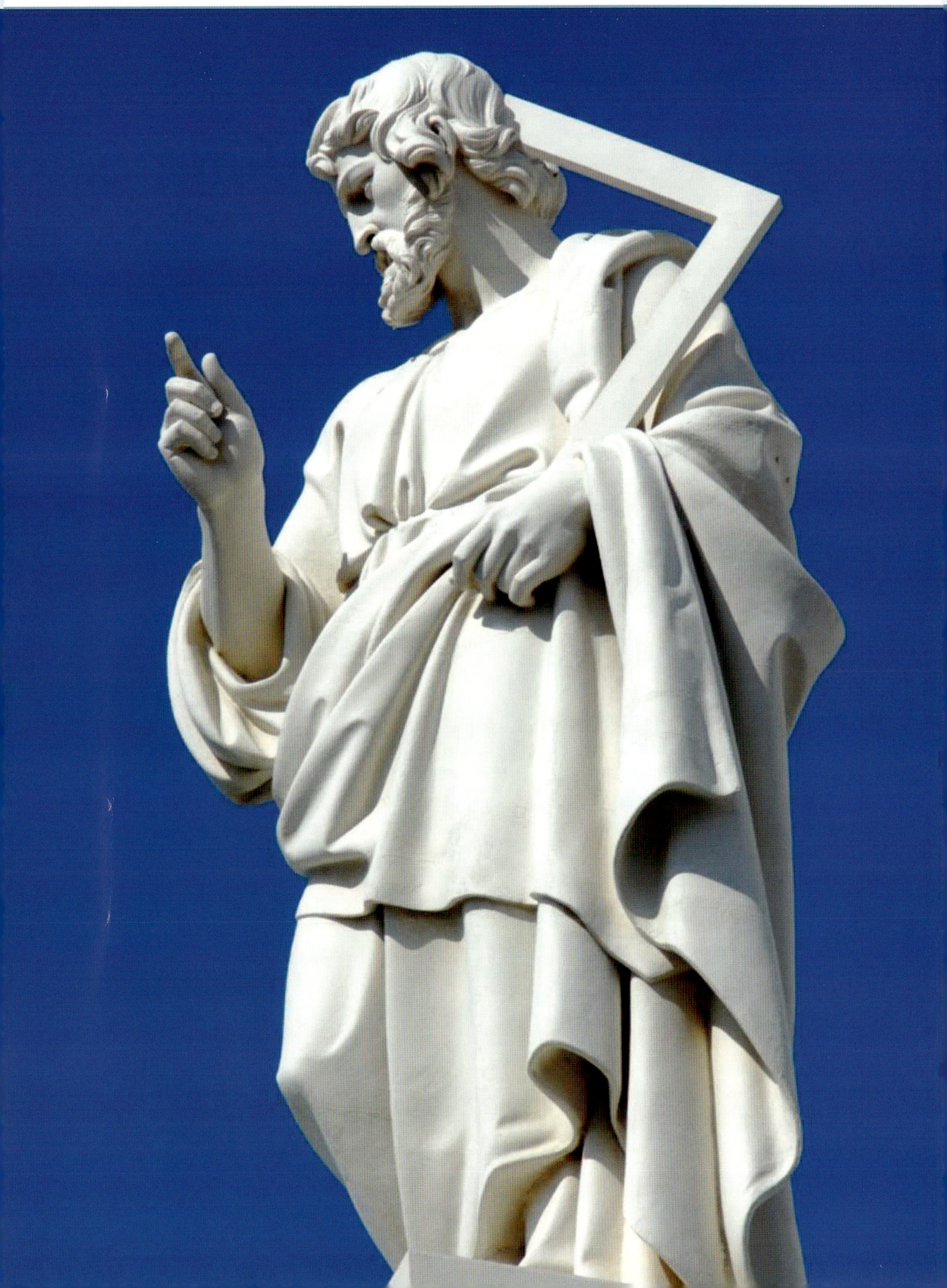

St Thomas the carpenter

And on this day Thomas the Apostle began to work like an artisan, and to preach in the country of India whereunto he went with Abnes the merchant. And Abnes went to salute Guendefor the king, and he told him concerning Thomas the carpenter whom he had brought with him. And the king rejoiced and said unto him, "What is thy trade?" And the apostle said, "I am a carpenter and an architect. And I can make walls of houses, and beds, and scales, and wheels (carts?), and ships, and oars, and royal palaces." And the king rejoiced, and he took Thomas to a place where he was going to build a palace, and he said unto him, "When wilt thou have built (the house)?" And the apostle said, "After two months (I will begin on) the new moon of the month Khedar, and I will finish in the month of Miyazya". And the king marvelled and said unto him, "Every house is built in the summer, then how can this house be built in the winter?" Then the king gave him much money both for himself and for those who were to work with him, and having taken it, he gave it to the poor and needy, saying, "I give what belongs to the king to another king."

Then the king sent his minister to the apostle to learn if the palace was finished, and the apostle said unto him, "Thy palace is finished, but there remaineth the roof to put on." And the king sent him money a second time, and he said unto him, "Finish quickly." Then when the king came and asked for the palace which Thomas had built, the apostle said unto him, "No palace hath been built; there are only the alms given to the poor of thy goods."

And the king was wroth, and he shut the apostle and the merchant up in prison until he could think out in what way he should kill them. That night Gadon the king's brother fell sick and died, and the angels showed him the palace, which Thomas had built for Guendefor his brother. He said unto them, "Who is this palace for?" And the angels said unto him, "This is for the king, and the Apostle Thomas who is in the prison house hath built it for him." When his soul returned to him Gadon told his brother this, and then they all vied with each other, and they went to the prison house and brought out the apostle and the merchant. And they believed on our Lord Christ, and were all baptised, both men and women, in the Name of the Father and the Son and the Holy Ghost, and they received His Holy Body and His Honourable Blood. Then Thomas laid hands on them and gave them the benediction, and departed from them.

The Coptic Synaxarium,
(Coptic Orthodox Calendar for Temket 9: Oct 19).

Gondopharus leaves St Thomas in charge of a huge treasure to build him a new palace, 13th c.; stained glass window, Chartres Cathedral, Chartres, France.

133

St Thomas the martyr

The Apostles cast lots as to where they should go, and to St Thomas fell Parthia.

St Thomas was taken to King Gondophares, the ruler of the Indo-Parthian Kingdom, as an architect and carpenter by Habban.

Remains of some of his buildings, influenced by Hellenistic architecture, indicate that he was a great builder.

According to tradition, St Thomas was a skilled carpenter and was bidden to build a palace for the king. However, the Apostle decided to teach the king a lesson by devoting the royal grant to acts of charity and thereby laying up treasure for the heavenly abode.

The journey to India is described in detail. After a long residence in the court at Taxila he ordained leaders for the Church, and left in a chariot for the kingdom of Mazdei. According to the Acts of St Thomas the Kingdom of Mazdai, in Southern India, was ruled by King Misdeus. Some Greek Satraps, the descendants of Alexander the Great, were vassals to the Indo-Parthian Kingdom.

The king Misdeus was infuriated when St Thomas converted the Queen Tertia's son Juzanes, sister-in-law Princess Mygdonia (a province of Mesopotamia) and her friend Markia. The King Misdeus led St Thomas outside the city and ordered four soldiers to take him to the nearby hill where the soldiers speared St Thomas and killed him there. After performing many miracles, he died a martyr.

Syphorus was elected the first presbyter by the brethren after the death of St Thomas while Juzanes the prince became the deacon. The names of the King Misdeus, Tertia, Juzanes, Syphorus, Markia and Mygdonia suggest Greek descent or Hellenised Persian descent.

During the rule of the Kushan emperor Vasudeva I (195 - 225), the bones of St Thomas were transferred to Edessa.

And on this day is commemorated the translation of the body of Thomas the Apostle. And countless signs appeared through his body, and they built a beautiful church for him on the river, and they laid the body of the saint therein.

The Coptic Synaxarium,
(The Coptic Orthodox Calendar for Tahisas 18: December 27).

Right: St Thomas with a pike; Georges de la Tour (1593-1652); oil on canvas; 1625-1630; Musée du Louvre, Paris, France.

St Thomas is frequently depicted with a set square or a compass, as these are the tools of a builder, and with a spear (signifying the wound in Jesus' side where doubting Thomas laid his hand, or the spear that caused his death as a martyr).

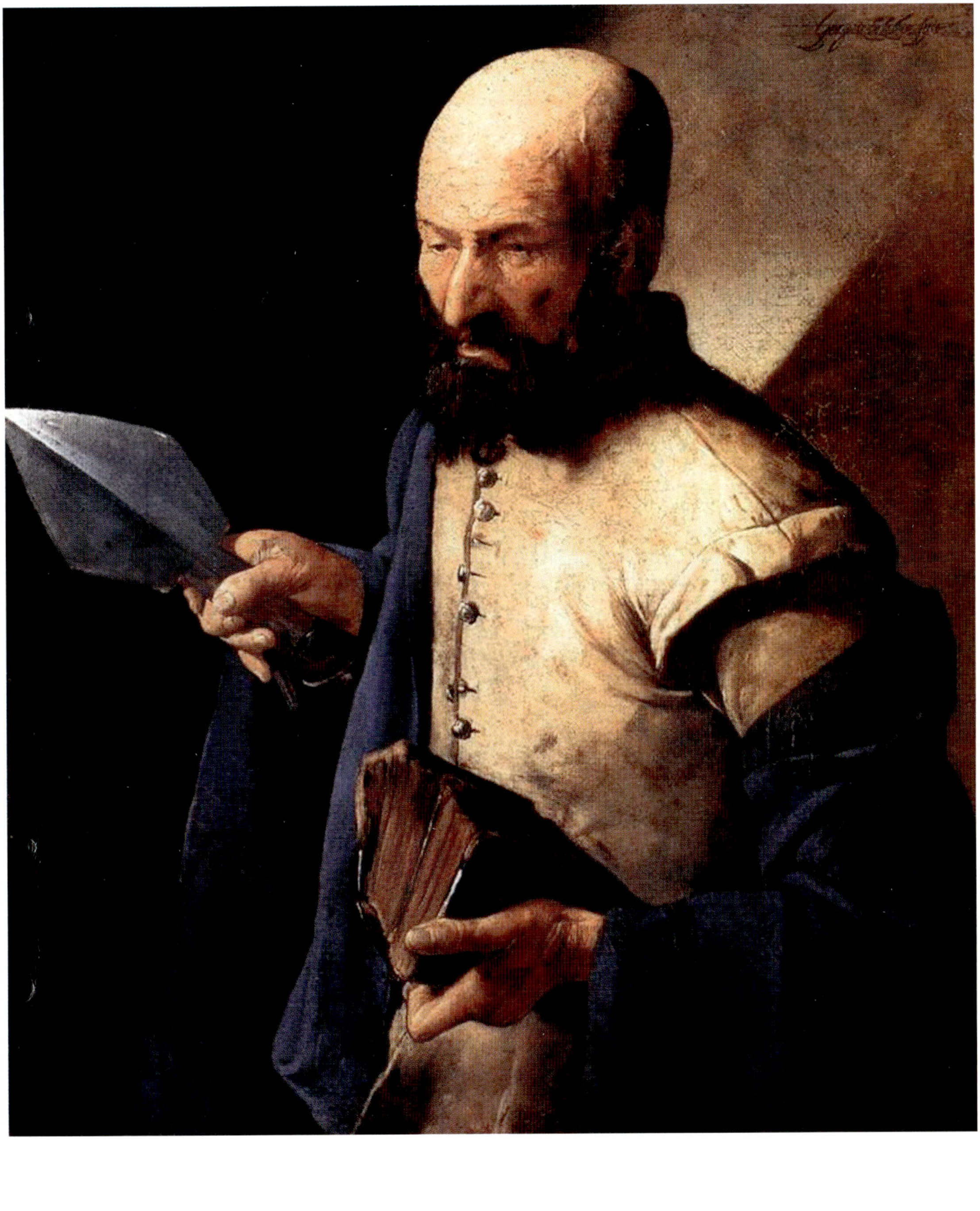

St Thomas and Arsonia

Terracotta statue of a bejewelled lady, 1st c. AD., the archaeological museum Samos, Greece (2010).

On this day Saint Thomas became a martyr, after he had preached in the country of India and Kantara. And this saint having arrived in the country of India, made himself a slave of a certain governor, whose name was Lucius; now that governor was a friend of the king. And he asked Thomas, saying, "Tell me what handicraft thou knowest." And Thomas said unto him, "I am an architect, and I can build temples and palaces. I am also a carpenter and I can make implements for use in the fields, and seats, and other things (in wood). I am also a physician, and I can heal the sick who are smitten with sores."

And when his master heard the words of Thomas, he was pleased exceedingly, and said, "I have gotten a slave who will be of use to the king." And at that time that governor set out to go to the king, and he left Saint Thomas to build in the house. And Saint Thomas began to teach the mistress of the governor the way of God, and he commanded her to walk in purity, and he made her to understand the mystery of the Son of God; and she believed on his words, and many of the men of the house also believed. And when Thomas's master returned from the king, and saw Saint Thomas the apostle, he said unto him, "O wicked slave, where is the fine work which thou didst tell me thou wouldst make for me?" And Thomas answered and said unto his master, "My lord, I have not lied unto thee. As for the temples and palaces which I have built (for thee) they are the souls who have become temples for the King of glory, and the ploughing implements which I have fashioned for thee are the Holy Gospels which shall plough up the thorny growth and weeds of sin. And the medicines, and the means of healing, are the Holy Mysteries, the Body and Blood of our Lord Jesus Christ, which heal those who have been poisoned with the deadly poison of sin." And when the governor heard this he commanded the soldiers to lay him down on the ground, and to tie his hands and feet together with ropes, and to drag him along on the lower part of his back, and to tie him by these ropes to a stake, and to cut off his skin with knives, and to fill the inside of his body with salt, and vinegar, and the dust of burnt bricks; and they did as the governor commanded, and the saint endured all these things with the endurance which was from God. And when his mistress saw them flaying him from the window of her house, she fell down straightway, and delivered up her soul (to God). And when Lucius knew that his wife was dead, he was exceedingly sad. And as for Saint Thomas, the apostle, God cooled his wounds and healed his body. And Lucius said unto him, "Behold, my wife hath died through thee, and if thou wilt raise her up from the dead, I will believe in thy God." And Saint Thomas, the apostle, came to her, and he laid his skin upon her, saying, "O Arsonia, in the Name of our Lord Jesus Christ, rise up!" And she opened her eyes straightway, and she rose, and stood up, and did homage to Saint Thomas, the apostle; and when Lucianus (sic) saw this, he believed on our Lord Jesus Christ.

And all the men of his house and all the men of the city believed on our Lord Jesus Christ, and Thomas baptised them in the Name of the Father and the Son and the Holy Spirit; and he appointed bishops and priests over them, and built churches for them. And (he remained) with them for four months, and confirmed them in the True Faith, and on everyone who was sick, no matter what the sickness was, he laid his skin, and he became healed straightway.

The Ethiopian Synaxarium,
(the Coptic Calendar for Ginbot 26:
3 June).

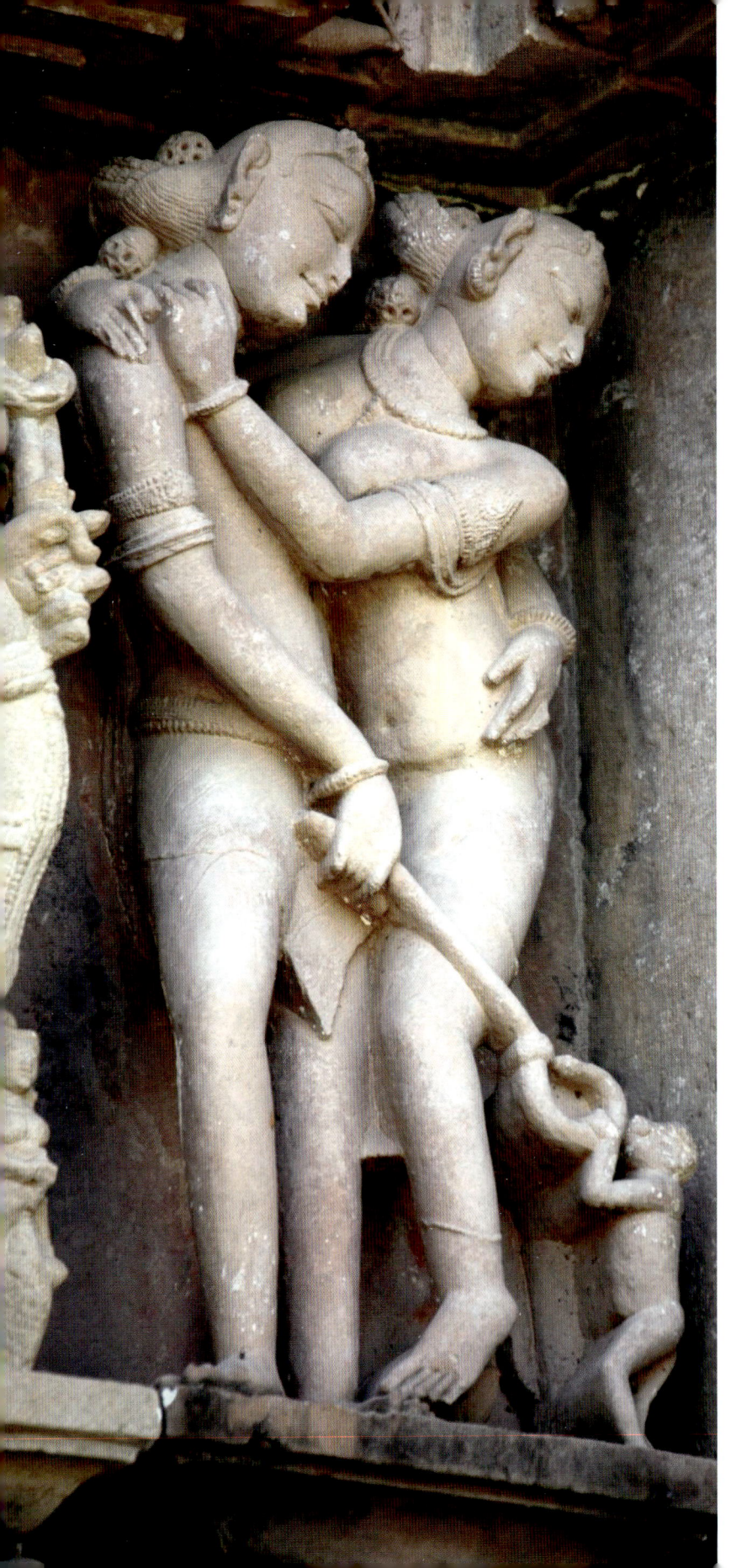

St Thomas and the miracle of the dead man

And on this day Thomas made manifest a miracle when he went forth to preach where our Lord commanded him to go.

And when he drew nigh thereto, and had come within two stadia of the city, he turned aside from the road and saw by chance a dead young man, and his appearance was very godly.

And the apostle said, "My Lord, was it that I might experience this trial that Thou didst bring me hither? But Thy Will be done."

And having said this he prayed much for the dead man, and straightway there came forth from the side of a stone a great serpent which lashed the ground with its tail, and cried out with a loud voice, saying, "What have I to do with thee, O apostle of Christ, thou hast come to annul my work?"

And the apostle said unto him, "Yea, speak." And the serpent said, "There was a beautiful woman (who came) from the vineyard, and I saw her and loved her.

Marble figures of two lovers, 14th c. AD, Hindu temple, Khajuraho, India (2014).

Then I found this young man kissing her, and consorting with her on the day of the Sabbath; but it is unnecessary for me to describe before thee all the wickedness, which he committed.

I knew that he was an associate of Christ, and therefore I killed him." And the Satan who ruled over the serpent told the apostle all the evil, which he used to do to the children of men.

Then the apostle anathematised him in the Name of Jesus Christ, and commanded him to withdraw the poison from the (dead) man. And straightway the serpent blew himself out, and burst asunder and died, and the young man leaped up and embraced the feet of the apostle and recovered.

And in this place the apostle made the people to believe, and he built them a church.

Then the apostle went into the city with the young man whom he had raised from the dead, and as they were standing and talking to the people of that place, a young ass came and stood before him, and he opened his mouth and said, "O associate of Christ, and apostle of the Most High, who knoweth the things which are hidden, thou companion of the Son of God, come return thou to Him that sent thee, God. Get up, and mount upon my back, and rest until thou enterest the city."

And when the apostle heard him he marveled exceedingly, and he praised God, and said unto the ass, "To what race dost thou belong that thou speaketh such deep mysteries?" And the ass said unto him, "I am a descendant of the offspring of the ass which was in the service of Balaam, and the ass whereon thy Lord and Teacher rode was descended from him, and was my father. Now as for me, I have been sent to give thee rest and for thee to mount upon"; and the apostle refused to mount upon him.

And when the ass had made many entreaties to him, the apostle mounted upon him, and he came to the gates of the city with many people following him; and he alighted from the ass, and said unto him, "Depart, and take heed whither thou departest," and straightway the ass fell down and died.

And those who saw this were dismayed, and they said unto the apostle, "Make him to live and raise him up." And the apostle said unto them, "I could raise him up by the power of my God, but it is better for him so"; and he commanded them to dig a hole in the ground, and to bury him, and then he gave them the salutation of peace and departed from them.

The Ethiopian Synaxarium,
(the Coptic Orthodox Calendar for Yekatit 2:9 February).

St Thomas and the Woman in the Tavern

Painted marble statue of a well-to-do Roman lady, 1st c. AD, the National Museum, Athens, Greece (2015).

And on this day Thomas the apostle worked a miracle for the woman who was killed in a tavern. There was a certain young man who used to do an unseemly thing, and he took a piece of the sacramental bread to put into his mouth; and his two hands withered, and he was unable to put (the bread) into his mouth.

And the man who saw him told the holy apostle what had taken place, and the apostle called him. And he said unto him, "Tell me, my son, what thou didst do. Be not ashamed, for the grace of God hath admonished thee."

And the man bowed down at his feet, and he said unto him, "I have done an abominable thing, though I thought I was doing a good one. I loved a certain woman who served in a tavern, and I said unto her, "Remain pure, even as thou hast taught me that thou art pure". And he said unto him, "Tell me, my son, what thou didst do. Be not ashamed, for the grace of God hath admonished thee."

And when she refused I took a sword and killed her." And the apostle said unto him, "How couldst thou let anger make thee to commit the act of the Serpent?" And straightway the holy apostle commanded one to bring him water, and he prayed over the water, and said unto the man, "Dost thou believe in our Lord Jesus Christ? Wash thy hand"; and the man washed his hand and it was healed and became as it was before. Then the apostle said unto him, "Come, lead me to the dead body."

And the young man went with the apostle, and brought him unto the place where he had stabbed the woman. And when the apostle saw her he was very sorry, for she was very beautiful; and he commanded the young man to bring her out, and to lay her on a bed, and the people did as he commanded. And he laid his hand upon her, and prayed, and having finished his prayer he said unto the young man, "Go and say unto her, holding her hand, 'I with my hand killed thee, and with my hand Christ raiseth thee, up through Faith.'"

And the young man drew nigh unto her, and he said to her, "I believe in our Lord Christ," and as he did so he drew the woman's hand [to him], and she leaped up and sat down, and many people who were there saw her. And she looked at the holy apostle, and left her bed, and bowed down at his feet. And she took the hem of his garment, and said unto him, "Where is the other one who was with thee, and who committed me to thee?" And the apostle said unto her, "Where didst thou arrive? Tell me." And she answered and said unto him, "A man who was wholly black, and wearing foul raiment, took me and carried me into a place of darkness, wherein there were many pits; and there was a horrible smell there. And I saw a pit of fire, which blazed, and a wheel of fire, and souls were bound to that wheel. And I also saw another pit of fire, which was filled with boiling filth and worms, and there were souls, which were being rolled therein.

And I also saw a place of darkness, which was very dense. And he who was guiding me said unto me, 'These are the souls of liars, and plunderers, and stealers, and murderers, and of those who never visited the sick, and who did not remember the Law of God; therefore they are rewarded according to their works.'" And the apostle said unto those men who were there, "Do ye hear what this woman saith? This is not the only punishment which God hath in store for the wicked, but there is worse than this. And turn ye to God, and forsake the working of sin, and the evil mind, and dwell in Faith, and with a meek spirit and with holiness, and ye shall receive grace from Him." And all the people believed in God, and they collected much gold in order that he might give alms to the poor, for the people were wont to give alms. And the fame of him arrived in all countries and cities, and the people took up all those who were sick or diseased, and those who were possessed of evil spirits, and those who were lunatics, and those who were tormented as they lay on their beds, and brought them and laid them down in the place where the apostle was. And he healed them all by the might of our Lord Jesus Christ.

The Ethiopian Synaxarium,
(The Coptic Orthodox Calendar for Hamle 1: 8 July).

4.
The Red Sea:

Oman

Cotton, silk and spices

The island of Soqotra

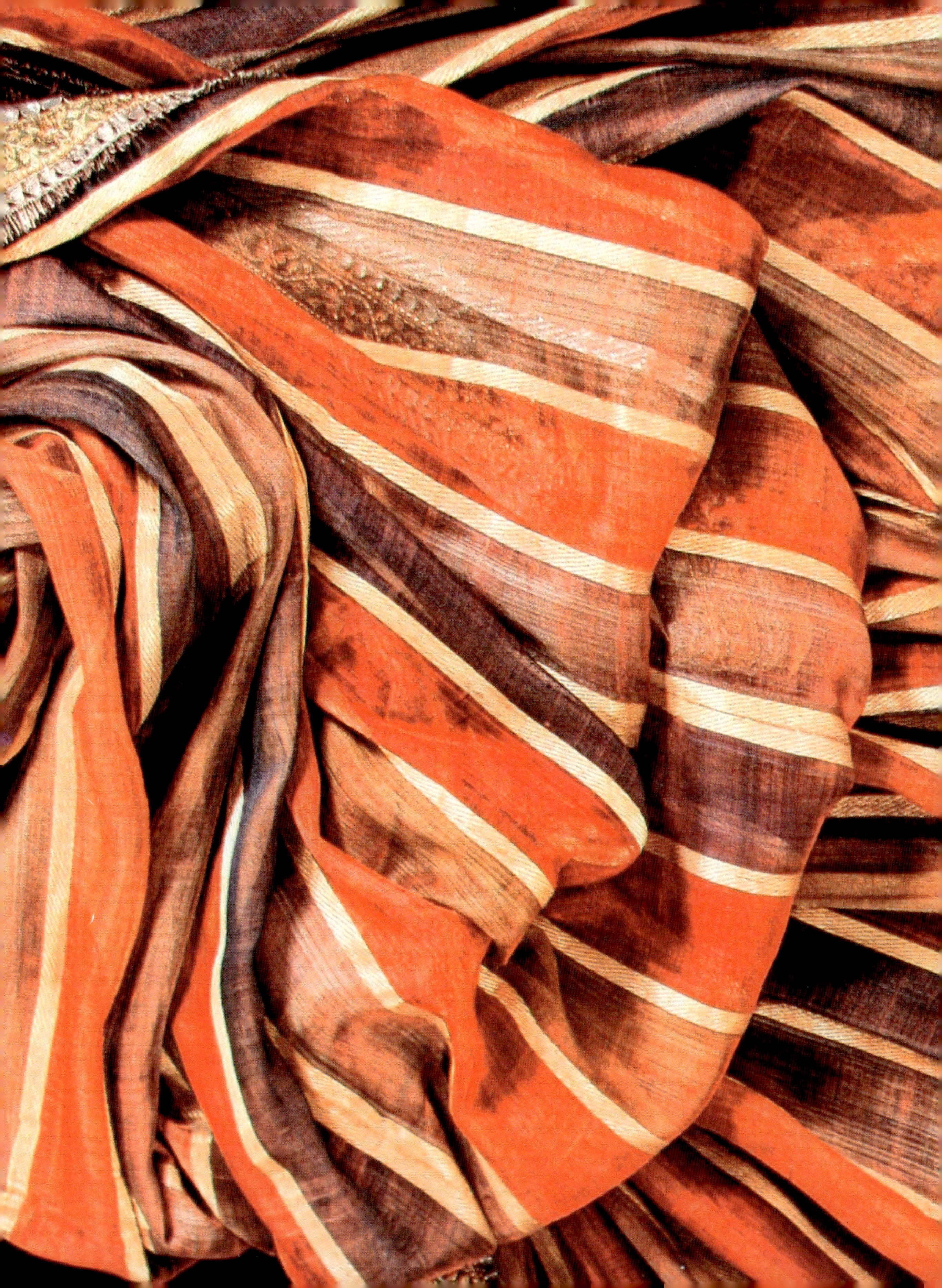

The Red Sea

The Red Sea near Suez, Egypt (2005).

Very few Greeks sailed across the Erythraean Sea before Alexander the Great's expedition in Asia. Herodotus alludes to the fact that around 520 BC Scylax of Caryanda (a Greek city in Asia Minor) was sent by the great King Darius I of Persia to follow the course of the Indus River and discover where it led. Scylax descended the river as far as its mouth. He then sailed westward across the Indian Ocean, entered the Red Sea and finally reached the Gulf of Suez. The entire journey took thirty months. However remarkable this voyage was, it does not seem to have led to a regular sea trade from Egypt to north-west India.

The name of Nearchus is widely renowned. He was one of the officers in the army of Alexander the Great. His celebrated voyage from what is now Pakistan to the north of the Persian Gulf after Alexander's expedition in India in 325 BC is preserved in Arrian's account of India entitled the *Indica*. Again this extraordinary achievement was not followed by regular sea traffic between India and the north part of the Gulf which belonged to the Seleucids - a dynasty founded by Seleucos, one of Alexander's successors - from around 310 BC until the mid-second century BC.

Pierre Schneider,
Maison de l'Orient et de la Méditerranée.
Lyon - Université d'Artois (Arras), France.

Frankincense and Myrrh

Arrian of Nicomedia (c. AD 85 - 160 was a Greek historian and philosopher. He served as an equestrian officer in Noricum and was appointed to the Senate, either by Trajan or Hadrian. The Anabasis of Alexander is considered one of the best sources on the campaigns of Alexander the Great. His other works include Discourses of Epictetus and Indica, all written in Greek. In reality the Greek presence in the Indian Ocean really began with the reign of Ptolemy II (reigned 283-246 BC). At some point this powerful sovereign needed a great number of war elephants which he could not obtain from Indian kings, for his Seleucid enemy Antiochus would have been opposed to such an attempt. To cope with this issue Ptolemy II decided to have African elephants captured and trained for warfare in Egypt, which was an extraordinary undertaking. He sponsored expeditions and founded hunting bases on the coast of Sudan and Eritrea to transport elephants by ship to Egyptian Red Sea ports. His son and successor Ptolemy III (reigned 246–222 BC) energetically continued his father's work.

The Ptolemaic explorations, however, had opened the way to sea trade. In the early second century BC merchants were probably heading to Eritrea, northern Somalia.

Frankincense granules, Oman.
Photograph: Wink Ogilvie (2010).

Myrrh, the Via Dolorosa, Jerusalem, Israel (2014).

Previous page: Benares silk skirt, woven thread with gold; Benares, India (2009).

Oman

The old port, Muscat, Oman. Photograph: Wink Ogilvie (2005).

In the centuries immediately preceding and following the birth of Christ, the great civilisations of the world - Roman, Indian and Chinese - were connected by commercial and diplomatic exchanges. These contacts began to decline in the 3rd century AD and were eventually cut off. But each civilization remembered that beyond the mountains and the deserts to the east or to the west lay other great civilisations. During the 1st and 2nd centuries AD, the prosperous years of the *Pax Romana*, the peoples of the Roman Empire maintained trade contacts extending far beyond the imperial boundaries.

Chinese silk, which the Romans believed was produced from the leaves of trees, was sold in the market quarter of Rome, and Indian cotton was converted into cloth at Alexandria. Contacts between West and East had progressively increased after 334 BC, when Alexander the Great invaded Asia, until a chain of intercommunicating states stretched across Eurasia from the Atlantic to the Pacific.

After Alexander's death, the Seleucid and Ptolemaic kingdoms of the Hellenistic Age maintained trade contacts with India over two routes, one by land and the other by sea. The most frequented route was the caravan road that began in Syria or Asia Minor, crossed Mesopotamia, then skirted the Iranian plateau to either Bactra (modern Balkh) or Kandahar before crossing the Hindu Kush to reach Taxila in India. The sea route began either at the Red Sea ports of Egypt or at the head of the Persian Gulf and moved along the coast to India.

Spices

Settlers from the Rome continued to live in India long after the decline in bilateral trade. Large hoards of Roman coins have been found throughout India, and especially in the busy maritime trading centres of the south. The South Indian kings reissued Roman coinage in their own name after defacing the coins to signify their sovereignty. The Tamil Sangam literature of India records mentions of the traders, and even Aden, in order to load aromatics (mostly frankincense and myrrh). One such reads: "The beautifully built ships of the Yavanas came with gold and returned with pepper, and Muziris resounded with the noise.

The Rome-India trade also saw several cultural exchanges which had lasting effects for both the civilisations and others involved in the trade. Traces of Indian influences appear in Roman works of silver and ivory, or in Egyptian cotton and silk fabrics used for sale in Europe. The Indian presence in Alexandria may have influenced the culture, but scant records remain about the manner of that influence. Clement of Alexandria mentions the Buddha in his writings and other Indian religions find mentions in other texts of the period.

Christian and Jewish settlers from the Roman Empire continued to live in India long after the decline in bilateral trade.

Spices in the market, Istanbul, Turkey.
Photograph: Nicholas Talbot-Rice (2014).

Portrait of a patrician lady, Pompeii, fresco covered in ash in the volcanic eruption of AD 79. The National Archaeological Museum, Naples, Italy (2014).

Trade goods to satisfy the patrician ladies of Rome

By the late first century BC, after Egypt and Syria had succumbed to Rome, Roman capital and appetite for the luxury goods of India - ivory, pearls, spices, dyes, and cotton - greatly stimulated trade with the East. By this time, however, the existing trade routes had serious disadvantages. The Parthians, whose kingdom extended from the Euphrates to the borders of Bactria, were levying heavy tolls on the caravan trade, and the Sabaean Arabs of southwest Arabia had cut off the Red Sea route at Aden and were in control of much of the overseas trade with India. From Aden, the Sabaeans sent Indian goods north by caravan to Petra, which grew rich as a distribution point to Egypt via Gaza and to the north via Damascus. Augustus broke the hold of the Parthian and Arab middlemen on the Eastern trade by establishing direct commercial connections by sea with India. By 1 BC, he had reopened the Red Sea by forcing the Sabaeans out of Aden and converting it into a Roman naval base. Ships were soon sailing directly to India across the Arabian Sea from Aden, blown by the monsoon winds from May to October. The monsoon blows from the south-west across the Arabian Sea, while the counter monsoon blows from the north-east between November and March.

Finest woven, printed cotton dupatta, Gujarat, India.

The island of Soqotra

Endemic tree species *Dracaena cinnabari*, the island of Soqotra, Yemen.
Photograph: Jane Taylor (1995).

The small island of Soqotra is part of Yemen and has long been a part of the Aden Governorate. It lies 150 miles east of the Horn of Africa and 240 miles south of the Arabian Peninsula. The island is very isolated and a third of its plant life is found nowhere else on earth. It has been described as "the most alien-looking place on Earth". Soqotra appears as Dioskouridou in the *Periplus of the Erythraean Sea*, a 1st-century AD Greek navigation aid. A local tradition holds that the inhabitants of Soqotra were converted to Christianity by Thomas the Apostle in AD 52. In the 10th century, the Arab geographer Abu Muhammad al-Hasan al-Hamdani stated that in his time most of the inhabitants of Suqotra were Christians. The were no Catholics, they were all Orthodox Christians and until the 13th century, the Bishop of India was responsible for the Christians of Soqotra.

Socotra is also mentioned in *The Travels of Marco Polo*; Marco Polo did not pass anywhere near the island but recorded that "the inhabitants are baptised Christians and have an archbishop" who, it is further explained, "has nothing to do with the Pope in Rome, but is subject to an archbishop who lives at Baghdad". They were Nestorian Christians but also practised ancient magic rituals despite the warnings of their archbishop.

Cucumber tree (*Dendrosicyos socotranus*), Hadibu, Soqotra, Yemen. Photograph: Jane Taylor.

The inhabitants of Soqotra

A wheat-eater, South Arabian, 1st c. BC - 1st c. AD alabaster. (Masterpiece Fair 2015).

Greek, Roman and Jewish merchants all changed ships for India and beyond in Soqotra, taking advantage of the newly discovered monsoon winds. Likewise Indian traders reaching the West.

The Red Sea port of Berica is now a desert, but also traded with Kerala.

The Chinese were long term allies of the southern Indian states. They gave way to the Arab traders who in turn controlled the western trade in the sea till the arrival of the European powers. These pre-Islamic Arabs from the Oman coast were the main suppliers of spices to Europe. They never revealed the source of these spices and even spread the stories of great birds protecting these spices in their nests in the unapproachable mountains of Arabia and Ethiopia.

A number of inscriptions, drawings and archaeological objects have recently been found on Soqotra island: further investigation showed that these had been left by sailors who visited the island between the 1st century BC and the 6th century AD.

Most of the texts are written in the Indian Brāhmī script, but there are also inscriptions in South Arabian, Ethiopian, Greek, Palmyrene and Bactrian scripts and languages. These 250 texts and drawings constitutes one of the main sources for the investigation of Indian Ocean trade networks in the first centuries of our era.

Opposite: Anthropomorphic stele, South Arabian, first c. BC - first c. AD, alabaster with white limestone and bitumen inlay. (Masterpiece Fair 2015).

Photographs reproduced courtesy of the Ariadne Galleries, London and New York.

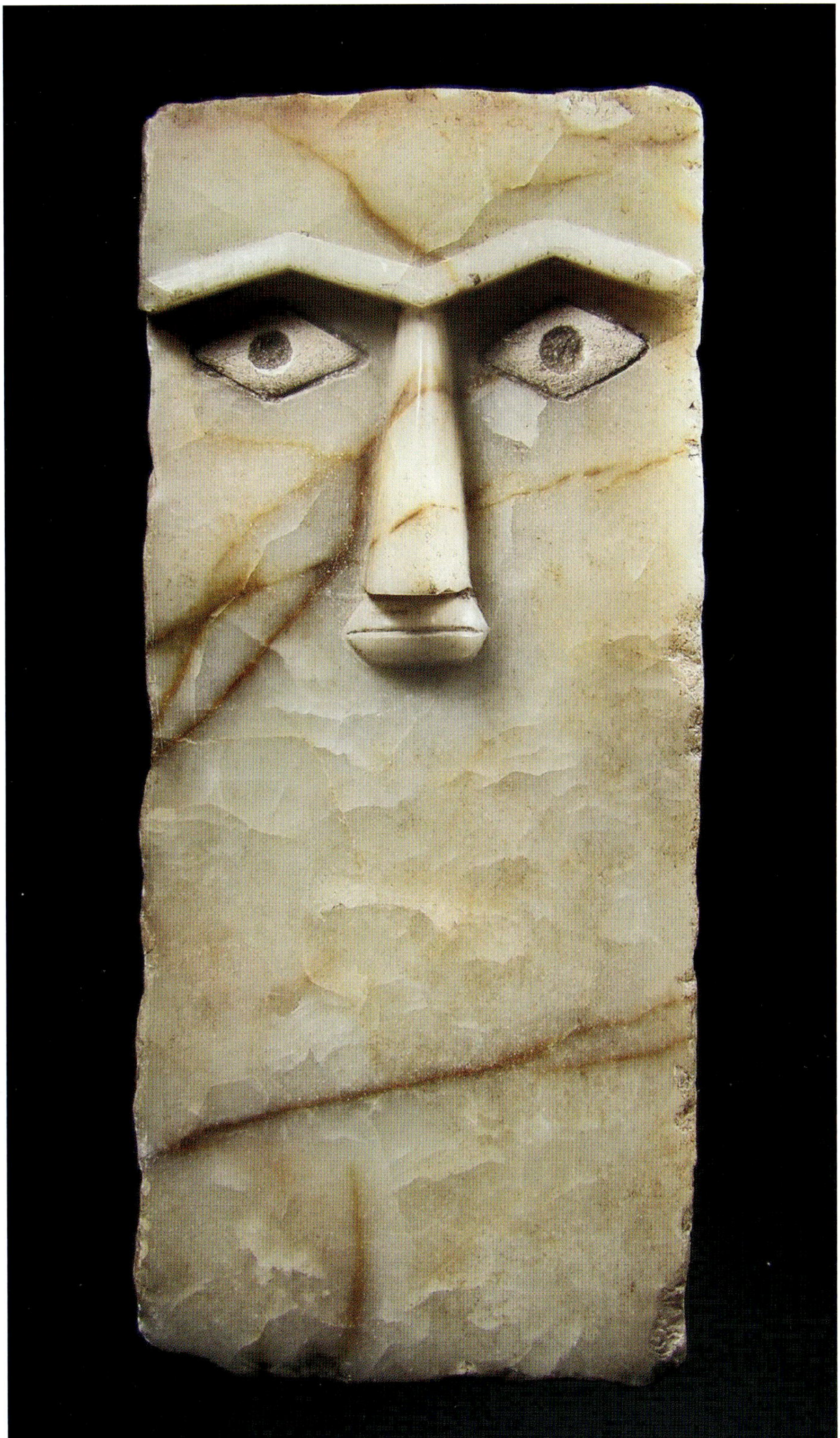

Habban the merchant and St Thomas set sail

Soqotra lies some 150 miles east of the Horn of Africa and 240 miles south of the Arabian Peninsula. The island is very isolated and a third of its plant life is found nowhere else on the planet.

The ancient city of Patala (Thatta) lay at the mouth of the Indus River. While Patala was well-known to mariners and traders of the Ancient Mediterranean, by the European Middle Ages, mapmakers no longer knew its location.

Pliny the Elder (Gaius Plinius Secundus, AD 23 - 79) referring to "the island of Patale, at the mouth of the Indus", wrote in Historia Naturalis: "Also in India as well as at Aswan in Egypt) at the well-known port of Patale the sun rises on the right and shadows fall southward".

The geographer Strabo (c. 64 BC - c. AD 24) said: "The Indus falls into the southern sea by two mouths, encompassing the country of Patalênê, which resembles the Delta in Egypt". He noted: "All these (nations) were conquered by Alexander, and last of all he reduced Patalênê, which the Indus forms by splitting into two branches... Patalênê contains a considerable city, Patala, which gives its name to the island".

In the late second century BC, Agatharchides of Cnidus recorded merchants from Patala, or as he called it, Potana, coming to the island of Soqotra to trade with Alexandrian merchants. The second century AD author Dionysius Periegetes said in his Orbis Descriptio: "This river (the Indus) has two mouths, and dashes against the island enclosed between them, called in the tongue of the natives, Patalênê".

Siltating has caused the Indus to change its course many times since the days of Alexander the Great, and the site of ancient Patala has been subject to much conjecture. Ahmad Hasan Dani, director of the Taxila Institute of Asian Civilizations, Islamabad, concluded: "There has been a vain attempt to identify the city of Patala. If 'Patala' is not taken as a proper name but only refers to a city, it can be corrected to 'Pattana', that is (Sanskrit for) a city or port city par excellence, a term applied in a later period to Thatta (onetime capital of Sindh), which is ideally situated in the way the Greek historians describe".

Did Habban and St Thomas sail from Soqotra to Patala and up the Indus to reach the Parthian capital of King Gondophares at Taxila, just ten miles from the river - a major Zoroastrian and Hellenistic city in which he would have felt very much at home?

St Thomas and Habban the merchant sailing to India; stained glass window, 12th c. Chartres Cathedral, Chartres, France.

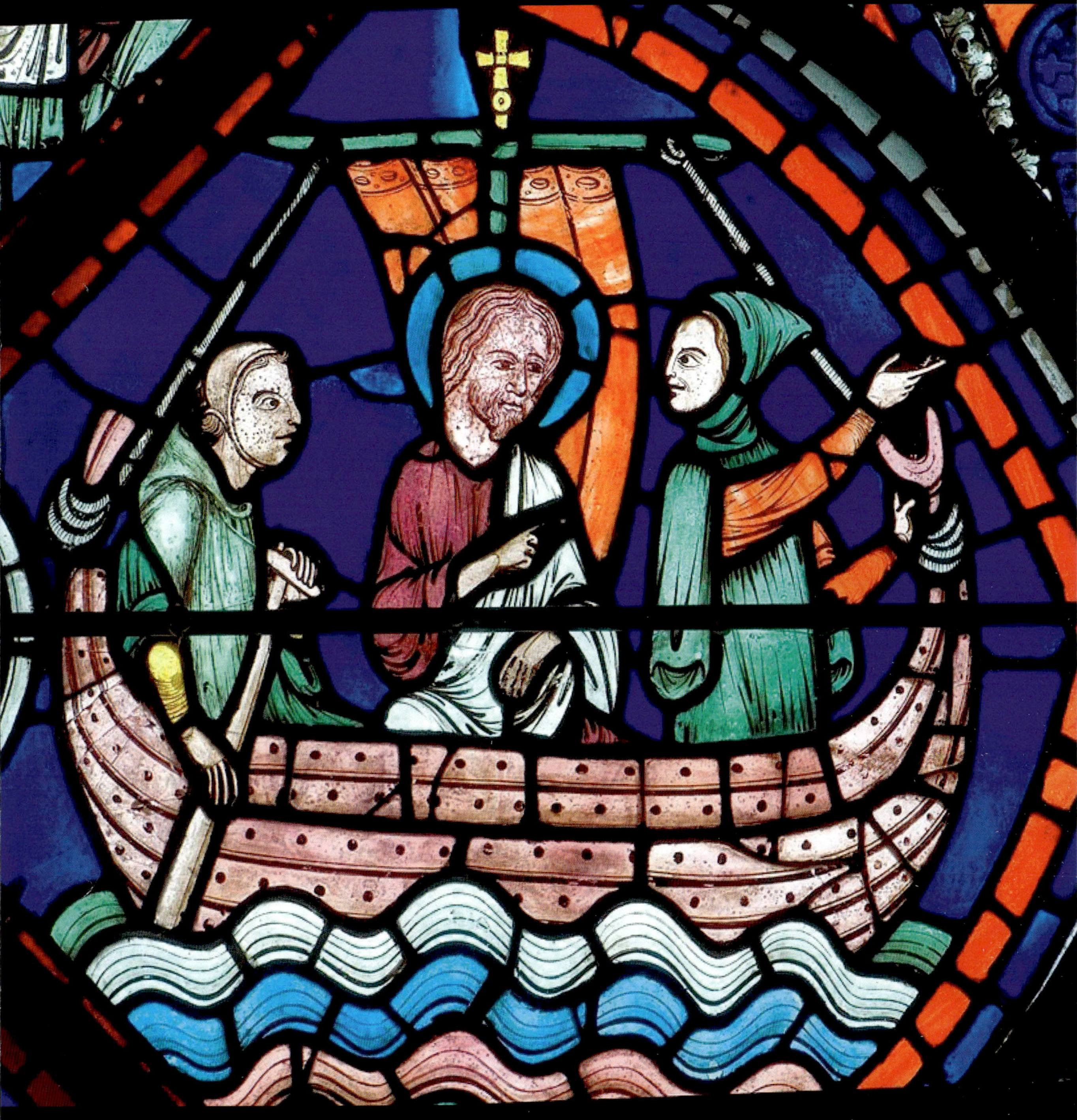

St Thomas calms the storm

Coptic textile of an Egyptian priest, 1st c. AD, the Benaki Museum, Athens, Greece (2013).

There was a certain God-fearing priest of the country of Egypt who went to the country of India to trade. And on the twenty-sixth day of the month of Genbot, which is the night of the festival of Saint Thomas, the apostle, he saw many people assembling on the bank of the river, wherein was an island on which Saint Thomas was, and at that moment a mighty wind storm came, and swept the water away.

And all the people set out and went into the church of Saint Thomas, which was on the island, and they found the verger of the church had died at that very moment; and they swathed him for burial, and buried him, and they prayed all that night.

And on the following day, which was the twenty-seventh day of the month of Genbot, and the festival of Saint Thomas, they partook of the Offering. And when the consecration was over, and the prayer of breaking the bread was said, they placed the Holy Body of our Lord in the hand of Saint Thomas, the apostle, the hand being alive and undecayed, and the people came one by one to receive the Holy Mysteries from his hand. And as they were receiving the Offering, there came a certain man from among the laity to receive, and the palm of the saint's hand was closed tightly over the Holy Body. And they all cried out "Kyrie-eleison" many times, and they prayed for a long time, and (then) the palm of the saint's hand opened, and administered the Holy Mysteries to that man, and all the people likewise received the Holy Mysteries; and they went out from the church, and returned to their houses in the peace of God. And at that very moment the storm of wind returned and brought back the water to its former place and height; and this has happened each year and it happeneth at the present day. Salutation to Thomas, who was prepared to thrust his hand into the wound made by the spear in the Lamb.

The Coptic Synaxarium,
(Coptic Orthodox Calendar for Genbot 26: 3 June).

Stormy waters over India (2016).

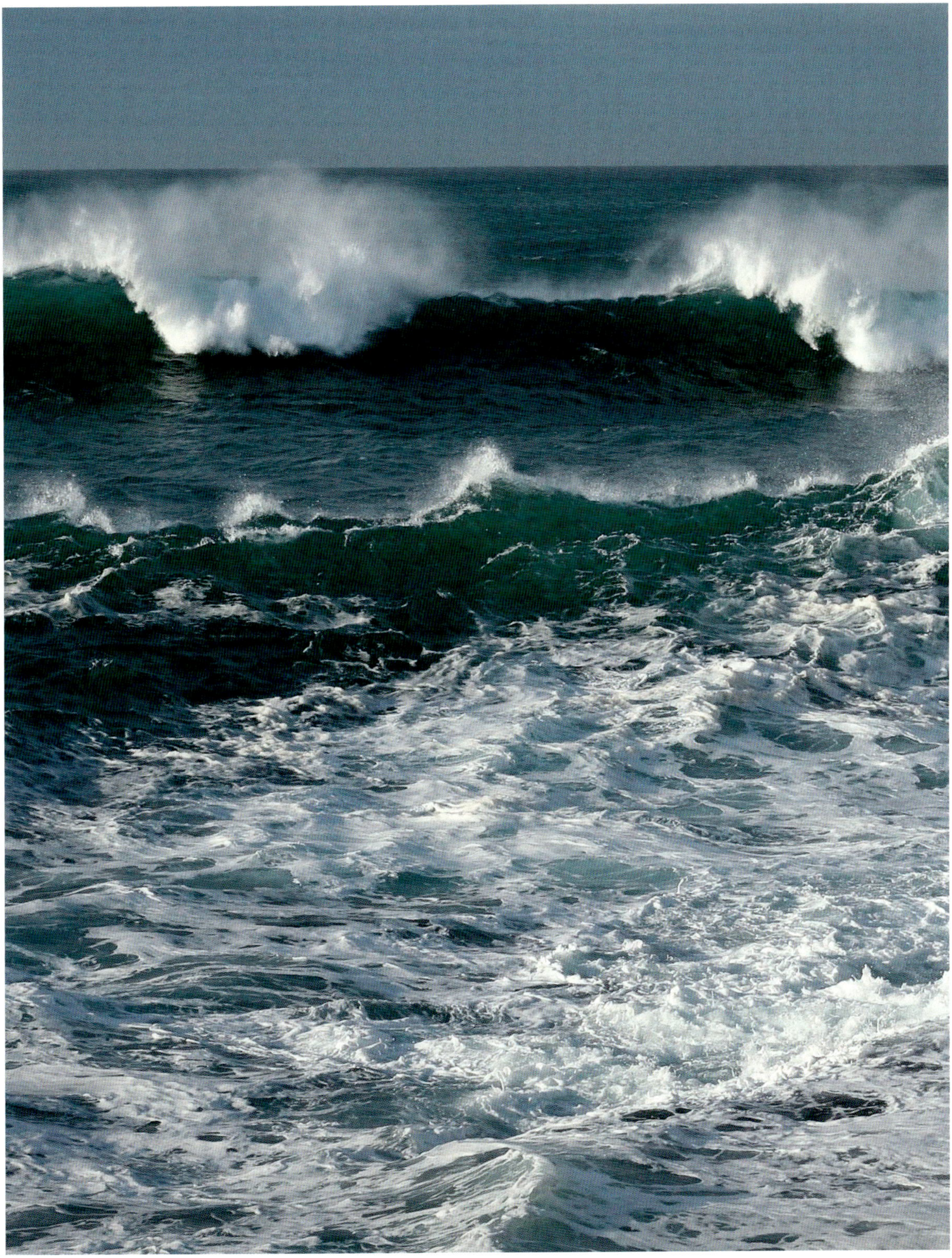

Shipping

Egyptian, Greek, Roman and Jewish merchants all changed ships for India and beyond in Soqotra, taking advantage of the newly discovered monsoon winds. Likewise Indian traders reaching the West. For many centuries, the sailors of Gujarat called the maritime route near Soqotra "Sikotro Sinh", meaning the lion of Soqotra that constantly roars - referring to the high seas near Soqotra.

The region was known to Roman and Greek traders, as shown by both Roman maps (such as the Tabula Peutingeriana), descriptions of traded goods such as silk, pepper and peacocks by writers such as Pliny and Ptolemy, and the discovery of Roman coins in southern India. It was known to Jewish traders, and small Jewish communities were already established by the time of Jesus; these were swelled considerably by refugees following the destruction of Jerusalem in AD 70.

St Thomas travelled by sea and landed on the coast of Kerala (also known as the Malabar coast) in 52 AD and preached to the Jewish community and locals of high standing. He established seven churches or "communities" and travelled overland around various kingdoms including those ruled by King Gondophares in Parthia.

Model of an Egyptian ship, 1st c. BC. The Israel Museum, Jerusalem, Israel (2014).

Traditional *dhows* like this have been built in Mandvi, the Rann of Kutch, India since ancient times. The design has not changed over centuries. (2010).

A *dhow* is the generic name of a traditional sailing vessel with one or more masts with lateen sails used in the Red Sea and Indian Ocean region. Historians are divided as to whether the *dhow* was invented by Indians or Arabs. Typically sporting long thin hulls, dhows are trading vessels primarily used to carry heavy items along the coasts of the Eastern Arabia, East Africa, Yemen and some parts of South Asia (Pakistan, India, Bangladesh). Larger dhows have crews of approximately thirty, smaller ones typically of around twelve.

The Indian presence in Alexandria may have influenced the culture, but few records remain about the manner of that influence. Clement of Alexandria mentions the Buddha in his writings and other Indian religions find mentions in other texts of the period. In view of these contacts, we can understand why Ptolemy's second century AD map of the world shows considerable knowledge of the geography of India.

3,000 ships a year came from the Red Sea ports to Muziris, for pepper and other spices. The maritime Silk Route was by sea via Kollon to Muziris.

Kutch had good sea relations with Kerala.

5.
Greek and Roman Mediterranean sea routes to India:

Trade winds

Greek, Ptolemaic and Roman accounts

Roman fishing boats and shipping entering a port; mosaic floor, 1st c., Rome, Italy (2012).

Greek navigators

Hindu boatman, Benares, India (2013).

According to Poseidonius, later reported in Strabo's Geography, the monsoon wind system of the Indian Ocean was first sailed by Eudoxus of Cyzicus in 118 or 116 BC. Poseidonius said a shipwrecked sailor from India had been rescued in the Red Sea and taken to Ptolemy VIII in Alexandria. The unnamed Indian offered to guide Greek navigators to India. Ptolemy appointed Eudoxus of Cyzicus, who made two voyages from Egypt to India. The first, in 118 BC, was guided by the Indian sailor.

After Eudoxus returned with a cargo of aromatics and precious stones a second voyage was undertaken in 116 BC. Eudoxus navigated the second voyage, sailing without a guide.

Strabo, whose Geography is the main surviving source of the story, was sceptical about its truth.

Modern scholarship tends to consider it relatively credible. During the second century BC Greek and Indian ships met to trade at Arabian ports such as Aden (called Eudaemon by the Greeks). Attempts to sail beyond Aden were rare, discouraged, and involved a long and laborious coast-hugging journey.

Navigators had long been aware of the monsoon winds. Indian ships used them to sail to Arabia, but no Greek ship had yet done so. For the Greeks to acquire the expertise of an Indian pilot meant the chance to bypass the Arabian ports and establish direct commercial links with India. Whether or not the story told by Poseidonius of a shipwrecked Indian pilot teaching Eudoxus about the monsoon winds is true, Greek ships were in fact soon using the monsoon winds to sail to India. By 50 BC there was a marked increase in the number of Greek and Roman ships sailing the Red Sea to the Indian Ocean. "Another Greek navigator, Hippalus, is sometimes credited with discovering the monsoon wind route to India. He is sometimes conjectured to have been part of Eudoxus's expeditions."

Eudoxus of Cyzicus,
c. 130 BC.
Greek navigator who explored the Arabian Sea for Ptolemy VIII, king of the Hellenistic Ptolemaic dynasty in Egypt.

Greek boat, mosaic floor, first century AD. The Israel Museum, Jerusalem, Israel (2016).

The monsoon winds

The Indians and southern Arabians had probably known these winds for a long time, but their discovery was ascribed by the Greeks to a navigator called Hippalus or Eudoxus (depending on the sources) who learned how to use the monsoon winds. Once they had succeeded in that, they were able to bypass the Arabian ports and establish direct commercial links with India. Whether or not the story of Eudoxus is true, by 70 - 50 BC there was a marked increase in the number of Greek ships sailing across the Red Sea and Indian Ocean to Indian ports, as we are informed by several inscriptions and also by Strabo. Shortly after Octavian's (the future Augustus) victory at Actium in 31 BC and the annexation of Egypt, many more merchants would sail to India. Strabo singles out only India, but ships also plied from Egypt to India, East Africa and South Arabia. They left from and returned to Myos Hormos and Berenikê (Bender el Kebir/Medinet el-Haras), the latter being a major trading port.

Merchants heading for Africa left Egypt in July. They reached Cape Guardafui, Rhapta, in the vicinity of Dar es Salaam - their final stop. Merchants involved in Indian trade, also started their trips in July so that they could reach Bab-el-Mandeb in September, at the right time to be carried by the southwest monsoon. They sailed either to the mouth of the Indus (Barbarikon) and northwest India (Barygaza, on the Gulf of Cambay) or to Muziris in south-west India - where a shrine of Augustus stood. The route so helped enhance trade between the ancient Roman Empire and the Indian subcontinent that Roman politicians and historians are on record decrying the loss of silver and gold to buy silk to pamper Roman wives, and the southern route grew to eclipse and then totally supplant the overland trade route.

Roman and Greek traders frequented the ancient Tamil country, present day Southern India and Sri Lanka, securing trade with the seafaring Tamil states of the Pandyan, Chola and Chera dynasties and establishing trading settlements which secured trade with South Asia by the Greco-Roman world since the time of the Ptolemaic dynasty a few decades before the start of the first century AD and remained long after the fall of the Western Roman Empire. Strabo records that in Antioch, Emperor Augustus received an ambassador from a South Indian king called Pandyan of Dramira. The country of the Pandyas, Pandi Mandala, was described as Pandyan Mediterranea in the *Periplus* and *Modura Regia Pandyan* by Ptolemy.

"The route between the Roman world and India, which was Rome's source for large quantities of fine muslins, pearls and spices, was well established."
The route between Rome and India was indeed old and established and the travellers went the other way too, to Alexandria and Rome from India.

A rich matron awaits the arrival of silks, cottons and spices from India. Fresco covered in ash in the volcanic eruption of Pompeii in AD 79. The National Archaeological Museum, Naples, Italy (2014).

The Indus

The River Indus, Pakistan.

The River Indus runs from just inside China, on the Tibetan Plateau, south through Pakistan to the Arabian Sea some 60 miles south-east of Karachi. The river marks the separation between the Persian Plateau and the Indian subcontinent. The name Indus is of Greek origin, dating from the time of Alexander the Great, whose armies crossed the river in about 326 BC. As early as 300 BC, the term "India" was applied to all lands east of the Indus.

The Brahmanical period would trace the gradual extension of the Aryan race over Northern India, from their first occupation of the Punjab to the rise of Buddhism, and would comprise the whole of the prehistoric, or earliest section of their history, during which time the religion of the Vedas was the prevailing belief of the country.

The Buddhist period of India embraced the rise, extension, and decline of the Buddhist faith, from the era of the Buddha, to the conquests of Mahmud of Ghazni, during the greater part of which time Buddhism was the dominant religion of the subcontinent.

The Indus forms the delta of present-day Pakistan mentioned in the Vedic Rigveda as Sapta Sindhu and the Iranian Zend Avesta as Hapta Hindu (both terms meaning "seven rivers"). The river has been a source of wonder since the Classical Period, with King Darius of Persia sending his Greek subject Scylax of Caryanda to explore the river as early as 510 BC.

Megasthenes's book *Indica* derives its name from the river's Greek name, "Indós", and describes Nearchus's contemporaneous account of how Alexander the Great crossed the river. The ancient Greeks referred to the Indians (people of present-day India and Pakistan) as "Indói", literally meaning "the people of the Indus". Both the country of India and the Pakistani province of Sindh owe their names to the river. The Indus River provides key water resources for the Punjab, which accounts for most of Pakistan's agricultural production, and Sindh. The word Punjab means "land of five rivers" which are the Jhelum, Chenab, Ravi, Beas and Sutlej, all of which finally flow into the Indus.

The ultimate source of the Indus is in Tibet; the river begins at the confluence of the Sengge and Gar rivers in the ranges of Mt Kailas.

The River Indus near Taxila, Pakistan.

Strabo's account

Strabo's mention of the vast increase in trade following the Roman annexation of Egypt indicates that the monsoon was known and manipulated for trade in his time. The trade started by Eudoxus of Cyzicus in 130 BC kept increasing:

"At any rate, when Gallus was prefect of Egypt, I accompanied him and ascended the Nile as far as Syene and the frontiers of Kingdom of Aksum (Ethiopia), and I learned that as many as one hundred and twenty vessels were sailing from Myos Hormos to the subcontinent, whereas formerly, under the Ptolemies, only a very few ventured to undertake the voyage and to carry on traffic in Indian merchandise."

Strabo,
64/63 BC – c. AD 24.
Book II: 5.12.

The western Indian Ocean bore several names in the antiquity: "Erythraean Sea" (Greek: *Erythra thalatta* ; Latin: *mare Rubrum*) or Indian Sea (Greek: *Indikon pelagos*; Latin: *Indicum mare*). The modern Red Sea was generally called either 'The Arabian Gulf' or 'The Erythraean Sea".

Roman shipping with a crocodile, marble sarcophagus panel, Rome, Italy (2012).

Herodotus' account

Gharials are found on the banks of the River Indus.

"But as to Asia, most of it was discovered by Darius. There is a river, Indus, second of all rivers in the production of crocodiles. Darius, desiring to know where this Indus empties into the sea, sent ships manned by Scylax, a man of Caryanda, and others whose word he trusted; these set out from the city of Caspatyrus and the Pactyic country, and sailed down the river toward the east and the sunrise until they came to the sea; and voyaging over the sea west, they came in the thirtieth month to that place from which the Egyptian king sent the above-mentioned Phoenicians to sail around Libya (i.e., Africa). After this circumnavigation, Darius subjugated the Indians and made use of this sea. Thus it was discovered that Asia, except the parts toward the rising sun, was in other respects like Libya."

Herodotus,
484-425 BC.
The Histories, IV: 44.

Muziris

A collection of glass beads, Roman, 1st c. AD, found at Muziris, Kerala, India (2016).

"If the wind, called Hippalus, happens to be blowing, it is possible to arrive in forty days at the nearest market of India, called Muziris. This, however, is not a particularly desirable place to disembark, on account of the pirates which frequent its vicinity, where they occupy a place called Nitrias; nor, in fact, is it very rich in products. Besides, the road-stead for shipping is a considerable distance from the shore, and the cargoes have to be conveyed in boats, either for loading or discharging."

Pliny the Elder,
AD 23-79.
Historia Naturae VI:26.

By the time of Augustus up to 120 ships were setting sail every year from Myos Hormos to India. So much gold was used for this trade, and apparently recycled by the Kushan Empire for their own coinage, that Pliny the Elder complained about the drain of specie to India.

"Minimaque computatione miliens centena milia sestertium annis omnibus India et Seres et paeninsula illa imperio nostro adimunt: tanti nobis deliciae et feminae constant: quota enim portio ex illis ad deos, quaeso, iam vel ad inferos pertinet? India, China and the Arabian peninsula take one hundred million sesterces from our empire per annum at a conservative estimate: that is what our luxuries and women cost us. For what fraction of these imports is intended for sacrifices to the gods or the spirits of the dead?"

Pliny the Elder,
AD 23-79.
Historia Naturae XII: 41, 84.

Augustus Caesar, bronze statue, 1st c. AD.
The National Museum, Athens Greece (2015).

Augustus Caesar

Roman exports to India

Greek amphora sent to Muziris. The Muziris Museum, Kerala, India (2016).

Gold and silver had to be continually exported from Rome to Asia. Late in the first century AD, Pliny estimated that India, China, and Arabia drained away annually at least 100 million sesterces (around 2.5 billion pounds in 2015), declaring: "That is the sum which our luxuries and our women cost us."

Wine in amphora was sent to Muziris for the consumption of Greek and Roman traders who spent several months waiting there for the monsoon winds to take them back to Europe.

The discovery of large hoards of Roman coins that have been found throughout India, and especially in the busy maritime trading centres of the south supports Pliny's statement. This serious drain was one of the factors in the general economic decline of the Roman world in the third century AD. The South Indian kings reissued Roman coinage in their own name after defacing the coins to signify their sovereignty.

The Tamil Sangam literature of India recorded mention of the traders. One such reads: "The beautifully built ships of the Yavanas came with gold and returned with pepper, and Muziris resounded with the noise."

Blue ribbed glass bowl, Pompeii, AD 70, the Archaeological Museum, Naples, Italy (2014).

Several similar ribbed glass bowls in blue, green and yellow have been excavated in Muziris, Kerala, and are in the small Muziris archaeological museum.

Indian trade with Pompeii

Among the archaeological findings in Pompeii, which was covered with ashes from the Vesuvius eruption of AD 79, a statuette of a goddess seems remarkably out of place. It represents the Indian goddess Lakshmi. It was definitively not manufactured in any part of the Mediterranean nor the Near or Middle East. Identical objects have been found in places like Tagara Bhogavardhana and they are evidence that the statuette found in Pompeii was made in India and exported all the way to that unfortunate city of the Roman empire. There are suggestions that, since it was found near the house of a dyer, it probably came together with an import of indigo dye.

The finding is further evidence of the flourishing trade existing in the first century AD between the Mediterranean areas and very distant Asian countries. At that time travelling within the Roman empire was extremely easy, safe and relatively fast. There was a developed postal system, at the service of the imperial public administration but in fact used by everyone. Messages could reach even very distant parts of the empire amazingly fast.

Travelling beyond the limits of the empire was equally safe and relatively easy, due to the trade routes in the Persian Gulf and Indian Ocean. Rome, with its immense wealth, was a very important trading counterpart for the Eastern oriental merchants. Rome was a net importer and the added value along the route made the trade extremely attractive and worthy of protection and promotion by the imperial authorities. The Romans even established trading posts in India. A well known one was identified in Arikamedu, near the modern Pondicherry. Roman coins, amphoras and other objects have been found in that area. A subject of the Roman empire who wanted to travel from the safe shores of the Mediterranean to such distant lands would have not met any particular difficulty. He could have chosen the land trade routes, followed by caravans that came even from more distant lands, like China, or the sea routes, probably faster although limited by the seasonal winds, from Malabar to the Red Sea and back.

St Thomas could have reached Alexandria from Judea with great ease and then from there to any of the trading stations on the Red Sea, where a ship would have taken him to Malabar.

I do believe that St Thomas was obeying the prompting of his Saviour when he decided to take the gospel so far. Maybe St Thomas saw cultic objects similar to the Lakshmi statuette and was determined to break the hold of pagan worship on those distant but worthy souls. We will never know for sure, but there is no doubt that the door was open and the way to India was an inviting and easy path for St Thomas, the first apostolic missionary to the East.

Dr Giancarlo Elia,
2015.

Lakshmi goddess of wealth, modern bronze statuette.

Black Gold

Peppercorns growing on the vine in Dr Kurian Thomas's garden, Kerala, India (2016).

When Augustus became head of the Roman world, the Tamil and Kushan rulers sent him congratulatory embassies. At least nine other embassies from India visited the Roman emperors, and Roman-Indian trade greatly increased. Indian birds (particularly talking parrots, costing more than human slaves) became the pets of wealthy Roman ladies, and Indian animals (lions, tigers, elephants and buffaloes) were used in the wild beast shows of Roman emperors.

To satisfy the Roman world's insatiable appetite for luxury goods, Western trade with the East grew immensely in the first two centuries AD. But because such Roman exports as wool, linen, glass and metalwork to the East did not match in value Rome's imports of silk, spices, perfumes, gems and other luxuries, the West suffered seriously from an adverse balance of trade.

The Rome-India trade, which was very strong in the first c. AD, also saw several cultural exchanges which had a lasting effect for both the civilisations and others involved in the trade. Traces of Indian influences appear in Roman works of silver and ivory, or in Egyptian cotton and silk fabrics used for sale in Europe.

Then as now, the very best quality of pepper grows in the area between Kollon and Muziris in Kerala. It is harvested in December and January and keeps for several years if dried properly. In antiquity, pepper cost the same as gold in weight, hence its name: Black Gold.

The Romans acquired their taste for pepper from the Copts in Egypt; till then they used garum paste (a fermented fish sauce) to flavour their food.

The Nazarins had a monopoly of the pepper trade and used the money they raised to build churches.

It was certainly possible that St Thomas came to Kerala: 3000 ships a year plied their trade on the maritime Silk Route by sea from the Red Sea ports via Kollon to Muziris, to buy pepper and other goods.

(Coffee comes from a flower in March-April and is not indigenous to Kerala, but is grown at 6,000 feet in the Nilgiri Hills to the north-east in Karnatica.)

Pepper drying in Dr Kurian Thomas' garden, Kerala, India (2016).

Dr Kurian Thomas's Peppercorns ready to sell, Kerala, India (2016).

Exotic birds

Roman mosaic panel of a songbird and a peacock, first c. AD, Masterpiece Fair, London (2013).

Patrician Roman ladies had a passion for exotic birds, especially those which sang like this yellow-vented bulbul, Ranthambhore, Rajasthan, India (*right*).

Photograph: Jim Wheeler (2014).

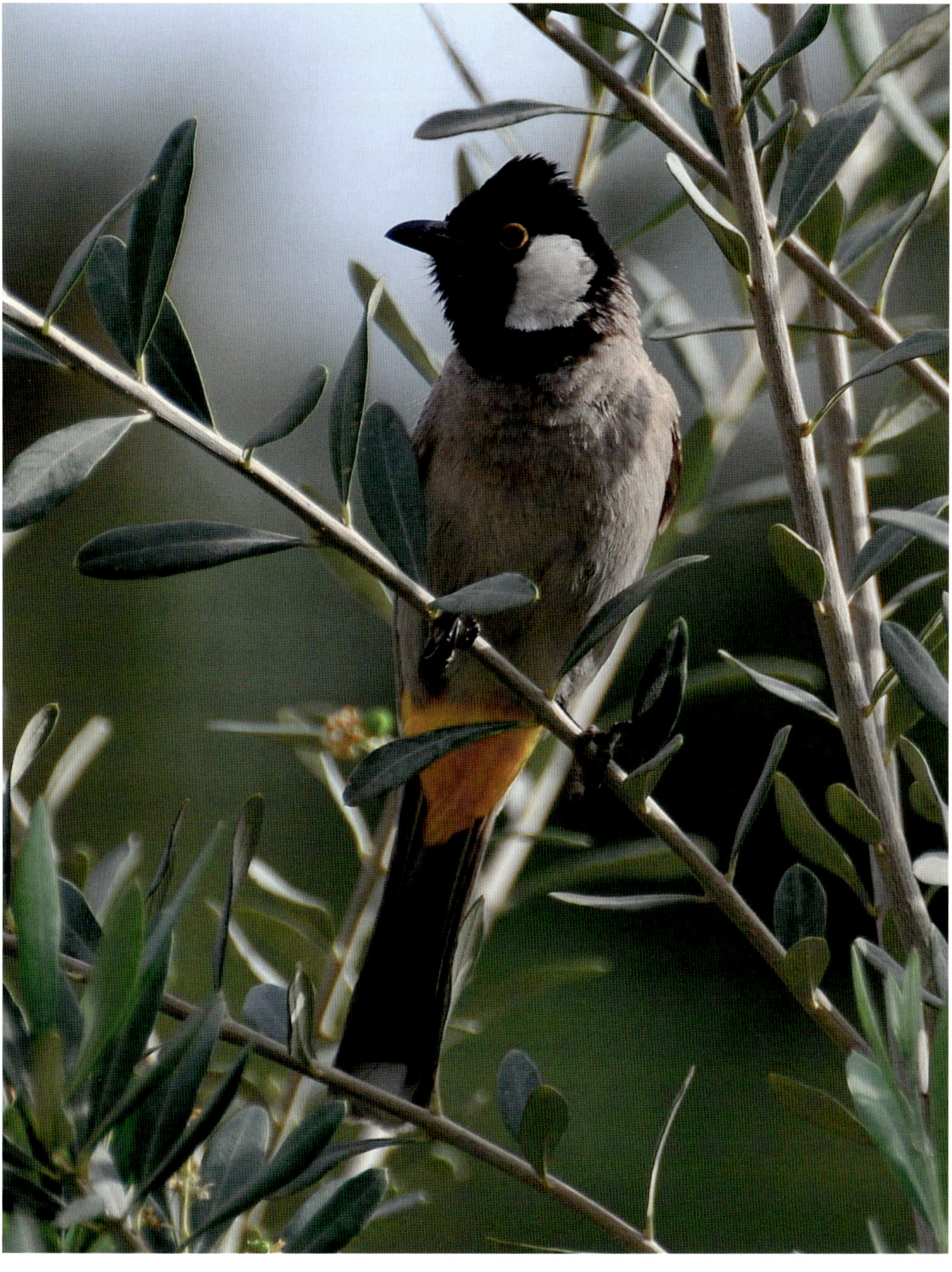

Tigers for the Colosseum

Wild animals to serve the blood-thirsty Emperors' constant "bread and circuses" entertainment in the Colosseum were shipped back from India to Rome in large numbers. Housed in cages, and fed a constant supply of raw meat, they must have suffered greatly on the long sea journey to Rome.

Damnatio ad bestias (condemnation to beasts) was a form of Roman capital punishment in which the condemned were killed by wild animals. This form of execution, which first came to ancient Rome around the 2nd century BC, was part of the wider class of blood sports called *Bestiarii*. The act of *damnatio ad bestias* was considered entertainment for the people of Rome. Killing by wild animals, such as lions, tigers and rhinoceroses formed part of the inaugural games of the Flavian Amphitheatre in AD 80. Between the first and third centuries AD, this penalty was applied to the worst criminals, slaves, and early Christians. The custom was brought to ancient Rome by two commanders, Lucius Aemilius Paullus Macedonicus, who defeated the Macedonians in 186 BC, and his son Scipio Aemilianus, who conquered the African city of Carthage in 146 BC and borrowed the practice from the Carthaginians. It was originally applied to such criminals as defectors and deserters in public, its aim being to prevent crime through intimidation and was rated as extremely useful: it soon became a common procedure in Roman criminal law. The sentenced were tied to columns or thrown to the animals.

The practice of throwing Christians to the lions dates from the Great Fire of AD 64 which Nero blamed on the Christians. This was reflected by the 2nd c. Christian writer Tertullian who states that the general public blamed Christians for any general misfortune and after natural disasters would cry "Away with them to the lions!"

The most popular animals in the arena were lions, which were imported to Rome in significant numbers specifically for *damnatio ad bestias*. These Asian lions are still bred in the Gir National Park in Gujarat, India; today there are some 523 left in the wild.

At the time of Augustus, tigers were to be found in abundance in jungles all over India. Today there are 48 tiger reserves in India, all governed by Project Tiger. The nearest reserve to Muziris would have been just up the Periya river in Kerala.

Poaching is a major threat to tiger populations and today (2017) there are some 3,062 wild tigers left in India.

Right: Machali, the most famous tigress in Ranthambhore National Park, Rajasthan, India. Photograph: Aditya Singh (2014).

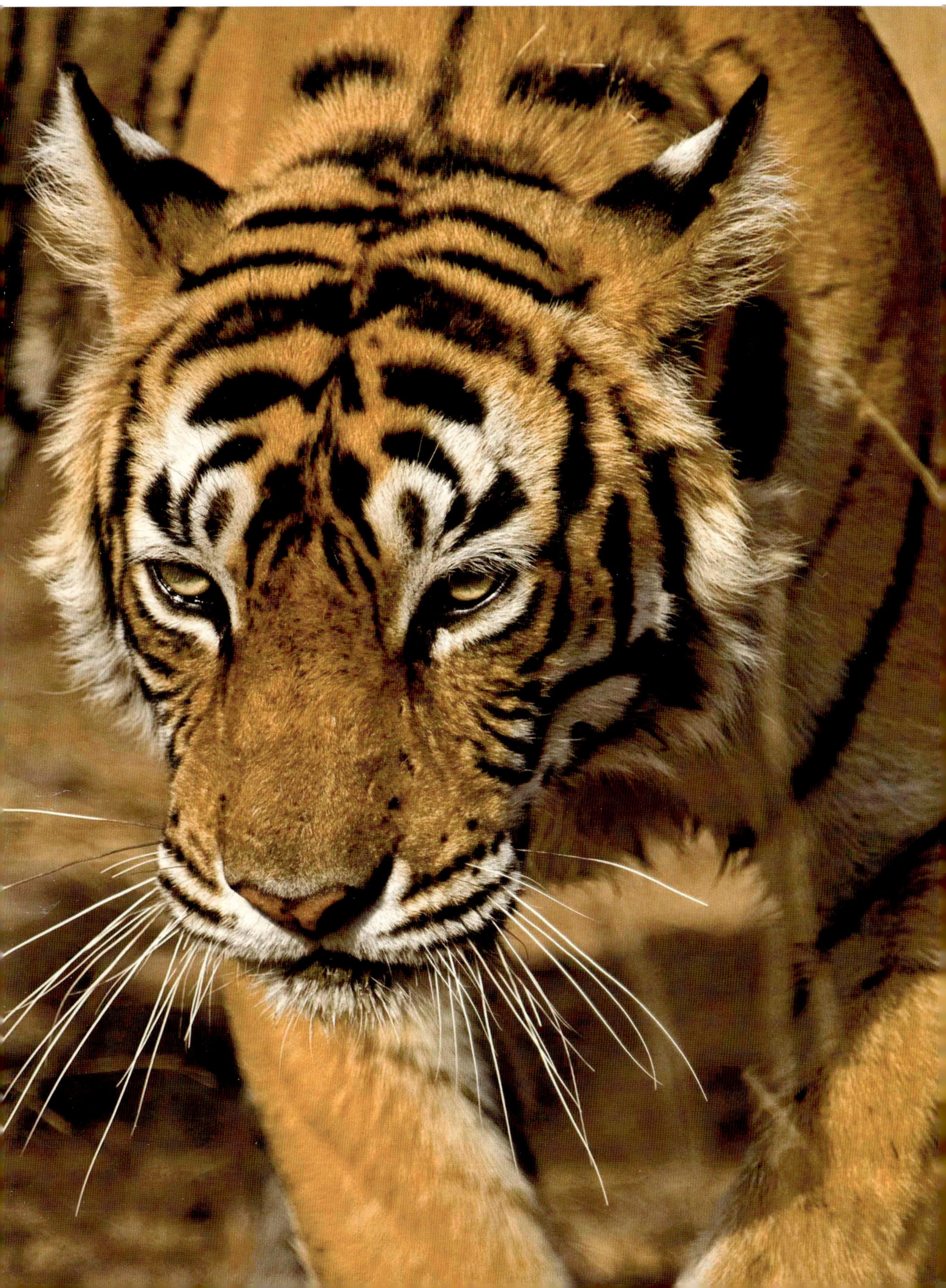

6.
6.
Kerala:

Muziris

The seven and a half churches founded by St Thomas

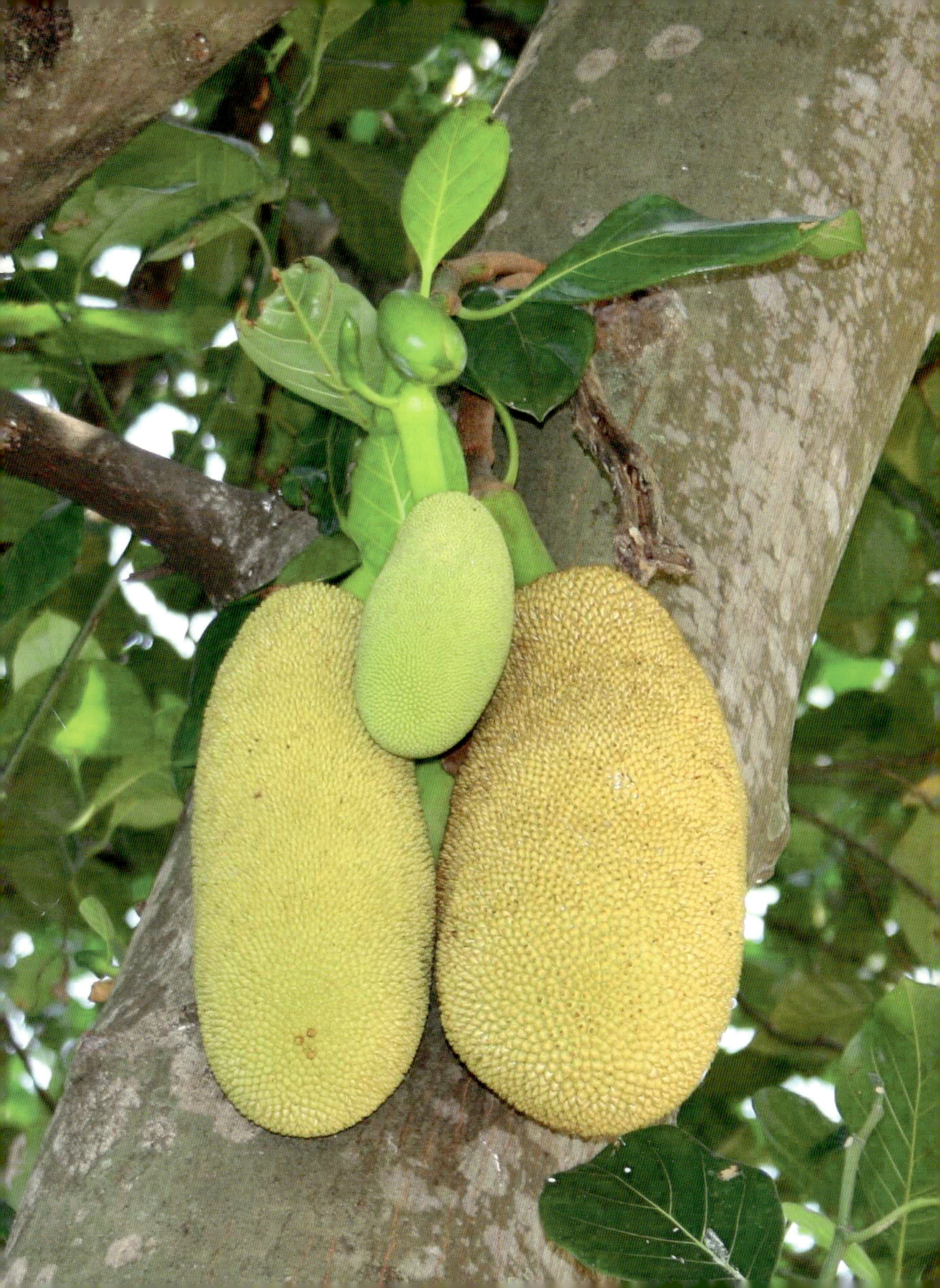

The Dravidians

With the exception of a short period during the Mauryan Empire, the vast tableland of south India - the Deccan - and its fertile coastal plains remained outside the main forces of political change in the north. The Dravidian peoples of this area, with their dark skin and small stature, differed in appearance, language and culture from the Aryan-speaking peoples of the north. Gradually, however, as Brahmin priests and Buddhist monks infiltrated the south, Hinduism and Buddhism were grafted onto the existing Dravidian culture.

Politically the south remained divided into numerous warring states, the most interesting being three Tamil-speaking (a Dravidian dialect) kingdoms in the far south. Tamil folk poetry, which describes the people at work and at play, is justly famous. By the 1st century BC, the Tamil Lands had become an intermediary in the maritime trade extending eastward to the East Indies and westward to the Hellenistic kingdoms.

The peace and prosperity that the Kushans brought to much of northern India ended in about AD 220. The collapse of the Kushan state was followed by a century of chaos and almost total obscurity before a new era of unified imperial rule, which rivalled that of the Mauryas, began in India under the Guptas. In the meantime another great civilisation had arisen in China.

Previous page: Breadfruit, Sri Lanka (2014).

Opposite: Two Dravidian matrons in the temple at Madurai, Tamil Nadu, India (2013).

185

The Malabar coast

Fish slab, Cochin, Kerala. India (2016).

St Thomas arrived on the Malabar coast during the Chera Empire. In total he spent eight years here. The Cheras were an ancient Dravidian royal dynasty of Tamil origin who ruled in areas of Tamil Nadu and Kerala from c. 270 BC to c. AD 710. This encompassed a wide area that included Venad, Kuttanad, Kudanad, Pazhinad, and others so that they governed the area between Kanyakumari in the south to Kasaragod in the north. This included Palghat, Coimbatore, Salem and Kollimalai. They established a capital at Vanchi, known by the Romans as Muziris, the bustling trade centre between the Red Sea ports and India and China.

Vedic influence seemed to have been minimal before the advent of Brahmanism. The Cheras had no particular religion - even the caste system was absent from their society - but ancestral worship was popular. The war goddess was known as Kottavai, but there no structural temples existed. Instead, images of gods were kept in the open air, probably under a tree (which echoes Indo-European practice in Europe, notably amongst the Celts and Germanics. So did the Dravidians copy the practice from similar Indo-European arrivals in northern India or did it predate both groups?). Unlike the later La Tène Celts, an established priesthood was conspicuously absent from Chera society. Structural temples only came into existence after the arrival of the Brahmins.

Agriculture was the main occupation for the great majority of the populace. Tools and tackles were made of iron, and fishing, hunting, spinning, weaving, carpentry, and salt manufacture were all important. Precious stones, pearls and spices were exported from Kerala. Ports included Muziris, Tyndes, Barace, and Nelaynda. The ruler's income depended on the war booty he collected, plus land revenue and taxes. This individual was called "ko", or "kon", or "kadumko" (meaning 'great king'), and these kings were generally known by their titles, which were based on personal peculiarity, a singular habit, or an important achievement.

By 100-50 BC the Greek kingdom of Bactria had fallen and the remaining Indo-Greek territories had been squeezed towards Eastern Punjab. India was partially fragmented, and the once tribal Sakas were coming to the end of a period of domination of a large swathe of territory in modern Afghanistan, Pakistan, and north-western India. The Greeks who had gained these lands were very soon to be overthrown in the north by the Kushans, while still battling for survival against the Satavahanas of India.

Fish slab, Cochin, Kerala, India (2016).

Hinduism

The world's oldest surviving religion is polytheistic Hinduism. The life cycle from birth to death is exemplified by this wonderful 10th century *Nataraj* (Dancing Shiva).

Hindus have to born into a caste, and so however much someone might be attracted to Hinduism and wish to practice it, conversion is impossible.

Being a Hindu is different from being a follower of any other religion. Hindus are not required to carry out any rituals or pray at any specific times or on any specific day of the week.

Hindus believe that the whole world was created equal by the creator as Brahmins, or the uppermost caste, and then in consequence of their acts became distributed into different castes.

Caste-ism, although identified with Hinduism, has been followed on the subcontinent by other religions also including Muslims and Christians.

The basic division into castes is:
1. Brahmin - the priestly and religious teacher class.
2. Kshatriyas - the warrior and ruler class
3. Viashyas - the trader and merchant class.
4. Shudras - the labourer and service provider class.

Outside and beneath these four castes are the untouchables – renamed by Gandhi-ji as *Harrayans* or Children of God.

Movement up and down in caste with each new birth takes place according to a person's "*Karma*" so a Shudra may become a Brahmin and a Brahmin may fall away from his status and become a Shudra in the next life according to how they have lived the previous life.

Most Hindu households will have a small temple room in their homes and this is where they pray so there is no need to visit any temple except on special occasions.

Hinduism is the historic Vedic religion known as "*Sanatan Dharma*" which literally translated means "Living tradition" and has evolved out of thousands of years of practical observation and theoretical study of the phenomenon of the birth - death cycle.

Vijay Kapur,
New Delhi,
2010.

Nataraj (dancing Shiva) 10th c. Chola bronze, the Archaeological Museum, Chennai, India.

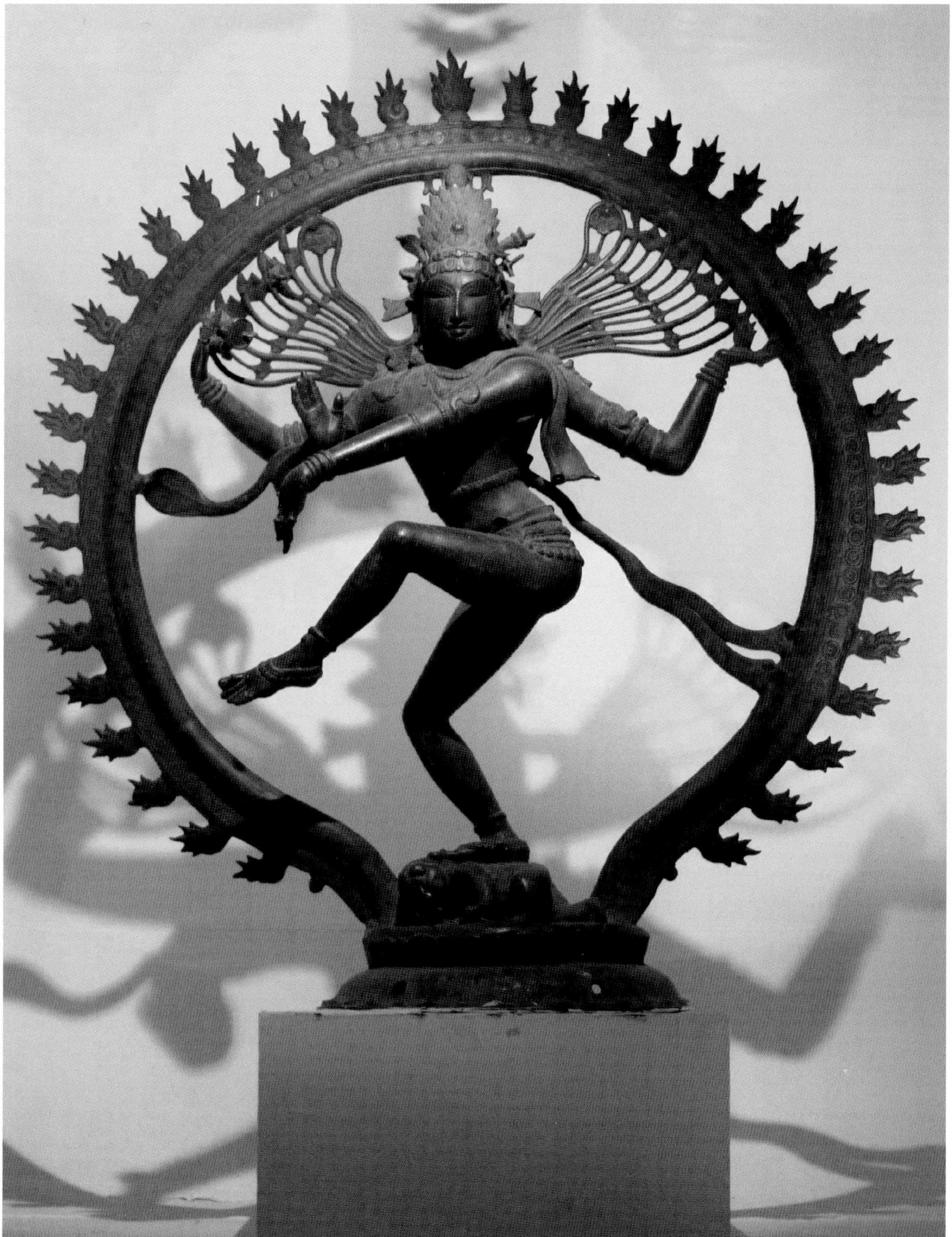

The Hindu cycle of birth and death

Hindus believe in the cycle of birth, death and rebirth. They believe that the *"Atman"* (the soul) is eternal and the *"Sharira"* (the body) is like clothes which when they get old, are changed.

So death is considered a stage of development: a change of body in the cycle of birth and rebirth which ends with *"Moksha"*- unity with God (or the cosmic spirit), when the life one has lived comes near to perfection in terms of daily morality, care of fellow beings and good deeds done.

The body is washed by relatives, dressed in fresh cloth and laid on a bamboo trestle bed. It is tied down to this and bedecked with flowers.

Only men attend funerals, always wearing white. The close male relations shave their hair and carry the body to the cremation ground which must be beside water, hopefully a river, especially the Holy River Ganges, or beside a *tank* or lake, where the family pundit conducts prayers, at the end of which the eldest son has to light the pyre and when the burning of the body is complete, to crack the skull to enable the soul to move on.

The ashes are gathered up when the pyre has completely died down. Three days later the eldest son collects the ashes and immerses them in the Holy River Ganges.

On the fourth day the *"Chautha"* ceremony is held at the home of the family and prayers are given to ensure the soul of the departed moves safely to the next world.

Young children are not cremated, but their bodies are put in the Ganges, as are those of *sadhus* (holy men).

If a wife dies with her husband still living, she is wrapped in her red wedding *saree* to show she never suffered the pangs of widowhood. If she is a widow, she wears white. All men are wrapped in a white cloth.

Many Hindus believe that the soul rests among the leaves of a pepel tree for 40 days after death, before reincarnating. Others believe it could be many years or even centuries before a soul chooses to do so.

And so the Hindu cycle continues as it has done for over nine thousand years.

Vijay Kapur,
New Delhi,
2010.

Hindu mourner with a shaven head and the "cow's tail", Benares, India (2015).

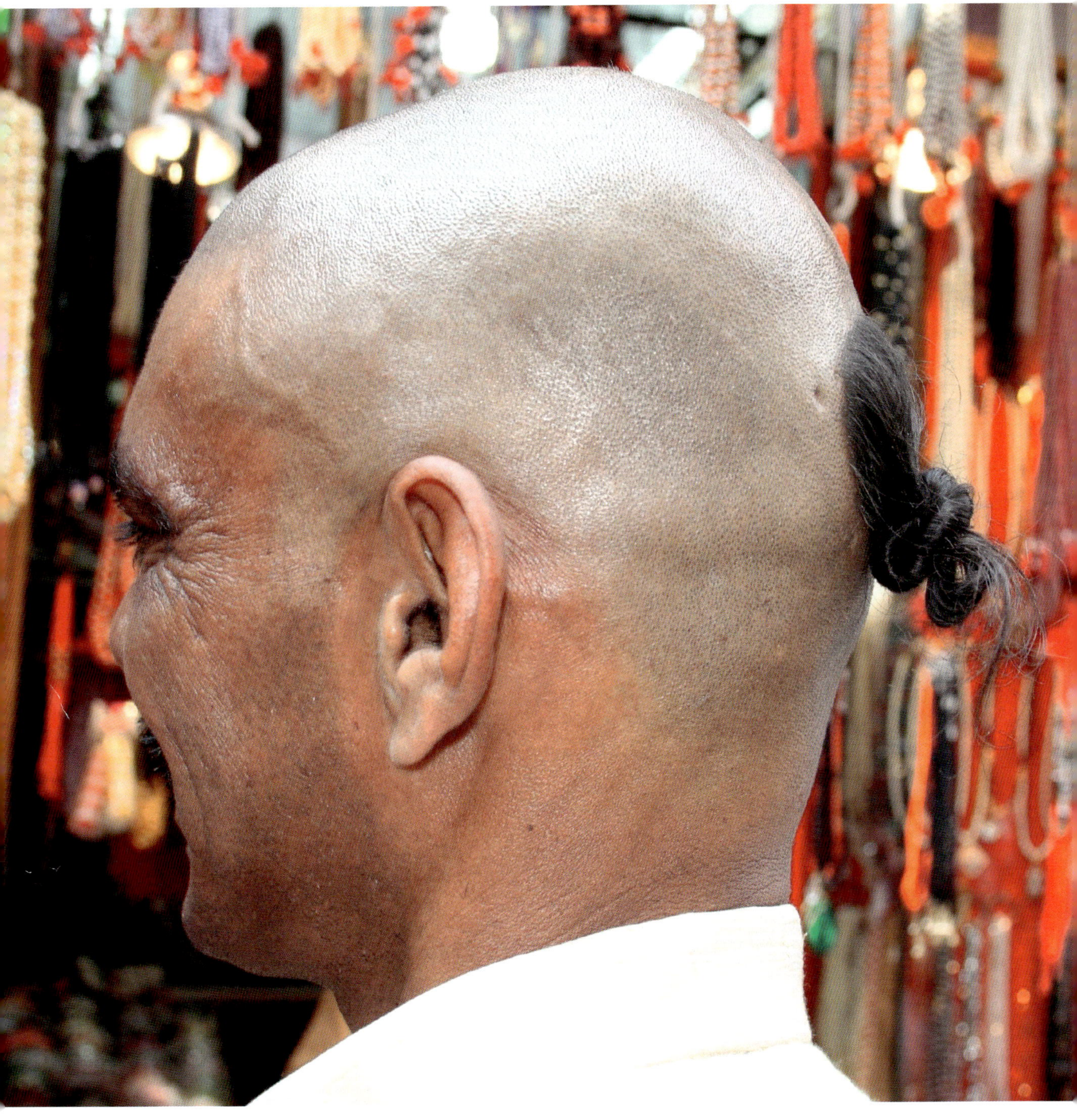

Coconuts

Coconuts, Colombo, Sri Lanka (2013).

Coconuts are native to the Asia-Pacific region of the world and have long occupied a place in Hindu religious practice, first appearing in Sanskrit literature in the fourth century BC. The two major Sanskrit epic tales, the Ramayana and the Mahabharata both feature coconuts. Kerala got its name from the coconut.

In India one of the most common offerings in a temple is a coconut. They play a vital role in all puja rituals. Aside from their use in cooking, coconuts with their life-giving milk are used in various Hindu ceremonies: it is cracked on the doorstep of a new house or on a new bridge; when a child is named and a great bonfire is made, a coconut is thrown into the middle; during a marriage proposal, it is sent by the girl's parents to the proposed groom: if he accepts it, then the engagement is fixed. (This is known as "having accepted the *nãriyal"*). It is used at a *haldi* ceremony before marriage when the bride holds a coconut. In the state of Kerala, the largest producer of coconuts in India, coconut flowers are planted in rice bowls and displayed during wedding ceremonies.

A coconut is always tied to a bier in six places before taking a body for cremation and burnt with the body on the funeral pyre and when a funeral pyre is made for a husband with a wife committing *suttee,* she is accompanied into the flames holding a coconut.

The Holy Cow

The origin of the veneration of the cow can be traced to the Vedic period (Second can be traced to the Vedic period (Second millennium–7th century BC). In Hinduism, the cow is revered as the source of food and symbol of life and may never be killed. In ancient India, oxen and bulls were sacrificed to the gods and their meat was eaten, but even then the slaughter of milk-producing cows was prohibited. Some scholars believe the tradition came to Hinduism through the influence of strictly vegetarian Jainism.

The cow continued to be especially revered and protected among the animals of India. Later, in the spiritually fertile period that produced Jainism and Buddhism, Hindus stopped eating beef: this was mostly for practical reasons as well as spiritual. The cow remains a protected animal in Hinduism today and Hindus do not eat beef. Most rural Indian families have at least one dairy cow, a gentle spirit who is often treated as a member of the family.

The five products (*pancagavya*) of the cow are milk which nourishes children as they grow up, curds, ghee butter, urine for disinfectant and dung (*gobar*) is a major source of fuel for rural households throughout India. They are all used in *puja* (worship) as well as in rites of extreme penance.

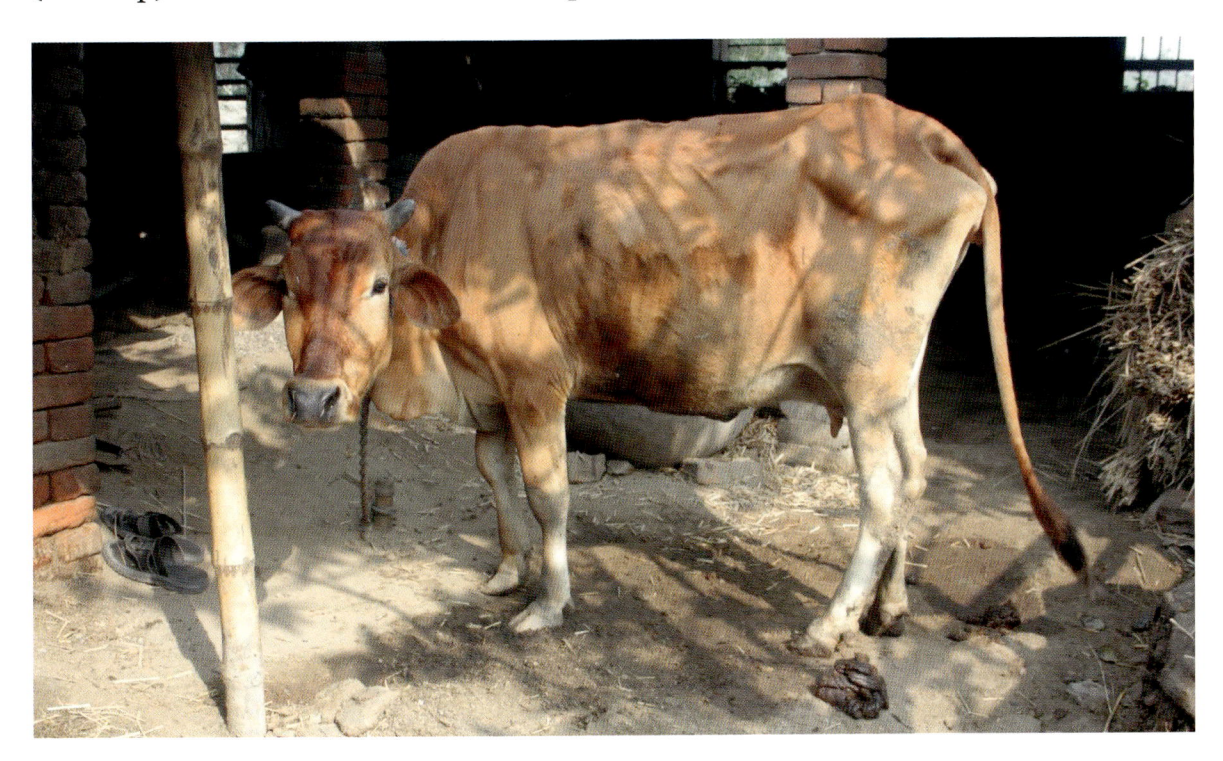

Domestic cow in its cowshed, Bihar, India (2016).

Indian comments on St Thomas

15 paise Indian postal stamp 1964.

The Government of India issued postage stamps to commemorate anniversaries of St Thomas' life and work in India. On one of those stamps Thomas is shown as an elderly man, with his facial hair very reminiscent of historic and contemporary hair and beard styles of older Indian men. This icon uses that stamp's image for the face of Thomas rather than using a more readily available youthful Mediterranean saint's face.

20 paise Indian postal stamp, 1972. The Mar Thoma cross.

You may be surprised to learn that Christianity came to India long before it went to England or Western Europe, and when even in Rome it was a despised and proscribed sect. Within 100 years or so of the death of Jesus, Christian Missionaries came to South India by sea. They were received courteously and permitted to preach their new faith. They converted a large number of people, and their descendants have lived there, with varying fortune, to this day. Most of them belong to old Christian sects which have ceased to exist in Europe.

Pandit Jawaharlal Nehru, 1889-1964,
First prime minister of Independent India: 1947-1964.

Remember St Thomas came to India when many of the countries of Europe had not yet become Christian, and so those Indians who trace their Christianity to him have a longer history and a higher ancestry than that of Christians of many European countries and it is really a matter of pride to us that it so happened.

Dr Rajendra Prasad, 1884-1963,
President of India: 1950-1962,
New Delhi on the St Thomas day celebrations, 18 December 1955.

Christianity has flourished in India from the beginning of the Christian era. The Syrian Christians of Malabar believe that their form of Christianity is Apostolic, derived directly from the Apostle Thomas. They contend that their version of the Christian faith is distinctive and independent of the forms established by St Peter and St Paul in the west. What is obvious is that there have been Christians on the west coast of India from very early times. They were treated with great respect by the Hindus, whose princes built for them churches. Christianity has been with us from the second century AD. It has not merely the rights of a guest but the rights of a native.

Dr S Radhakrishnan, 1888-1975,
President of India: 1962-1967.

Right: Hindu Sadhu, Madurai, India (2015).

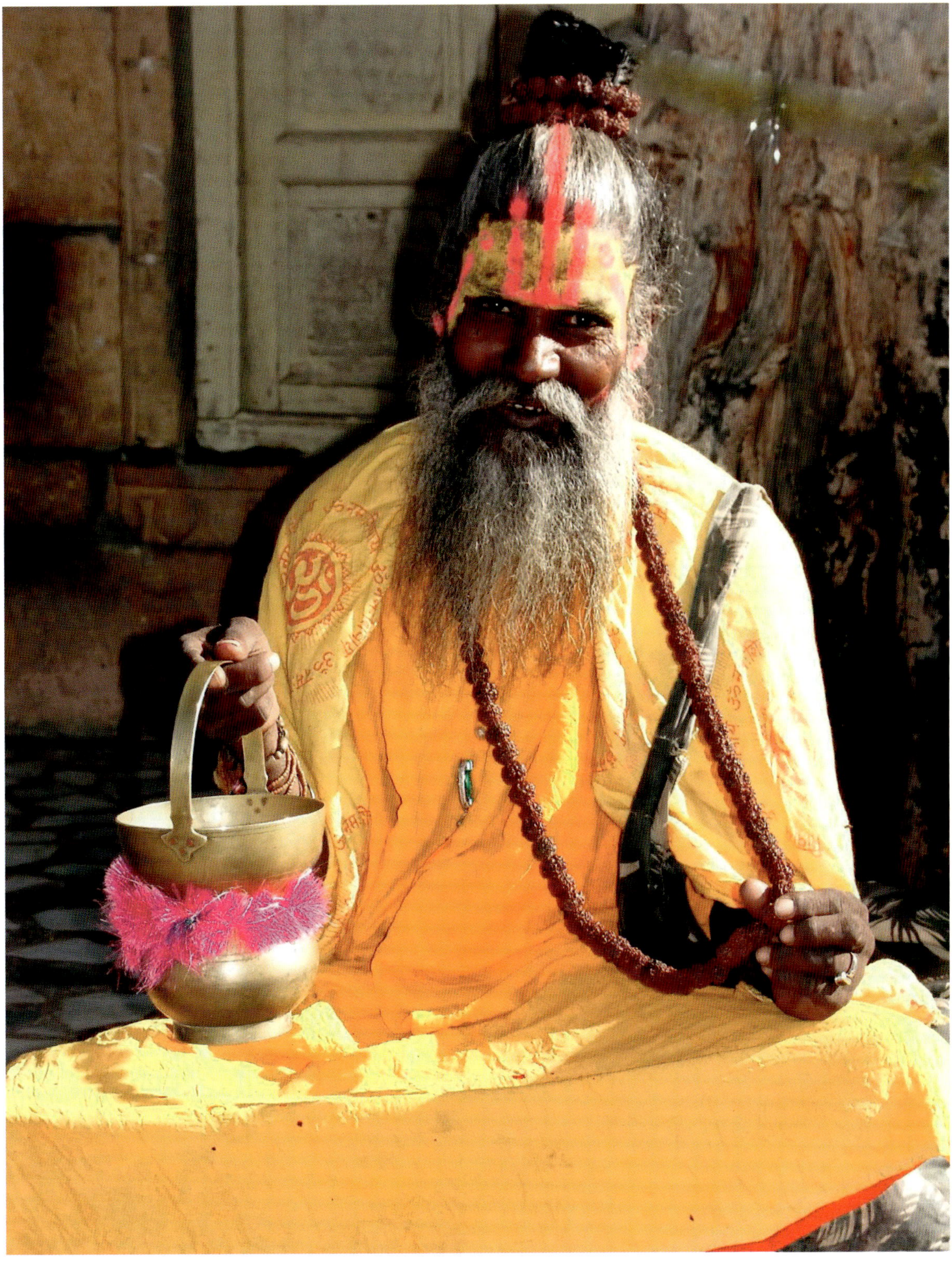

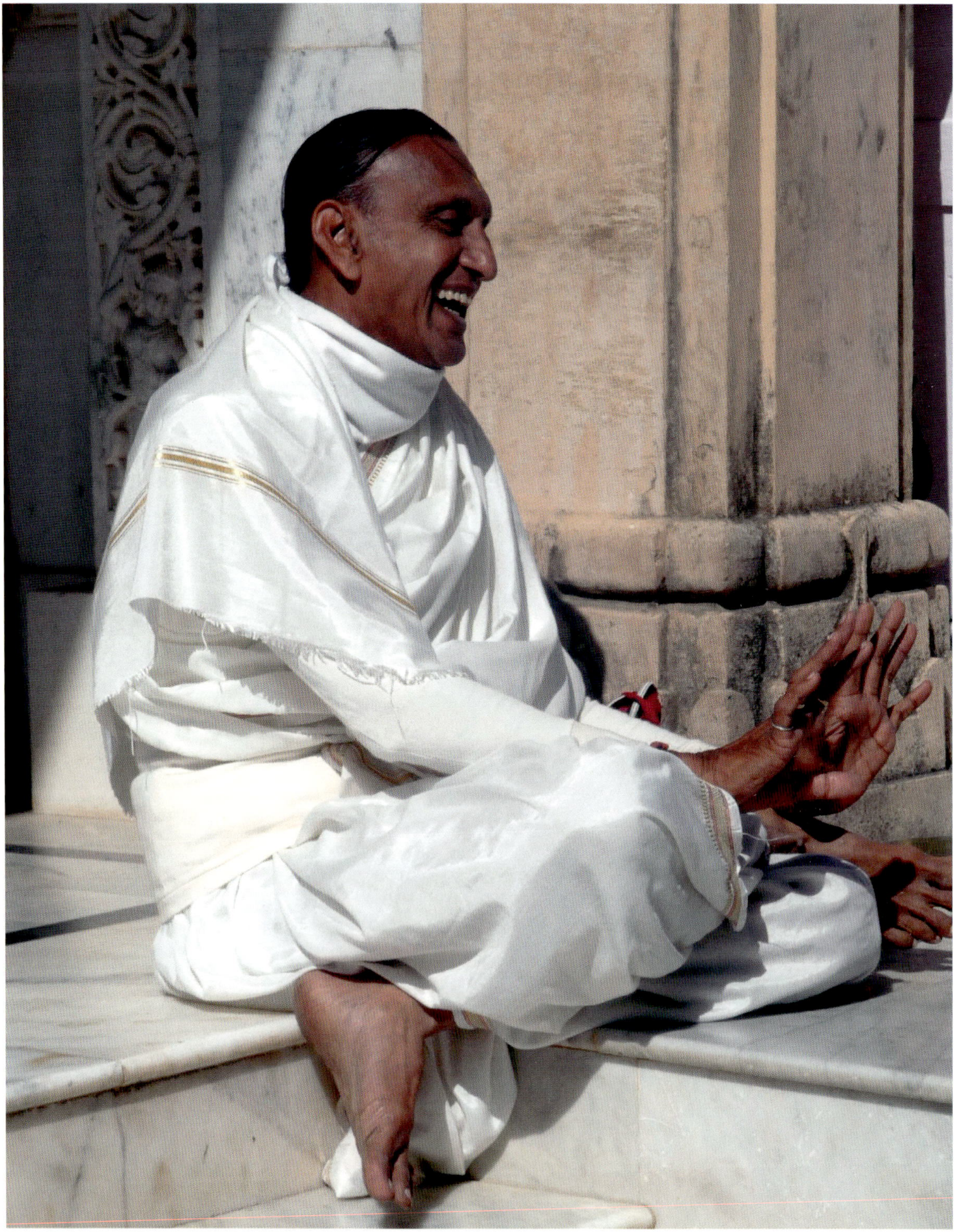

Jainism

Jainism is an ancient Indian religion that teaches that the way to liberation and bliss is to live a life of harmlessness and renunciation. It teaches a path to spiritual purity and enlightenment through a disciplined mode of life founded upon the tradition of *ahimsa*, non violence to all living creatures. Beginning in the 7th–5th centuries BC, Jainism evolved into a cultural system that has made significant contributions to Indian philosophy and logic, art and architecture, mathematics, astronomy and astrology, and literature. Along with Hinduism and Buddhism, it is one of the three most ancient Indian religious traditions still in existence. While often employing concepts shared with Hinduism and Buddhism, it must be regarded as an independent phenomenon. It is an integral part of Indian religious belief and practice, but it is not a Hindu sect and not a Buddhist heresy, as earlier scholars believed. The most illustrious of those few individuals who have achieved enlightenment are called *Jina* (literally "Conqueror"), and the tradition's monastic and lay adherents are called Jain ("Follower of the Conquerors") or Jaina. This term came to replace a more ancient designation, *Nirgrantha* ("Bondless"), originally applied to renunciants only. Mahavira, like the Buddha, was the son of a chieftain of the Kshatriya (warrior) class. At the age of 30 he renounced his princely status to take up the ascetic life. He spent the next twelve and a half years following a path of solitary and intense asceticism. He then converted eleven disciples (called *ganadharas*), all of whom were originally Brahmans. The community appears to have grown quickly. According to Jain tradition, it numbered 14,000 monks and 36,000 nuns at the time of Mahavira's death. While Mahavira had rejected the claims of the caste system that privileged Brahman authority on the basis of innate purity, a formalised caste system nonetheless gradually appeared among the laity in the south. The hierarchy differed from the Hindu system in that the Kshatriyas were assigned a place of prominence over the Brahmans and in its connection of purity, with a moral rather than a ritual source. Jinasena did not see the caste system as an inherent part of the universe, as did Hindu theologians and lawgivers.

In Jainism, a human being who has conquered all inner passions and therefore possesses omniscience, is called Jina (conqueror),distinguishes the soul (consciousnesses) from the body (matter). Jains believe that all living beings are really soul; intrinsically perfect and immortal. Souls in transmigration (i.e. the liability to repeated births and deaths) are said to be embodied in the body like a prison. Non-injury (*ahiṃsā*) and self-control are said to be the means to liberation. The liberated souls free from transmigration (*saṃsāra*) are worshipped as God in Jainism. Jain texts reject the idea of a creator or destroyer God and postulate an eternal universe.

Jain merchant, Palitana, Gujarat, India (2012).

The Jews in Kerala

The reception of the Queen of Sheba by King Solomon, English silk work embroidery, mid-17th c., courtesy of Witney Antiques, Oxfordshire, England (2016).

Jews from Babylon settled in South India in 973 BC from the time of King Solomon's first fleet and the first Jewish settlement in Kerala was soon after the Babylonian conquest of Judea in 586 BC. Mass migration followed the sack of Jerusalem in AD 70. In the historical tradition of the Malabar Jews, Cranganore is regarded as their original home and chief dwelling place. Jewish immigrants reputedly established their first foothold on the Malabar coast, and from there branched out into neighbouring towns and villages. Cranganore, the leading port and commercial centre in ancient and medieval India, is associated with the ancient port of Muziris, north of Cochin. Medieval travellers (including Benjamin of Tudela) refer to it as Shingli, Shinkali or Ginjalek. The Jews of Cranganore enjoyed cultural and religious autonomy under their leader, called the *mudaliar*, appointed by the rajah who was accorded a charter and privileges engraved on copper plates by the Hindu emperor, which are still in the hands of the Cochin Jews. The suggested date of these inscriptions ranges from the 4th to the 11th century AD.

Christian and Jewish settlers from the Roman Empire continued to live in India long after the decline in bilateral trade. Their number may have given rise to the widely circulated notion that the Jews had an independent kingdom in Cranganore. Given the fact that Muziris was an important port, it likely that the Jews of the town were engaged in trade. Another argument in support of this view is that when in 1341 the harbour of Cranganore became silted up and the town lost its significance as a port, the Jews moved to Cochin.

The conquest of Cranganore by the Portuguese in 1523 led to the complete destruction of the Jewish community. As a result there was another wave of emigration to other places in Malabar, from which the city of Cochin benefited in particular. The Jewish settlement in Cranganore was finally abandoned in 1565, when Jews moved permanently to Cochin and neighbouring areas, but the memory of the Jewish settlement in Cranganore/Shingli has survived until today.

Until recently there was a tradition of placing a handful of earth from Cranganore in the coffin of a deceased Cochin Jew. The Shingli form of pronunciation is a specific feature of the liturgy of the Cochin synagogue. Now there is no one left to bury them except the local Keralans. There are only 35 Jews left in Kerala (in 2016); they have all died or emigrated to Israel or America. A rabbi now comes to Cochin from Jerusalem to celebrate the major festivals.

Below: Jewish shop, Jew Street, Cochin, India (2013).

The Jews of Cranganore

The present Kodungallur was called Mahodayapuram, Makothevarpattanam, Muyirikkodu and Muziris by the Greeks and Romans; Shingly by the Jews; and Cranganore by the Portuguese. Recent archaeological findings reveal that the 3000-year old port city of Shingly or Muziris is closer to Paravur than the popularly accepted location in Kodungallur. Interestingly, Muziris had the first Jewish settlers around 961 BC. Cranganore was known as the "Jerusalem of East" or the "Little Jerusalem". Cranganore is said to have no fewer than 18 synagogues at the height of its glory. Tradition has it that in AD 70, when the Second Jerusalem Temple was destroyed by the Romans, some 10,000 Jews or 1000 families (including men and women) fled to Cranganore. An interesting folklore describes how they brought two of the original silver trumpets used in the Second Jerusalem Temple to Cranganore and these were blown by Levites on the eve of every Sabbath. Once when the Levites were late, the non-Levites usurped their privilege resulting in a quarrel that ultimately led to the destruction of the trumpets!

According to Syrian Christian traditions, St Thomas converted 40 members of the Jewish community in Cranganore, but a good number continued to follow their ancestral religion and gave Christians the name "Nazaranis". We know from the writings of the Arab traveller Ibn Wahab (AD 880) that a Jewish community existed in Cranganore in the 9th century AD. Benjamin of Tudela (12th century) refers to it as Shinkali or Ginjalek. From the 4th - 15th century AD, the Jews of Kodungallur had an independent kingdom ruled over by a Prince (Mudaliar) of their own race and choice.

Words of the 14th century Spanish Hebrew poet and traveller Rabbi Nissim ben Reuven (1320-1376) shares that feeling: "I heard of the city of Shingly, I longed to see an Israel king, Him, I saw with my own eyes!" Thus, Joseph Raban (4th Century) the first Jewish Mudaliar of Kodungallur and the recipient of the famous "Copper Plates", was followed by 72 leaders. The last leader, Joseph Azar (14th century), fled with a few faithful followers to Cochin after he had a fight with his brother and established the Kochangadi synagogue in 1344. Legend has it that Joseph Azar swam to Cochin with his wife on his back! This was the first major split inside the Jewish community of Kodungallur. David Reubeni, a Qabbalist of Rome and Lisbon, has cited many Jews living in Cranganore in 1524. Similarly, a letter sent from Israel to Italy by David di Rossi in 1535 records Shingly with a large Jewish population who followed the 12th century classic 'Mishneh Torah'. He calls Shingly Sindschell and reports that the town was exclusively inhabited by Jews who sold the king of Portugal, annually, 40,000 burdens of pepper!

Menorah, the synagogue, Cochin, India (2013).

Pliny describes the Indian ports

Muziris (Kodungallur) and Nelcyndis or Nelkanda (near Kollam) in South India, are mentioned as flourishing ports by Pliny the Elder (c. AD 23- 77) who gives a description of voyages to India in the first century AD. He refers to many Indian ports in his work *The Natural History*:

To those who are bound for India, Ocelis (on the Red Sea) is the best place for embarkation. If the wind, called Hippalus (Southwest Monsoon), happens to be blowing it is possible to arrive in forty days at the nearest market in India, "Muziris" by name. This, however, is not a very desirable place for disembarkation, on account of the pirates which frequent its vicinity, where they occupy a place called Nitrias; nor, in fact, is it very rich in articles of merchandise. Besides, the roadstead for shipping is a considerable distance from the shore, and the cargoes have to be conveyed in boats, either for loading or discharging. At the moment that I am writing these pages, the name of the king of this place is Caelobothras (Keralaputras).

Another port, and a much more convenient one, is that which lies in the territory of the people called Neacyndi, Barace by name. Here King Pandion (Pandya) used to reign, dwelling at a considerable distance from the market in the interior, at a city known as Modiera (Madurai). The district from which pepper is carried down to Barace in boats hollowed out of a single tree is known as Cottonara (Kuttanadu).

St Thomas is believed to have left north-west India when invasion threatened and travelled by vessel to the Malankara coast, possibly visiting southeast Arabia and Socotra en route, and landing at the former flourishing port of Muziris (modern-day North Paravur and Kodungallur) near Cochin (c. AD 51–52) in the company of the Jewish merchant Habban. From there he is said to have preached the gospel throughout the Malabar coast. The various churches (or communities) which he founded were located mainly on the Periyar River and its tributaries and along the coast, where there were Jewish colonies. He reputedly preached to all classes of people and had about 17,000 converts, including members of the four principal Hindu castes.

Dravidian fishermen on the banks of the Periyar river, Kodungallur, Kerala, India (2016).

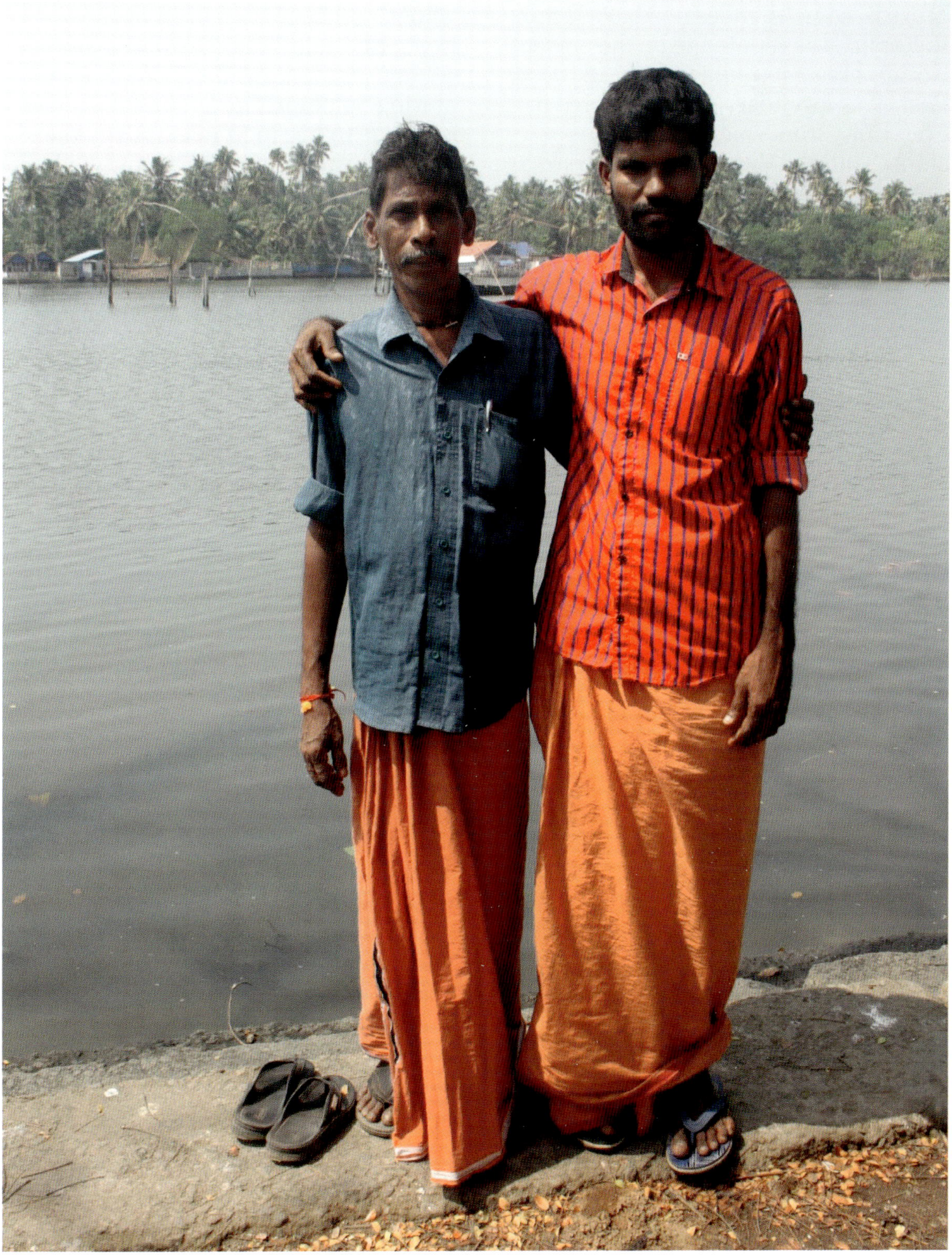

Muziris

Muziris, some 12 miles north of Cochin in Kerala, was reputed to be the ancient world's greatest trading centre in the East. This legendary seaport traded in everything from spices to precious stones with the Egyptians, the Greeks, the Romans and the rest of the world. The port dates back 3000 years or more: Muziris was the doorway to India for various cultures and races: Buddhists, Arabs, Chinese, Jews, Romans. But no Hindu would ever cross the "Black Water" (Kala Paru in Hindi), because it was believed that it would pollute them: the idea being that you do not mix with others!

Southern India's maritime trade with the West had existed since ancient times. Both Egyptian and Roman trade with India flourished in the first century AD. In AD 47, the Hippalus wind was discovered and this led to direct voyages from Aden and the island of Soqotra to the south western coast of India in forty days. The Cheras named this capital Murichipattanam (Muziris in Greek) and it soon rose to international fame, thanks to its extensive trading relations. The Cheras built several palaces and temples, typical of its traditional Dravidian culture. Being made of wood, alas, none now remain. Some very old houses and the community of Tamil Brahmins in the Kannankulangara and Mookkambi areas can still be seen.

St Thomas reputedly landed in the ancient port of Muziris in AD 52 with the Jewish merchant Habban. He would have found a large Jewish community who would have been his first converts to the new faith: there had been Jewish colonies in Kodungallur since the time of King Solomon and a handful of Jews continue to live in Kerala, tracing their ancient history; most have now died or emigrated to Israel.

From the 11th century AD onwards, the fortunes of Muziris declined due to its constant wars with the neighbouring Tamil state, the Cholas and in 1341 the port of Muziris was destroyed by a massive flood that forced the great Periyar river to change its course, realigning the coastline and choking the port of Muziris. Soon the Cheras moved their capital to nearby Thiruvanchikulam and renamed it Mahodayapuram. By the 14th century, after the hundred-year Chera-Chola war, the Cholas successfully raided Muziris and set the city on fire, destroying it for ever.

At Muziris, trade and religion grew together. The Paravur synagogue must have been the place of worship for the Jews that settled very close to the Parur market. Though the users of the synagogue have all but faded away, both the market and the synagogue still exist. The Parur market opening to the river Periyar still functions twice a week, a boat jetty has been constructed there, and the Jew Street still goes by that name, though one of its two pillars at the entrance has been knocked down.

Large commercial fishing boats unloading their catch, Cochin harbour, Kerala, India (2013).

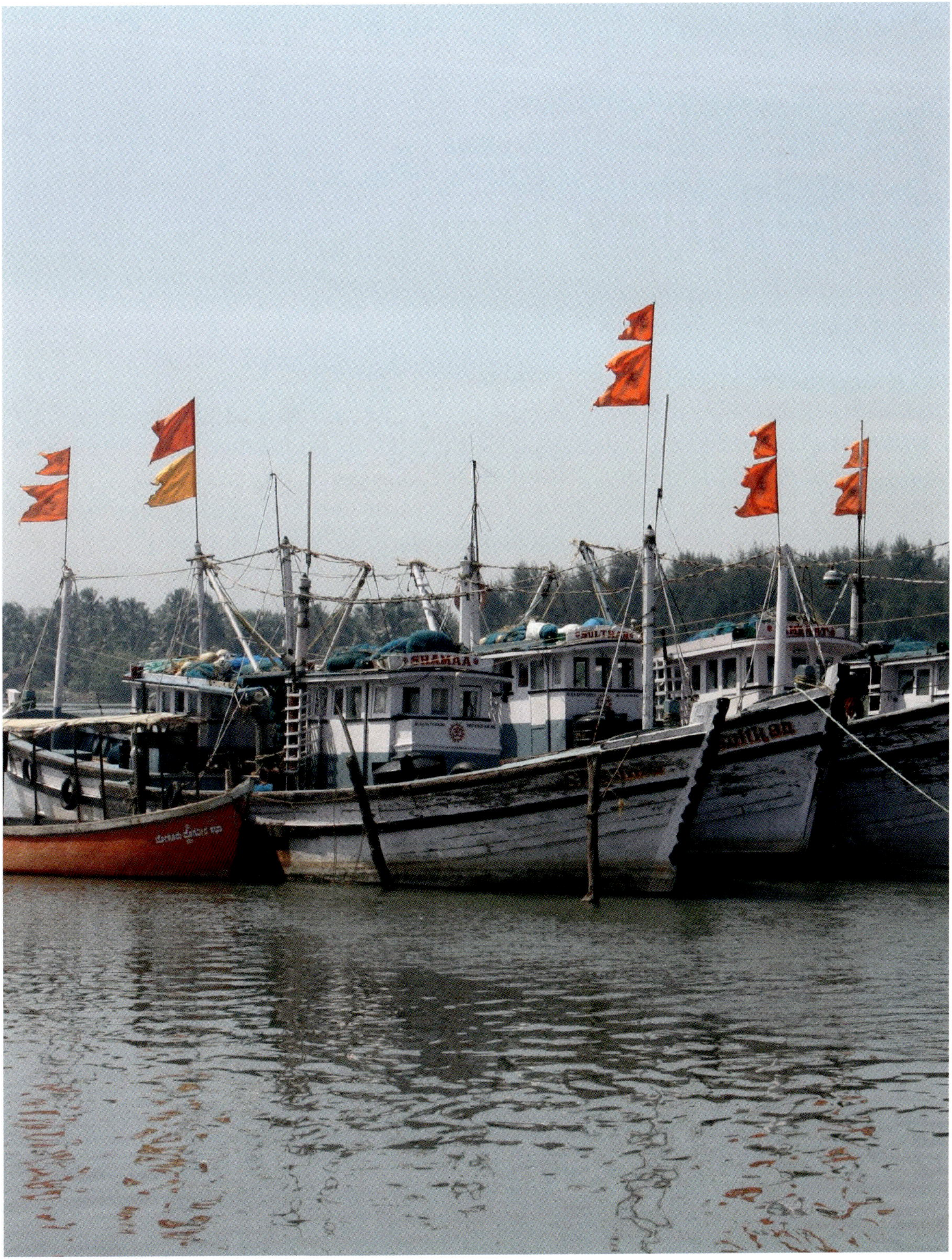
SHAMAA

Kodungallur

Above and *right*: The Mar Thoma Syro-Malabar Catholic Church, Kodungallur, Kerala, India (2016).

St Thomas the Apostle is believed to have visited India in two phases. The Syro-Malabar Church claims to have been founded by those directly baptised by the Apostle who landed in Kerala in AD 52. He successfully established seven and a half church communities, known in Malayalam as *ezharapalli*. Although he was persecuted continuously by Hindu radicals, his mission in India to spread the word about Jesus and his teachings was highly fruitful. A substantial part of the native population accepted Christianity with open arms. At that period and in the immediate centuries that followed, there were medium-scale migrations to Kerala from the Middle East (Persia and Israel) carrying both Jews and Christians who followed the Church of the East. These people settled in Kerala, intermingled with the population and had children. Such settlers along with the earlier converted native population, are collectively known as the St Thomas Christians or Nasranis or Syrian Christians because they follow the Syrian Rite.

St Thomas spoke the gospel first to the Jews who were living in and around Kodungallur, and then to the caste Hindus following the apostolic convention. The people, who were impressed by the exhortation and miracles of the divine personality, accepted Christianity. They were members of four reputed Brahmin families, Kalli, Kaliyankal, Pakalomattom and Sankarapuri. When it was known that they had embraced Christianity, other Namboothiri families found it disagreeable and they excommunicated the four families. The newly converted Christian Namboothiris who were originally priests in the Hindu temple started to conduct the Christian form of worship in the temple and later this temple was used as a church.

The place where St. Thomas landed in Kodungallur is now under the sea. After the biggest ever flood known in the history of Kerala in AD 1341, the port was washed away and a new island known as Puthu-Vypin was formed near Cochin in the Vembanad Lake. The modern church houses a holy relic of the saint's right arm.

"MY LORD AND MY GOD"

MARTHOMA PONTIFICAL SHRINE
AZHICODE, KODUNGALLUR

FOUNDATION STONE
MAR GEORGE ALAPPAT
BISHOP OF THRISSUR

BLESSING AND ENTHRONEMENT OF THE RELIC OF ST. THOMAS
HIS EMINENCE EUGENE CARDINAL TISSERANT

CMI DEVAMATHA PROVINCE, THRISSUR

The Syrian Orthodox Church of South India

Bishop Thomas Mar Athenasius of Cranganore with his priests.

The ancient, unbroken tradition is that St Thomas was the founder of the church in India. Our traditions are unanimous that he came here, and that is something we have held onto, despite persecution, for 1,700 years. Our spirituality is very close to that of the early church and we believe our church is as old as any Apostolic Church in the world. Our songs and traditions are quite clear about this. In the end it is these traditions that we base our belief on: not something on paper or stone which is secondary. It is our fidelity to St Thomas that is most important to us.

The Syrian Orthodox Church of South India.

Catholic and Syrian Orthodox churches are divided into "white" congregations, who claim to be pure descendants of Assyrians, and "black" congregations, who claim descent from native Dravidian Indians, converted personally by St Thomas.

Tradition traces the origin of Christianity in Kerala to the visit of St Thomas, one of the twelve apostles of Jesus Christ. It has been handed down from ancient time and is accepted by almost all the Syrian Christians of Kerala that St Thomas landed at the port of Cranganore on the west coast near Cochin in AD 52 in the company of a Jewish merchant Abbanes (Hebban). He preached Christianity first to the Jewish settlers in and around Cochin and then worked among the Hindus. The Apostle is believed to have founded seven and a half churches (or communities) of believers between c. AD 52 and 72 in Maliankara (Cranganore - Kodungalur), Palayoor (Chavakkad), Parur, Kokkamangalam, Niranam, Nilackal, Kollam and the Ara Palli "Half"church at Thiruvithamcode, for the use of the Christian converts and ordained presbyters.

St Thomas Christians currently number about 2½ million in 1500 parishes in the Kerala region, and they still use the ancient language Syriac as part of their liturgy. Syriac is a very close relative of the Aramaic spoken by Jesus and the Disciples, and is the liturgical language of the family of Syrian Orthodox churches.

Syriac clergy, from left to right: Gabriel Gregorius, Eusebius and Apron, Kerala, India.

Kana Thomas

Kana Thomas, modern portrait.

The identity of the St Thomas Christians is not exhausted by their being Indians and Christians, they are also Syrian. As the modern Indian scholar Fr Placid Podipara says: "They are Hindu or Indian in culture, Christian in religion and Syro-Oriental in worship". How they came under Syrian influence is to be found in stories preserved by oral traditions. They speak of the arrival of another Thomas: Thomas of Kana (*Knayi Thomman* in Malayalam), a rich Syrian Jewish Christian merchant from Persia who was escaping persecution under the Sassanian Emperor, Shapur II and who had relatives in Kerala. According to another version, he was a Christian Jew originating from Cana in Galilee and, according to another, even deriving his name generically from that place.

The Kerala tradition, which connects its events to precise dates, states that this happened in AD 345. This date is taken for granted both in oral conversation and in writing by the Knanaya, the modern Christians who claim to descend from Thomas of Kana and who variously belong to the Syro-Malabar Catholic Church, or the Orthodox Church of Syria and the Jacobites. However, the early Portuguese recorders of the various oral traditions give a wide range of datings. According to some, Thomas of Kana came even earlier so that he could still meet a servant of St Thomas, while others hold that he came later, namely in AD 752, some 700 years after the Apostle. The date AD 345 seems to be documented by a Syriac text written by a certain Fr Matthew in Malabar in 1730. It is said that he wanted to build a church in Muziris. Seventy-two families, a number that may simply represent a large, well-organised, strong group of people, with various clergy came with Thomas of Kana. It is said that they found the St Thomas Christians, known till then as Nazaranis, weak, dispersed and in great spiritual need. Thomas of Kana reorganised their fragmented communities and put them under the jurisdiction of the Persian church. Thus the link of the Malabar Christians with the Orthodox Syrian Church may originate from that time.

According to some historians, this relationship meant simply an alliance to the church of the East.

According to others, the Malabar Christians were under the impression that the orient belonged to the Patriarchate of Antioch, so that the Catholicos of Seleucia-Ctesiphon would be a representative of the Patriarch of Antioch. According to some other historians, the grafting of this powerful group with the existing fragmented Christians must have led to the identification of Kerala Christians with the St Thomas tradition to which they hold steadfastly to this day. The St Thomas of their stories may be the merchant Kana Thomas originating from Syria.

Important elements of the tradition are the famous copper plates that Thomas of Kana is said to have received from the King of Malabar, the Cheraman Perumal. In Kerala in the Middle Ages royal charters on privileges were written on copper plates, generally in *Grandha* or *Vattezhuttu,* "round script", characters. Communities belonging to different religions, including Jews, Christians and Muslims, possess their own copper plates. At present, some of the Christian copper plates are kept at important ecclesiastical centres, such as the Metropolitanate of the Mar Thoma Church in Thiruvalla and the Syrian Orthodox Catholicosate in Kottayam, and they are not shown to visitors. In the middle of the sixteenth century the Portuguese apparently acquired the very copper plates that were claimed to relate to the story of Thomas of Kana arriving in Cranganore and the privileges granted to him by the Cheruman Perumal. Unfortunately by the end of the same century, the plates were lost.

These traditions are also important formative elements of the Kerala Christians' identity and have an explicative value for their social reality. In fact, they may explain not only the Syrian affiliation, but also a division between "Southists" (*Thekkumbhagar*) and "Northists" *(Vadakkumbhagar)* Indian Christians. Both groups claim legitimate descent from Thomas of Kana, either through his two Syrian wives, or through a Syrian and an indigenous wife, or through two Kerala native wives, one of lower caste and ancestress of the Northists, one of higher caste and mother of the Southists. Only the Southists claim that they have preserved pure Syrian blood. The names are believed to come from the fact that once the two groups inhabited, respectively, the northern and the southern parts of the Christian quarter of Cranganore. The division is somehow indicative of the inter-caste relationships, not always peaceful, that exist among the Kerala Christians, not so differently from those among the Hindus.

The debate on the origins of the Kanaya, the time of the migration of the Syrian Christians to Kerala, the origins of other divisions and the mixing of the St Thomas's and Thomas of Kana's stories, is theoretically an unsolvable mystery.

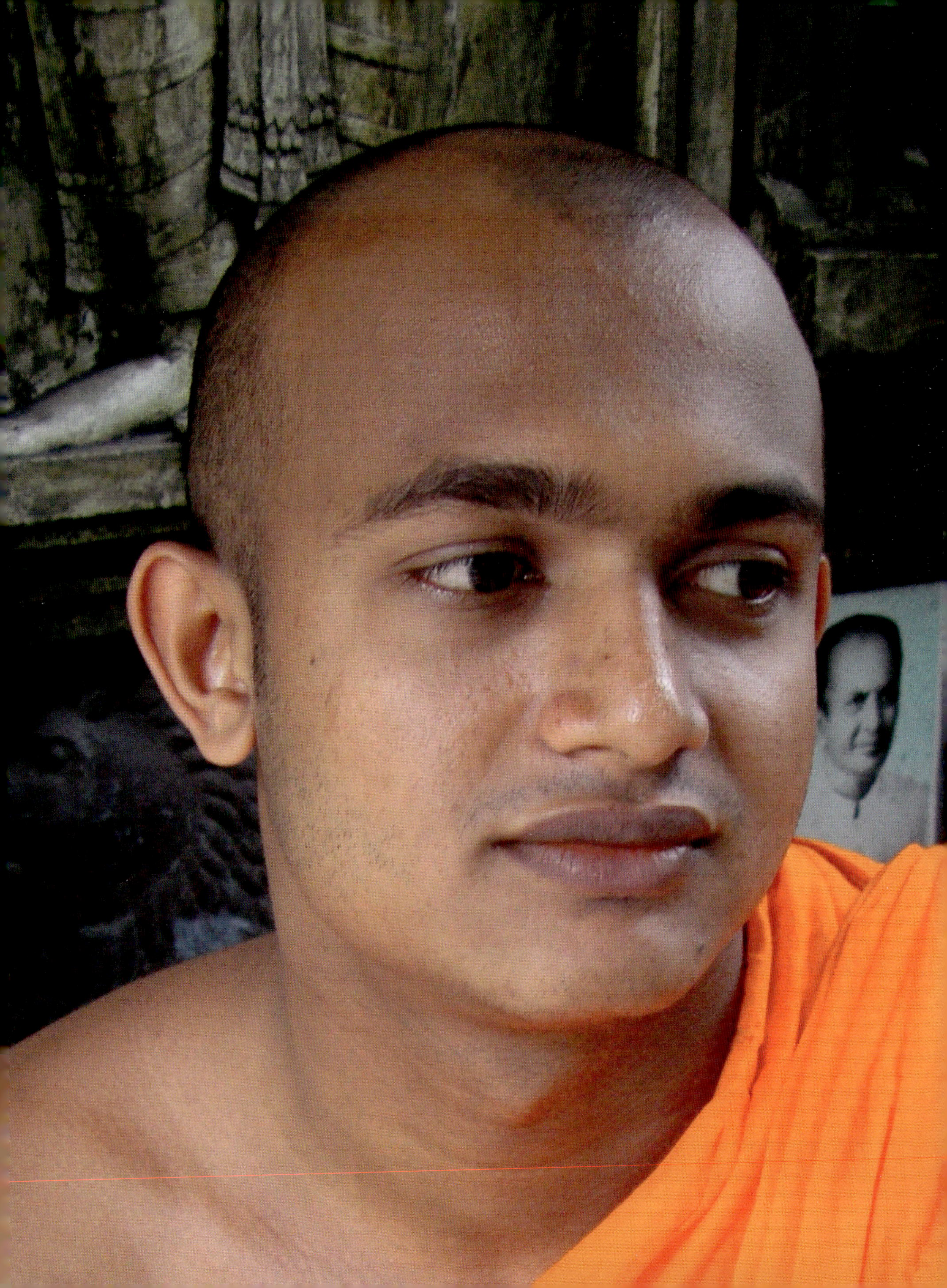

The St Thomas Christians

The St Thomas Christians refer to themselves in this way because their tradition holds that their ancestors, who came from the high castes of Hindu society, or were Buddhists, Jains or Jewish traders, were converted by the Apostle St Thomas, who landed in India in AD 52. There is no way scientifically to prove or disprove this tradition. One thing is certain: ever since the discovery of the monsoon winds in AD 45 by Hippalos, an Alexandrian ship-captain, the land and sea routes were open from the Mediterranean via the Persian Gulf to India, and there were intense contacts between these areas.

Buddhism was introduced in Kerala in the third century BC by the missionaries of Emperor Ashoka on their way south to Sri Lanka (which still is a Buddhist country). Jainism and Ajivaka philosophy also co-existed with Buddhism creating the great Sramana civilisation of the South that has given birth to the whole canon of Sangam writing. The Buddhist, Jain and Ajivaka seers introduced the Brahmi script and the art of writing in South India. All the early inscriptions now available are written in Brahmi script in the Tamil language. Many of St Thomas's early converts were Buddhists, who were as numerous in the south as the Hindus.

The tradition of Jesus's Apostle's missionary work in India is the principal formative element of the identity of a large and flourishing (at present over seven million-strong) community. At a certain stage of its history, this community entered into intense contacts with the Syrian Christian world.

Tradition tells us that this happened in AD 345, when Thomas of Kana, a rich Syrian merchant, landed in Cranganore, accompanied by seventy families. Their descendants, the endogamous Knanaya community, boast of having preserved pure Syrian blood. Thomas of Kana and the bishops who accompanied him established a permanent contact with the Syrian Church. So, if we are to believe tradition, ever since Thomas of Kana, the Malabar Church, consisting of an Indian and a Syrian component, has ecclesiastically and culturally belonged to the Syrian Christian world. Thus the St Thomas Christians constitute an unique community, whose native tongue is Malayalam, whose everyday culture and customs are typically Indian, and whose language of worship and of high culture has been Syriac for many centuries. For this high-caste Indian Christian community, Syriac held the same social function as Sanskrit.

Buddhist monk, Colombo, Sri Lanka (2015).

Hindus venerated Christian holy places

Hindu ladies, Tanjore, Tamil Nadu, India (2013).

The Thomas Christians lived in a society that has been able to accept them as one among its organic strata, while also accepting Christ and the saints as belonging to the many divinities legitimately worshipped by the different segments of Hindu society. It considered the Christians as one element belonging to the same society, and permitted them to practise their professions (mainly trade and agriculture and, to a lesser extent, military service), which were highly regarded by others. The Hindus also venerated the Christian holy places, and they still hold the priests of the St Thomas Christians in high esteem, considering them as holy men. This might not have always been the case, and the remembrances in the tradition about earlier persecutions may point to less tolerant periods and neighbourhoods. All this and much more is admirably expressed in the founding traditions of the community, connected to St Thomas.

According to the traditional structure, the Indian diocese of the Church of the East was governed by a Metropolitan sent by the Catholicos Patriarch, from Seleucia-Ctesiphon. At the same time, on the local level, in India Church affairs were governed by the Malabar yogam, that is, Assembly. There was also an indigenous Church of Malabar (called Jatikku Karthavian in Malayalam), which, according to Jacob Kollaparambil, means "the head of the caste".

According to the canons of the latter Church, the Archdeacon is the highest priestly rank: he is the head of all the clerics belonging to a bishopric; he is responsible for the entire worship of the cathedral church and represents the will of the bishop in his absence. One clearly understands how the appointment of an indigenous Archdeacon of All India served the needs of the ecclesiastical organisation of the Church of the East. While the Catholicos Patriarch of Seleucia-Ctesiphon reserved for himself the right to send his own prelates originating from Iraq to the Indian diocese, the continuous governance of his Indian flock was secured by the indigenous Archdeacon serving as the head of all the priests in Malabar and representing the bishop's will.

The history of the St Thomas Christian community before the arrival of the Portuguese colonisers, has few sources other than local traditions. Documented history begins with the arrival of the Portuguese. The European documentation beginning with this period already permits a fairly detailed picture of the social status, the life and the customs of the Christians whom they found upon their arrival in southern India, and in principle all the following, colonial, history of the community can be traced. However, here as well, although to a lesser extent, history is inextricably interwoven with oral tradition. At the moment when the Portuguese arrived on the Malabar Coast, the Christian communities that they found there had had longstanding traditional links with the East Syrian Christians in Mesopotamia.

The Margam Kali dance

Margam Kali- a Nasrani dance form in which songs praising or chronicling the life and experiences of St Thomas are sung. The lamp used by Syrian Christians is of Hindu origin but has a Chaldean cross on the top of it, one of the unique symbols of Nasranis, having both Indian and Syriac Influences.

Margam Kali is one of the ancient group dances of Kerala which was practised by St Thomas Christian men and is now danced by girls. It is difficult to trace the exact origin of the dance form and the compilation of the lyrics. These dance forms were in practice among the St Thomas Christians before the arrival of Portuguese missionaries in Kerala in 1498. In the traditional style, the performance of Margam Kali is divided into two parts, Vattakkali (round dance) and Parichamuttu kali (sword and shield dance) with singing a particular ballad known as Margam Kali pattu (The Song of the Way). This dance form describes the introduction of Christianity or the Christian way (Marga) of worship into Kerala.

The Margam Kali pattu text comprises fourteen stanzas which narrate the life and work of St Thomas the Apostle in Kerala. It retells how the Apostle landed in Malabar, how he healed the sick, won converts, how he established churches or communities and undertook missions to China and how in the end he died a martyr in Mylapore.

Margam Kali, as a performance art form of St Thomas Christians has undergone changes in its structure and appearance with the Portuguese influence and with the developments among the Christians due to the emergence of ecclesiastical jurisdictions. The literal translation of the word Margam (Margam) is 'way' or 'path'. In olden days those who embraced the new faith was called ' Margamkar' or 'Margam Vasikal". The term "Marga" is a derivation of the Pali word "Magga"'and has always been used among the St Thomas Christians of India.

It is very difficult to fix the origin of this dance form. It has been suggested that the Margam Vaasikal (followers of Margam - St Thomas Christians) in order to propagate and sustain their faith performed the elements of their passage in Pattu tradition and then gradually resorted to dance traditions. The earliest form of these dancing traditions of the native Christians involves circular movements while singing in gathering. Pallippaattu, Margam Kali and Vattakali were some of these performing traditions of the early St Thomas Christian community.

In both the Margam Kali and Parisamuttu Kali, an old-fashioned brass lamp was placed on the floor, and the dancers, usually twelve in number, used to go round it, with measured steps, singing religious songs about St Thomas the Apostle, and the Virgin Mary. Some of the songs now used are modernised versions of ancient songs.

Converting the Indians

What can a Jew, who has just found his Messiah and is now one of the main protagonists of a revolutionary, drastic renewal movement, share with Buddhists, Hindus and Jains who have never heard of the God of Israel?

St Thomas was prompted by the Holy Spirit to travel all the way to India and bring the gospel to those very distant people. He found a religious system much older than the faith of Abraham and based on a complex variety of beliefs, practices and tradition, far from the much simpler and almost monolithic Judeo-Christian faith.

He brought with him faith in a personal God, who revels Himself to man, wants to be known by man, who is so relational that He became a man to redeem men and bring men in a close, intimate, eternal relationship with Himself. In front of Thomas there was pantheism, polytheism, pandeism, monism, atheism and even more "isms", somehow originating from an impersonal God, unattainable by man.

What was the main attraction of the gospel for the people Thomas met in India? According to tradition and judging by the fruit, the vast number of St Thomas Christians in India who trace their origins to the apostle, Thomas was successful.

What was the driving force, what was his secret, what was his method, at the base of such a successful mission? Thomas had the power of the gospel, as Paul says in Romans 1:16. He had it in his heart and he knew that in his words there was the power of eternal salvation for everyone who believed his message. The gospel is powerful by itself, the core values of the gospel are simple and straight and contain in themselves the most extraordinary message ever given: "Christ in you, the hope of glory" Colossians 1:27.

It is the utter reversal of the ancient values that struck the hearts of those Buddhists, Hindus and Jains converted by Thomas: you do not have to give anything to those insatiable gods who ask and ask, instead you are free to take from this loving God who gives and gives. You do not have to reach high levels of illumination, instead you may know all that has to be known by revelation, you do not have to concentrate on yourselves to reach some level of liberation from cycles of reincarnation, rather you are able to know your God because He wants to be known by you, you do not have to look at distant impersonal inscrutable unpredictable impenetrable capricious gods who can be approached only through millions of anthropomorphic or zoological manifestations, rather you simply receive one personal loving Father in your own heart.

It was a very drastic, dramatic revolution that was produced by the encounter of the Jewish mind and heart with the Hindu spirit.

Dr Giancarlo Elia, 2016.

Shivite priest, Konarak, Orissa, India (2016).

Arthat St Mary Cathedral, Kunnamkulam

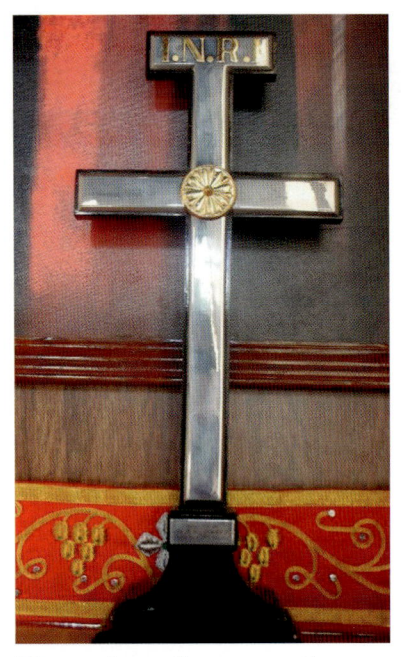

The Arthat Orthodox Cathedral of St Mary is the chief centre of the Malankara Orthodox Syrian Christians in Kerala. In the past, the town was called Kunnankulangara. Most of the oldest and wealthiest Christian families are to be found in Kunnamkulam.

The prominence given to this church by the early historians, circumstantial evidence, and the later historical records bear witness to this tradition. It is a permanent monument of St Thomas' mission in Kerala. The Christian community associated with the Church is believed to be the most ancient Christian community in South India, even earlier than the Niranam Christian congregation.

The uniqueness of this region is that the Christian Church was established in this part of Malankara at the same time or little bit earlier than the Christian faith was established in Rome, Antioch and Alexandria. The ancient name of Arthat was Chettikulangara. The Church is now under the Kunnamkulam Diocese of the Malankara Orthodox Syrian Church. It is the most prominent church and Thalappalli of all the churches in the diocese.

The present Palayur village is at sea level, and during the formative years of the Christian era, was believed to be under the sea. The nearness to the sea, the sandy soil, and the presence of oceanic fossils also bear witness to this fact. But Arthat is the first high land from the sea level in the Paloor region, which was known as Jewish Hill or 'Juda Kunnu'.

The modern silver cross, the Arthat Orthodox Cathedral, Palayur, Kerala, India (2016).

Embroidered sanctuary curtain, the Arthat Orthodox Cathedral.

Right: The Arthat Orthodox Cathedral of St Mary, Palayur, Kerala, India (2016).

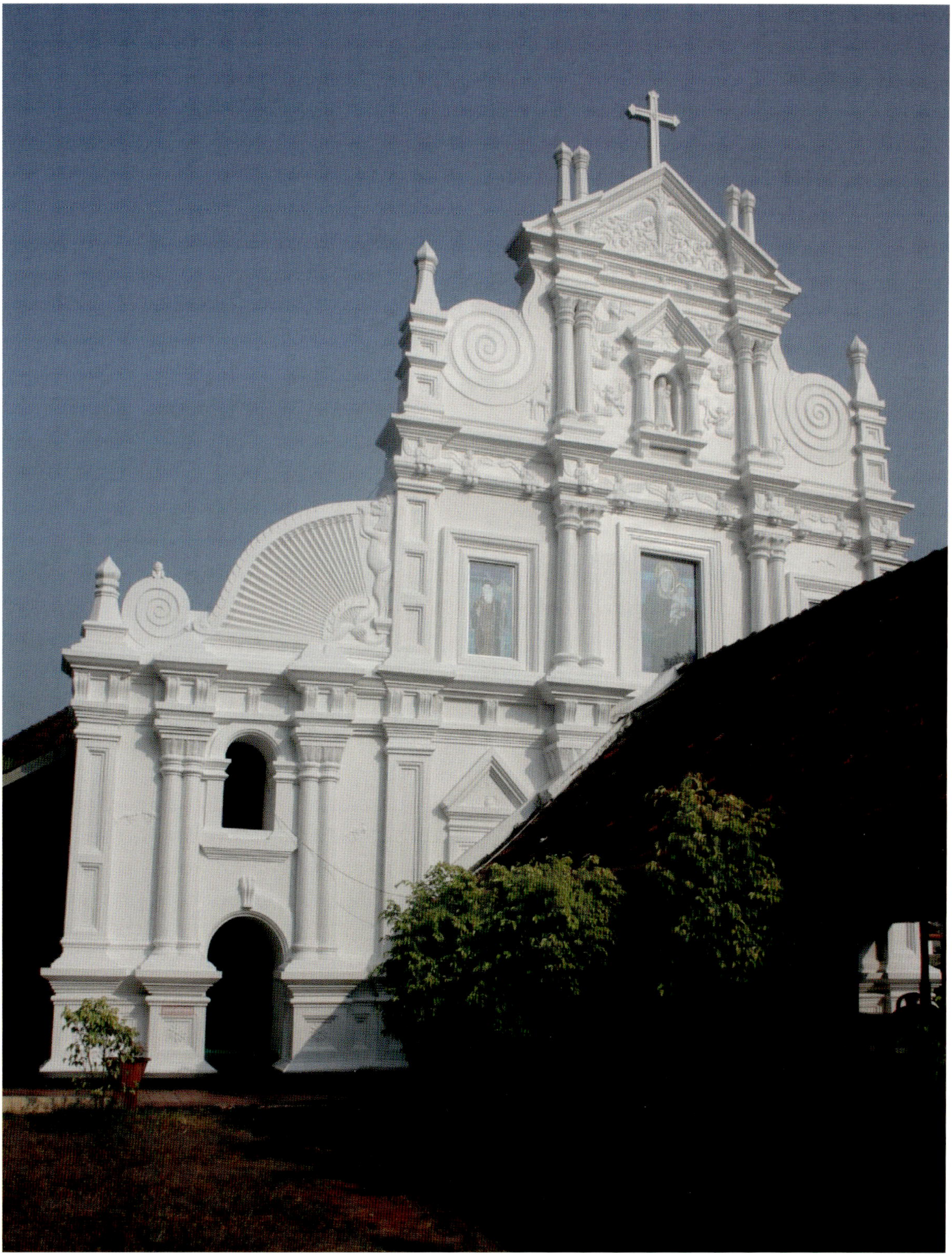

Palayur

The Cross, Syro Malabar Catholic Archdiocesan church of Palayur, Kerala, India (2016).

St Thomas travelled by boat through the backwaters from Muziris (Kottakkavu or Kodungallur) and landed at Palayur which was a stronghold of both the Brahmins and the Jews. He came to visit the Jewish merchants at Palayur at "Judankunnu" (meaning the hill of Jews) to preach the Christian gospel to them. This spot has since become dry land but its position as a boat jetty, locally known as "Bottukulam", has been preserved as a monument to St Thomas.

Of the seven churches originally established by St Thomas, only three namely, Palayur in the Syro-Malabar Catholic Archdiocese of Thrissur, Kottakkavu in the Syro-Malabar Catholic Major Archeparchy of Ernakulam-Angamaly, and Niranam in the Malankara Orthodox Diocese of Niranam can claim continuity, while the remaining four churches have undergone several changes in their locations.

It is said that a Hindu temple that was abandoned by the Brahmins was converted into the present church. Further, as proof of Jewish settlements existing when St Thomas arrived here in AD 52, ruins of a synagogue could be seen near a Hindu temple, close to the church. Temple remnants in the form of broken idols, sculptures and relics of the old temple can also be seen near the precincts of the church, in addition to two large *tanks* near the west and east gates of the church.

It is also said that the conversion of Brahmins has resulted in such an aversion among the Nambudiri Brahmins that they do not even accept cold water or tender coconut water anywhere in the vicinity of the church. It is recorded that St Thomas stayed in India for 17 years: four years in Taxila (now in Pakistan), about six years on Malabar Coast, and seven years at Mylapore in Tamil Nadu.

In 1607 the Italian Jesuits received permission to construct a more convenient church around the existing old structure for the parishioners of Palayur.

The Syro-Malabar Catholic Archdiocese of Thrissur, Palayur, Kerala, India (2016).

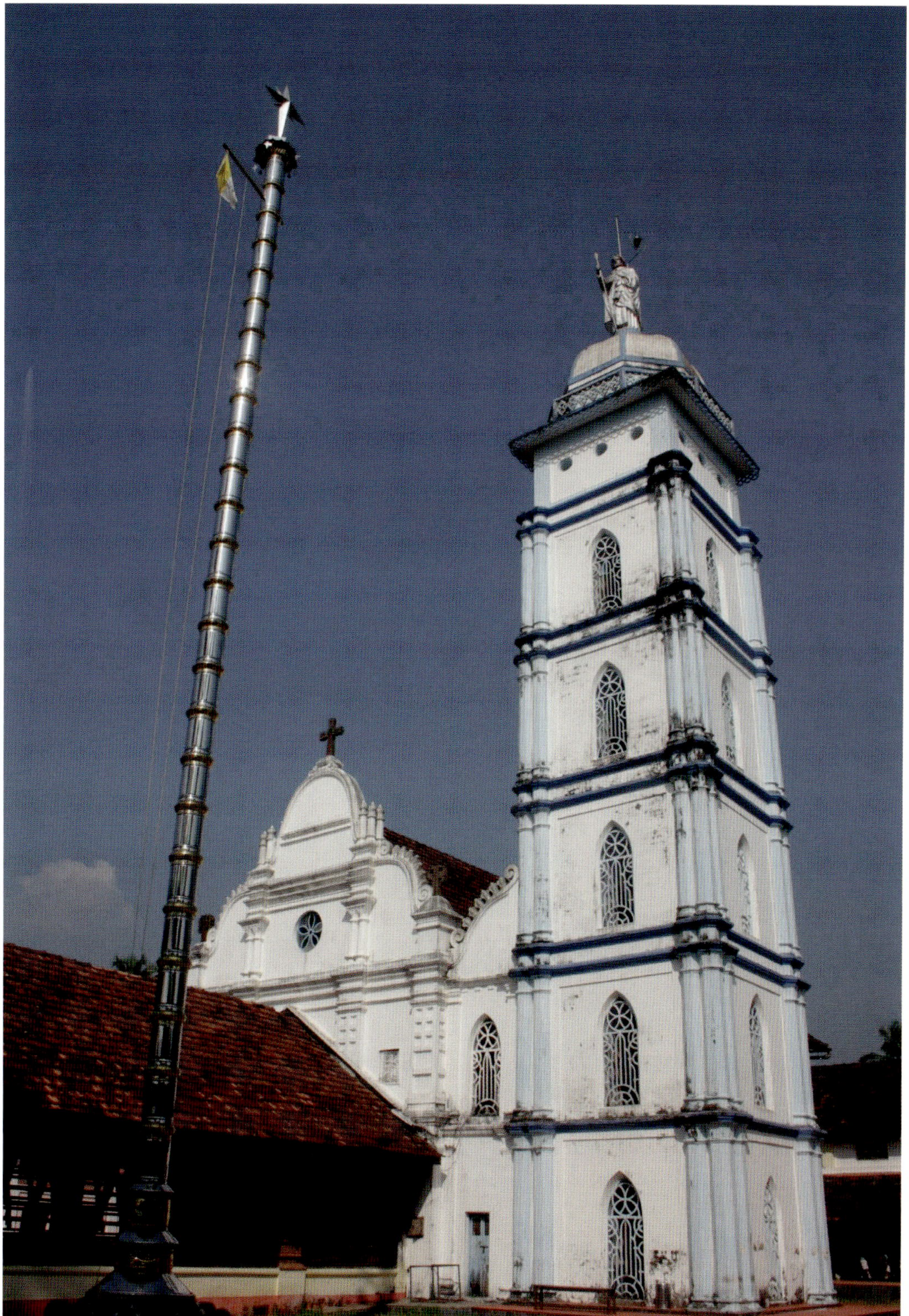

Oral traditions

Oral traditions, and their transmission from one generation to another, lie at the heart of most religions. In Judaism, the Oral Torah, as complementing the written Torah in the Pentateuch, was held to be of Divine origin. Our Lord Jesus Christ left no written records, yet within a few years of His Ascension, His disciples recorded the eye-witness memories of His acts and teachings. Holy Tradition, as understood by the Church, was both written and oral, and indeed, the Holy Bible itself is the fruit of that oral tradition. The Prophet of Islam, being unlettered, dictated the revelation he had received, whilst his acts and thoughts, on even quite pedestrian matters, were later dutifully recorded by his companions. In cultures where only a minority were literate, words spoken and deeds done had profound significance and the religious communities, to whom these traditions belonged, faithfully preserved them in order to pass them on as a "living" tradition.

By the time that the Roman Emperors issued their edicts of toleration for Christianity (in 311 and 313), the new faith had already spread beyond the Roman Empire. Although there were local differences, the Christian Church emerged with a standard character, a common ministry and an emerging written canon compiled during the lifetime of the first generation of believers. By the early years of the third century the tradition of the apostolate of St Thomas in India-Parthia was already well known and is witnessed to by Clement of Alexandria, Origen, Hippolytus, Eusebius and the apocryphal Acts of Thomas.

The debate about how far the pious accretions of almost two thousand years have obscured the essential witness to St Thomas's ministry, should not be used to undermine a most ancient tradition almost certainly grounded in truth; whilst modern scholarship concerning the Indo-Parthian king, Gondophares, mentioned in those ancient stories, offers a corroborative testimony unavailable to the post-apostolic writers. Those who would readily dismiss this very ancient tradition are in danger of discarding an authentic witness which has survived from the earliest times. It has always seemed to me inconsistent that the Apostle Thomas is known to posterity as "Doubting" Thomas, as his bold proclamation of his belief in the Resurrected Christ as "My Lord and my God" is one of the earliest affirmations of the Lordship and Divinity of Christ. In our age of doubt and scepticism, Thomas's profession of faith has particular resonance, which draws from Christ the response, *"blessed are those who have not seen and yet believe."*

Abba Seraphim, Metropolitan of Glastonbury
& Primate of the British Orthodox Church,
2017.

The cross in the courtyard of the Marthoma church, Kottakkavu-Paravur, Kerala (2017).

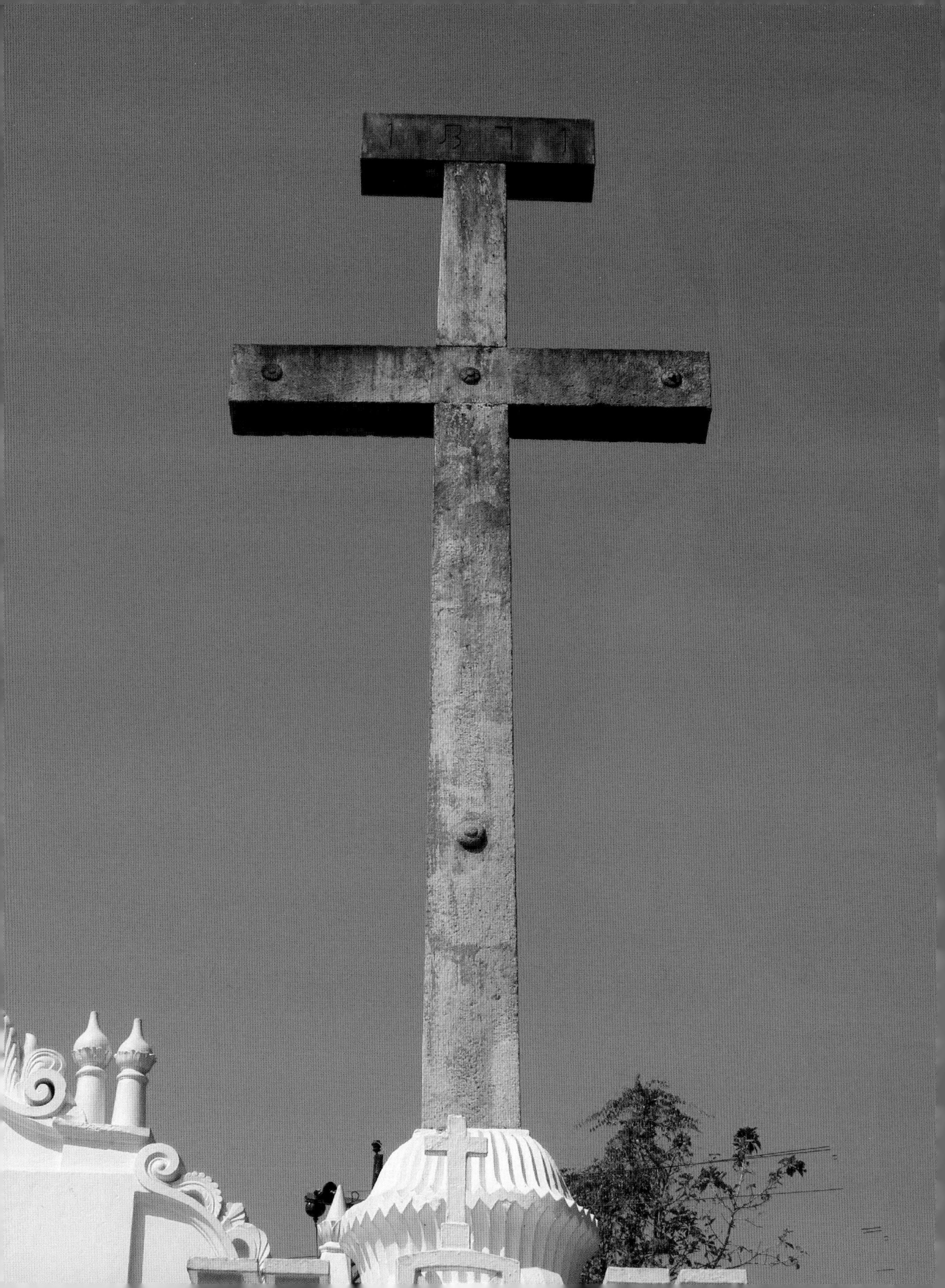

Kottakkavu-Paravur

The Marthoma church, Kottakkavu-Paravur, on the shores of the Vembanattu backwaters and the Periyar river, Kerala, India (2016).

The church at Palayur on the western shore of Lake Vembanattu in Chertalai (20 miles from Cochin on the way to Kottam), stands on the same spot where the Apostle first established a community. It continued to exist from the first c. and until the advent of the Portuguese, it was under the rule of local kings. It was visited and blessed by St Francis Xavier in 1542. In 1607 the Italian Jesuit Fr Fenichio received permission to construct a more convenient church around the existing old structure. Later, this church was attacked by Tipu Sultan. Renovations were done in 1952. The sacred relics from the old church are kept in a cell near the altar.

Palayur was a major trade centre and Jewish colony; many of them had settled in the 6th century BC to escape persecution in the Persian Empire. St Thomas's first converts were the Jews and Hindus of Cranganore, Palayur and Quilon. At Palayur, he organised the new converts and appointed priests from among the leading families. Palayur was the stronghold of the Nambudiri Brahmins when St Thomas arrived from Kodungallur, and a large number of them embraced Christianity. But some were adamant about their religion. It is said that they cursed the place which came to be known as the Sapakad (Cursed land), the present-day Chavakkad.

St Thomas travelled by boat from Kodungallur through the backwaters and reached the Vanchi Kadavu (Boat Jetty) of Palayur. This boat jetty still exists in the form of a large pond, called Bottukulam. Two large *tanks* on the west and east gates recall the ancient glory of the Hindu temple. Here he is said to have baptised 1,600 people.

St Thomas is said to have spent over a year here and to have established a cross for the Thambudhiries to pray before (but more probably this was done by Kana Thomas in the fourth century).

The Thomas churches were created by demolishing Hindu temples. Historical analysis reveal that this temple destruction was done by early Christian settlers. This destruction of temples and building of Thomas churches was done by Iranian Christian missionaries in the 8th and 9th centuries. This was the second major migration of Christian refugees into India from Iran. This temple destruction and subsequent creation of churches were later attributed to St Thomas, but it may not have happened until the arrival of Kana Thomas and his group of Syrian Christians in the fourth century.

There was a festival in progress at Kottakav-Paravur when St Thomas arrived. As he preached, a strong wind blew over a row of elephants and 1,170 Brahmins were baptised in the lake! (2013).

Kottailkavu

The altar, Kottailkavu Santhome Church, North Paravur, Kerala, India (2017).

According to the history and traditions of the Indian Church, St Thomas the Apostle who reached Kerala had established a church at "North Paravur" (then known as Kottailkavu). This historic site is located just a few miles south of the ancient port of Kodungallur (Cranganore).

The early Christian converts are believed to be the Jewish settlers who migrated to the India for trade purposes after the fall of Jerusalem in AD 70 and also some upper caste Hindus. North Paravur in the early centuries was the most prominent Christian centre in India and it still holds a unique position in the Malankara Church. A large Christian population, mostly Syrian Orthodox and Roman Catholics, live here. Angamaly, which was the headquarters of the Christian community for many centuries, is near the town of North Paravur.

The new church was built in the 19th century, due to the lack of space in the old church for conducting Mass and community functions. The parishioners have preserved the old church, which is behind the new one, the elephantine wall, called Aanamathil, on the adjacent western side and the Pilgrim Pond where the Apostle baptised the devotees and they continue to maintain them.

North Paravur

North Paravur is one of the oldest towns in Kerala, established in 52 BC when an ancient Tamil tribe, the Cheras, made the city its capital, thanks to the presence of a natural port. The mighty Periyar river flowed through this region, creating many small islands and making it one of the most fertile lands for agriculture.

As in the history of Christendom, many places such as Peshavar in Pakistan, Kalyan in Bombay, Paravur near the ancient port of Muziris, Nilackal near Sabarimala, Mylapore, Thrissinapalli, Dindigul in the former state of Madras, and Chang'an in China where the ancient Christian presence held by the Church of the East (probably Nestorian/Chaldean Christians) existed from the first century onwards, later lost their presence due to forced migration of people either due to persecution by local rulers or due to Muslim invasion or due to the outbreak of fatal endemic diseases.

As these eastern churches in many of these places had Nestorian connection they were considered heretic by the mainstream western churches after the arrival of the Portuguese in 1498, which, alas, resulted in their disappearance.

Below: St Thomas baptised his many converts in the Pilgrim *tank* beside the church (2016).

St Mary's Orthodox Syrian Church, Kottayam

St Mary's Orthodox Syrian Church, an ancient Orthodox Syrian Church in Kottayam with His Holiness The Catholics of the East as its supreme head, better known as Kottayam Cheriapally, is one of the oldest churches in Kerala, rebuilt in 1579, the church is well preserved. The architectural style is European, with galleries, pillars, cornices and pediments. The walls are adorned with murals in Oriental and Western styles on biblical and non-biblical themes. Three Metropolitans of the Orthodox Syrian Church came from three Kottayam families.

The Tamil epic of Manimekalai, written between the second and third centuries AD (the Sangam Literature era), mentions the St Thomas Christian (Nasrani) people by the name Essanis, referring to one of the early Jewish-Christian sects within the Nasranis called Essenes. Christianity in India dates back to the days of St Thomas. Since then, it has flourished and added a new dimension to India's rich cultural heritage. With deep roots in the soil, Indian Christianity has developed an independent personality of its own - Christian in religion, Oriental in worship and Indian in culture. This local character has been sustained and enriched over the last two millennia.

Giani Zail Singh, President of India (1982–1987).
From his speech on October 26, 1983, inaugurating the Paurastya Vidyapitham, Vadavathoor, Kottayam.

St Thomas Orthodox Cathedral, Kottakkathu

Kottakkathu (or Karthikappally) and surroundings were once large Buddhist centres. "Sreemoolavasam", the legendary Buddhist shrine, is believed to have been located at nearby Trikkunnapuzha.

The St Thomas Orthodox Cathedral is one of the ancient churches in Kerala and was said to have been founded in 828. During the years 1729-1758, King Marthanda Varma of the princely state of Venad, attached Karthikappally to Travancore, his newly formed kingdom.

What made Karthikappally unusual and important was the proximity of an inland waterway or *thodu* which enabled a free flow of traffic, and thus Karthikappally evolved into a large trading centre.

The Cathedral keeps an immense archive of the local history in about 621 palm-written records. It recently became the centre of attention when archaeological evidence was unearthed in and around the cathedral, including two lithographic stones which have been identified as being over 500 years old. A well with an unusual structure in the churchyard attracts special attention.

The Kottakkathu Suriyani Palli St Thomas Cathedral of AD 829, rebuilt in 1581 and renovated in 2007. Kerala, India (2017).

Kokkamangalam

St Thomas reputedly stayed here for two years, preaching to the farmers. Until recently there were no roads: it was only possible to reach the church by crossing Lake Vembanattu in a boat.

St Thomas came to Kokkamangalam to convert the Hindu farmers and he established a cross here for the 1,600 Nambudhiries to pray before. The church still has some sacred oil, a miraculous portrait, and a holy relic given by Pope John Paul II in 1986.

The church was blessed when St Francis Xavier came here in 1542, but the church he visited has also been pulled down and a new one, known as the St Thomas Archdiocesan shrine, is being built for the 450 Catholic families (2,000+ people) who worship here.

Kuruppumeetil Gopalapillai, in his book *Kerala Mahacharithram* says: "Kokkomangalam was an important township in the Villarvattom Kingdom, which happened to be the only Christian Kingdom in ancient Kerala."

Left: The modern stone cross on the landing stage of Lake Vembanattu, Kokkamangalam, Kerala (2017). The ancient church was founded on the western shore of Lake Vembanattu in Chertalal.

Right: the precious relic of one of St Thomas's bones, given to Kokkomangalam from Ortona in Italy by Pope John Paul II during his visit to India in 1986. Note St Thomas's set square: the symbol of him as an architect. Kokkomangalam, Kerala, India (2016).

Niranam

St Mary's Syrian Orthodox Church, known as Niranam Valiyapally, Niranam, Kerala, India (2016).

This is said to be the first place where St Thomas founded a church on his arrival in Kerala in AD 54 and he gave it the name of St Mary, the Mother of God. It is also known as Melkuttanadu and is set between two branches of the River Pamba near Thiruvalla and Edathua in the district of Alleppey. The church has been rebuilt four times, most recently in 1912 and was renovated in 2000. Inside are five altars: one each to St Mary, St Thomas, St George, St Behnam and St Stephen, and with elaborate tombs for two Metropolitan saints.

The church has a well from which St Thomas reputedly used to drink, a granary (which is now a museum) and the cross established by him for the new believers. Later, some adversaries of the new faith took out the cross and threw it into the nearby river. When St Thomas returned to Niranam two years later in AD 56, he heard about this and went in search of the cross. He found it at a place down stream and again founded the church at that place, which is believed to be its present location, beside the Sri Thrikpaleswara Temple of Lord Shiva.

The statue of the Virgin Mary is made of marble and pure gold. The church has a flag post and stone lamps similar to those seen in Hindu temples.

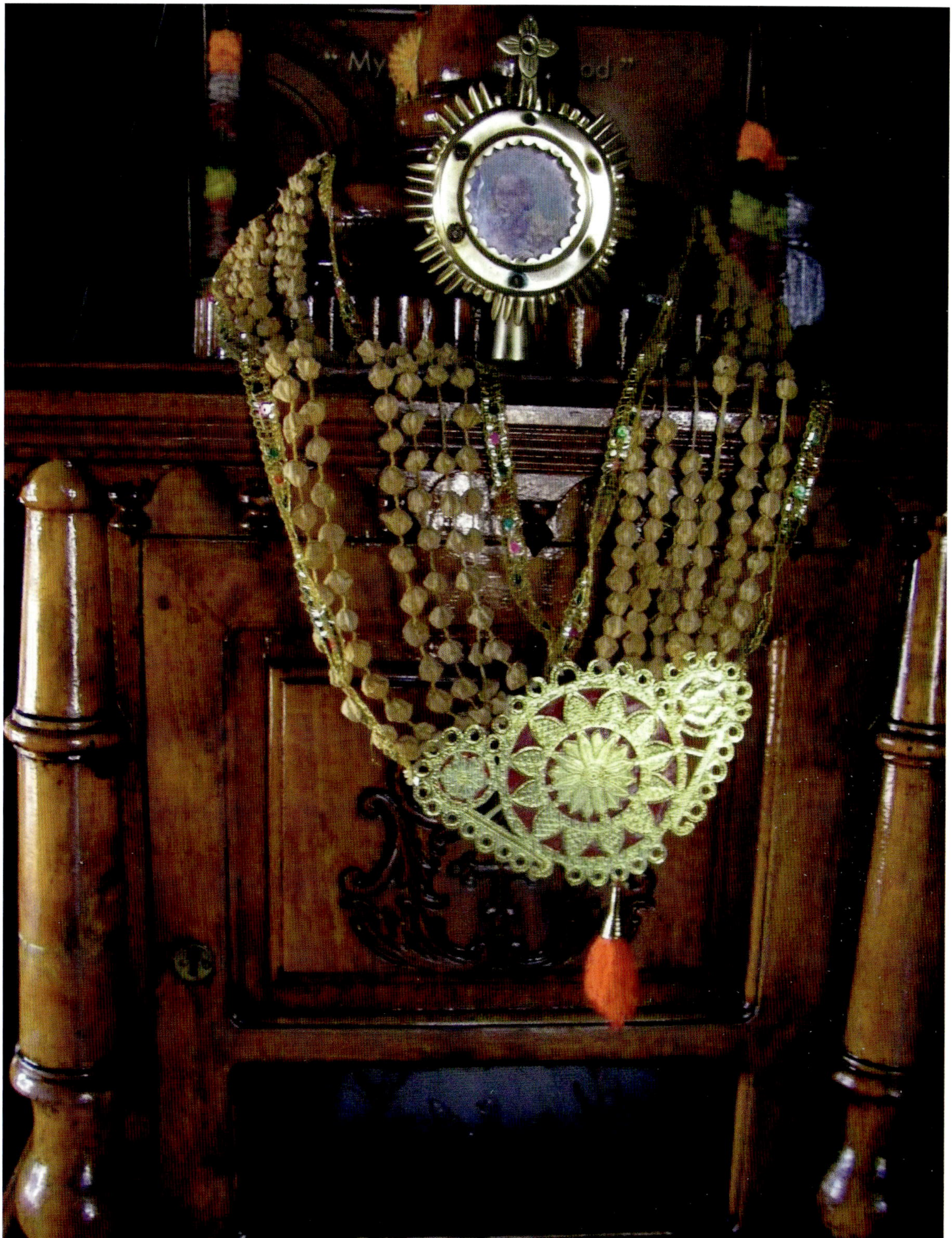

The altar. Niranam, Kerala, India (2017).

The miracle of the water standing up, fresco, Niranam, Kerala, India (2016).

The bathing ghats

In AD 190, Pantaenus from Alexandria visited the Christians in Kerala. He found that they were using the Gospel of Matthew in Hebrew. Around AD 522, an Egyptian Monk, Cosmas Indicopleustes, visited the Malabar Coast and he mentions Christians in Malabar (Kerala), in his book *Christian Topography*. This shows that until the 6th century these Christians had been in close contact with Alexandria.

Prior to the advent of Roman Catholic Christianity in India in the 15th century, Syrian and Persian Christians in Malabar were called Nestorians or Nazaranis or Nazarenes. The first name indicated the Christian doctrine they followed after the church founded by Thomas of Cana in Malabar was linked to the Nestorian Church of Seleucia in AD 450 and the second name linked them back to the first Jewish Nazarene Christians who fled to Edessa, Syria, prior to the fall of Jerusalem in AD 70. Jewish Nazarenes belonged to an ancient sect of which Samson and Jesus were the most famous members: Nazarene does not refer to the town of Nazareth in Israel, which did not exist till the third century AD.

The Christians built a small thatched hut to house the Cross, about a hundred yards to the west from the bank of the backwaters. When the community grew larger, a bigger church was built, yet another five hundred yards to the west, where the present church now stands.

The bathing ghats, Niranam, Kerala, India. St Thomas is said to have landed in Niranam, Kerala in AD 54 (2016).

The Mar Thoma Cross

Thomas crosses are unique to the St Thomas Christians, named by the Portuguese missionaries as they found these crosses widespread in almost all the St Thomas churches. According to the St Thomas Christian tradition, the Apostle Thomas planted crosses in the Christian communities that he established, but this is unlikely as the cross was not used as a Christian symbol in the first century! *The Acts of the Apostles* does not comment about any such acts by any Apostles despite the author of the *Acts of the Apostles*, St Paul himself, being a champion of the power of the Cross. The early Roman catacombs have no symbolism of the Cross.

The *Acts of Thomas* describe the Apostle performing miracles with a simple sign of cross. This may be a rejection of later developments from apostolic times. The Cross occupies a prominent place in the East Syriac tradition, especially in its liturgy and the Syriac Christian tradition developed a rich symbolism and use of the Cross.

As the Syriac word for cross, *sliba* means both the cross and the crucified, there is ample scope for compressing multi-level meanings in hymns on the cross. The Syriac Liturgy of Hours is particularly rich in this. The symbolism of the cross gained prominence in the Syriac tradition earlier than it did in the other traditions. The East Syrian Church had a great veneration of the cross. They considered the sign of the cross as one of the sacrifices.

As far back as AD 250, East Syrians erected crosses on their tombs. This shows that they venerated the cross very early on. St Helena was a Syriac Christian who discovered the wood of the True Cross.

The St Thomas' Cross or Mar Thoma Silba is the symbol of St Thomas' Christians. This cross was the only object venerated in the churches of St Thomas Christians when the Portuguese missionaries arrived. The most popular and the most ancient model is that of the Cross found on St Thomas Mount discovered by the Portuguese in the ruins of the church in AD 1547.

There are many legends in Kerala and Tamil Nadu of St Thomas planting crosses in the "churches" that he founded. This is not correct, as at the time of his visit he founded communities of believers rather than church buildings. It is much more likely that these first buildings were constructed by the Persian merchant Kana Thomas and his 72 Syrian families in the fourth century, together with erecting the first crosses. Most of the buildings have been rebuilt many times, some early ones are now under water, others are not necessarily in the same spot as when they were first built and the same applies to the crosses.

The Mar Thoma cross, Niranam, Kerala, India (2016).

239

Quilon

The bay of Quilon - Kollam; the shoreline has decreased dramatically since St Thomas landed here in AD 54.

"Most church historians, who doubt the tradition of Doubting Thomas in India, will admit there was a church in India in the middle of the sixth century when Cosmas Indicopleustes visited India."

His Grace Metropolitan Mar Aprem, Patriarchal vicar of the Assyrian Church, 2015.

A candle for St Thomas burns on a shrine on the bay where he landed, Quilon - Kollam, Kerala, India (2016).

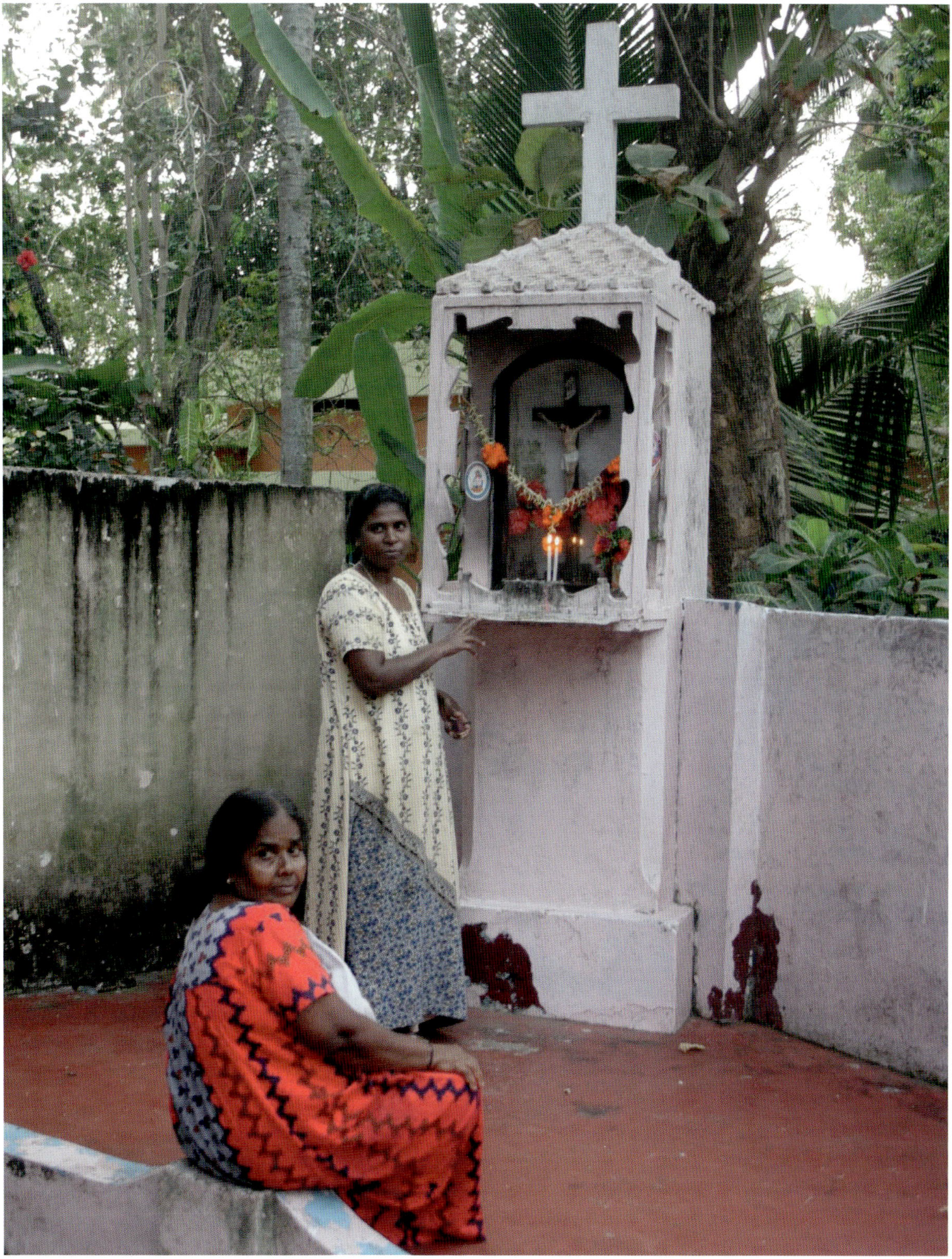

Quilon Port Church

Kollam or Quilon, formerly Desinganadu, is an old seaport and city on the Laccadive Sea coast in Kerala, India, on Ashtamudi Lake. Kollam has had a strong commercial reputation since the days of the Phoenicians and Romans.

The Apostle preached the Good News among the Jews of Quilon and then went to all castes of Indians and many of them were baptised.

Popularly known as Kollam Port Church, the Catholic Church of Our Lady of Purification has been rebuilt many times and is a replacement for one of the "seven and a half" churches founded by the St Thomas: the first church here was claimed by the sea long ago. A stone, popularly known as Palli Kallu (Stone of the Church) among the local fishermen, which is believed to be a part of the original church, can still be seen during the period of low tides.

In AD 522, Cosmas Indicopleustes (called the Alexandrian) visited the Malabar Coast. In his book *Christian Topography* he mentions Syrian Christians in Malabar, and writes that in the town of "Kalliana" (Quilon or Kollam), there is a bishop consecrated in Persia.

Gregory of Tours (AD 594) gives an account of the monastery of St Thomas in India, based on the report that he had heard from a monk called Theodore who had visited that monastery.

St Thomas and St Francis Xavier

In 841, Suleiman, a Muslim traveller, mentions 'Bethuma' (House of Thomas), which can be reached in ten days from Quilon.

Fed by the Chinese trade, Quilon was mentioned by Ibn Battuta in the 14th century as one of the five Indian ports he had seen during twenty-four years in the course of his travels. Desinganadu's rulers were used to exchanging ambassadors with Chinese rulers and there was a flourishing Chinese settlement at Quilon. The Indian commercial connection with South-East Asia proved vital to the merchants of Arabia and Persia between the 7th and 8th centuries. The 9th century merchant Sulaiman of Siraf (in Persia) found Quilon to be the only port in India, touched by the huge Chinese junks, on his way from Canton to the Persian Gulf. Marco Polo, who was in Chinese service under Kubla Khan in 1275, visited Quilon and other towns on the west coast of Kerala, in his capacity as a Chinese mandarin.

When the Portuguese arrived in the 16th century, they found no less than 16,000 Thomas Christian families in Quilon.

Monument to St Thomas and St Francis Xavier, marking the fourth century of St Francis Xavier's visit and the nineteenth since the death of St Thomas in AD 72; Our Lady of Purification Catholic church, Quilon, Kerala, India (2016).

The Syrian Orthodox church, Quilon

In 822 two Nestorian bishops, Mar Sabor and Mar Proth, settled in Quilon (ancient Kollam) together with their followers; they came from the Mar Mattai monastery of Nineveh (Iraq) at the invitation of the Chera King Kuleshakara of Kollam, as an Authority for the Doctrine of the Trinity against the background of a Shivate Revival of Advaita Vedanta, propounded by Adi Shankara.

Two years later in 824, the Malayalam Era (also referred to as Kollavarsham) began and Kollam undoubtedly became the premier city of the Malabar region including Travancore and Cochin. In AD 825, two more bishops, Shappur and Arthrod, came to Kollam and the next era began with these East Syrian Saints who settled in Korukeni Kollam, near to the present city.

In AD 825 a great convention was held in Kollam (an important town at that time), at the behest of King Kulashekhara. Kollam and the Malayalam Era's alternative name of "Kollavarsham" is possibly as a result of the Tarisapalli Shasanangal, which refers to the gift of a plot of land to the Syrian church near Quilon, along with several rights and privileges to the Syrian Christians led by Mar Sapir Iso. It also signified the independence of Malabar from the Cheraman Perumals.

The present church has been rebuilt several times on this plot of land. It is the oldest surviving church in Quilon.

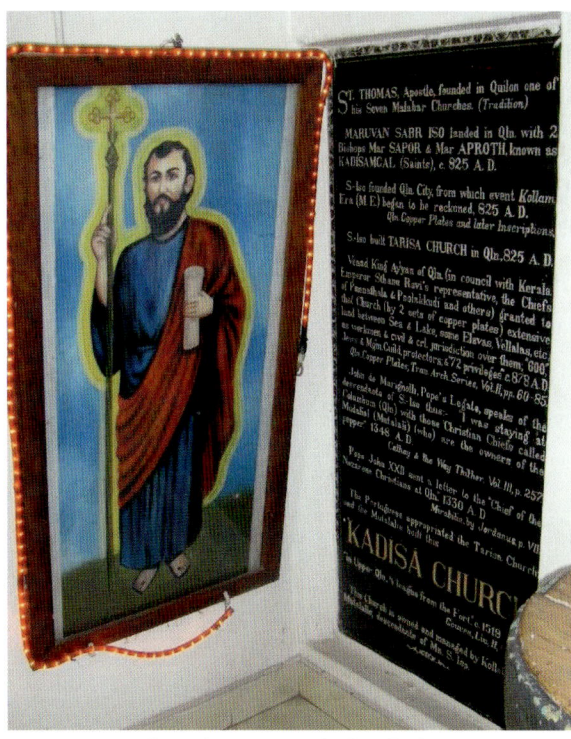

A portrait of St Thomas with the dedication panel of the Kadisa church, Quilon, India (2016).

In AD 849 King Kulashekhara granted the copper plate grants to Mar Sapir Iso whom he invited to Kollam from Nineveh and transferred to the Tarasa church: ("Tarasa" is a Syriac orthodox word and means true believer).

It is also believed that in an audience with the Chera king, Mar Sabor volunteered to create a new sea port near Kollam in place of the king's request to renew the almost vanished inland sea ports of Tyndis (now known as Kadalundi) or Nelcynda.

Left: Two Syrian monks outside the Kadisa Orthodox church, Quilon, India (2016).

The coastal fishing ports of Kerala

Fishing boats named after saints line the shore of this vibrant port with its small, brightly painted church of St Mary, just north of Covelong, Kerala, India (2000). The scene in this large, sheltered bay would have been similar in the early years when St Thomas visited this coast in AD 52.

Jewish traders were living along the coast of Kerala from the time of King Solomon. Later large numbers of them arrived in 586 BC and again in AD 72. Thriving Jewish colonies were to be found at the various trading centres, thereby furnishing obvious bases for the apostolic witness.

The sea shore, Thiruvithamcode

The seashore where St Thomas landed, 25 miles north of Cape Comorin. This is the furthest point south that he reached; here he founded the Ara Pally half-church in AD 52. Kerala India (2017).

The church in Thiruvithamcode is otherwise known as the "Ara pally" of St Thomas among the Christians and as "Thomayar Koil" among the native Tamil people. The name Ara pally has two meanings: "King's church" or "half church". The former school of thought argues that the term Ara was used to denote anything that relates to the King in Dravidian culture: Ara chan means King, Ara mana is King's residence, the tree Aal maram was called Ara yaal, and the bird Ara yannam were all given special importance in Dravidian culture.

The later group who call it a "half church" maintain that according to tradition, St Thomas did not establish the church here, but only kept a Cross for the migrant Christians from Mylapore on the Coromandel coast who fled due to persecution in the Chola Kingdom. It is believed that those who fled from Mylapore consisted of 64 families, mainly of the Brahmin Vellala chetty community, who accepted Christianity and St Thomas brought them to Travancore, crossing the Sahya Parvatham (Western Ghats) via the Aruvamozhy Pass. When they arrived in Travancore, the local Venad king received them and offered them land and food.

Right: St Mary's Orthodox church, the "Ara pally" half church, Thiruvithamcode, Kerala, India (2016).

The Ara Pally or "half" church

250

The Ara Pally or "half" church

St Mary's Orthodox church, the "Ara pally" half church, Thiruvithamcode, Kerala, India (2016).

Both these stories point to the common fact that the church was a gift from the Venad King. It is believed that he gave them 64 fragments of land in the northern part of the historical Venattu thitta and 64 houses were built at government expense. On further request, the king sanctioned another 24 cents of land for worship. It is at this place that the Church now stands.

The church is built in the traditional south Indian architectural style similar to ancient Jain temples. The church has three main parts built in the 17th century and a 20th century entrance hall. Its walls are built of locally quarried stone. On the southern side of the sanctum is a cross believed to be carved by the Apostle himself, although this is unlikely - it is more likely to have been carved by later believers.

The Ara pally church was unknown to many in Kerala until recently. Note that in this church there were no pictures or idols near the altar, other than a Persian cross until recently, which shows that this church was built much earlier and before the present liturgical practices were introduced. The church is now part of the Malankara Orthodox Church and has recently become a pilgrim centre, known as St Mary's Orthodox Church.

Right: Relics of St Gregory in front of a painting of St Thomas, the Ara Palli church.

Lotus Flower

The leaved cross

Primitive Christian groups used the image of the fish as their symbol. The Cross was an instrument of punishment before it became a sign of Christianity. Persians, Greeks and Romans executed people on crosses.

The Sign of the cross was reported to be used by Christians by Tertullian (AD 160-220). Early in the third century, Clement of Alexandria mentions the Cross, but it only emerged as the public symbol of Christians after the "Exaltation of the Holy Cross" by Constantine at the Battle of Milvian Bridge near Rome in AD 312.

The brass crosses where worshippers place their candles at the narthex of the Mar Thoma churches are in the traditioned Orthodox design, with an inverted dove descending on a cross which is supported on an upturned lotus flower. The lotus reflects the mingling of Buddhist culture with that of the early Thomas Christians. These handsome brass crosses hang or stand inside the churches. They are not like a typical crucifix but are always plain and never show Christ on the cross. In Eastern and Syrian Christianity, the plain cross is the symbol of the triumph of Christ's life over death.

These crosses are sometimes called Leaved Crosses, or Persian crosses, as they have a set of leaves at the bottom. The leaves usually flow upwards either side of the base of the cross, symbolising the cross as the tree of life, but on many of these Keralan crosses the leaves point downwards. This is indigenous to Kerala and comes from the original Buddhist influence on Christianity.

Right: The brass Mar Thoma cross in the narthex of the Ara pally "half church", Kerala (2017).

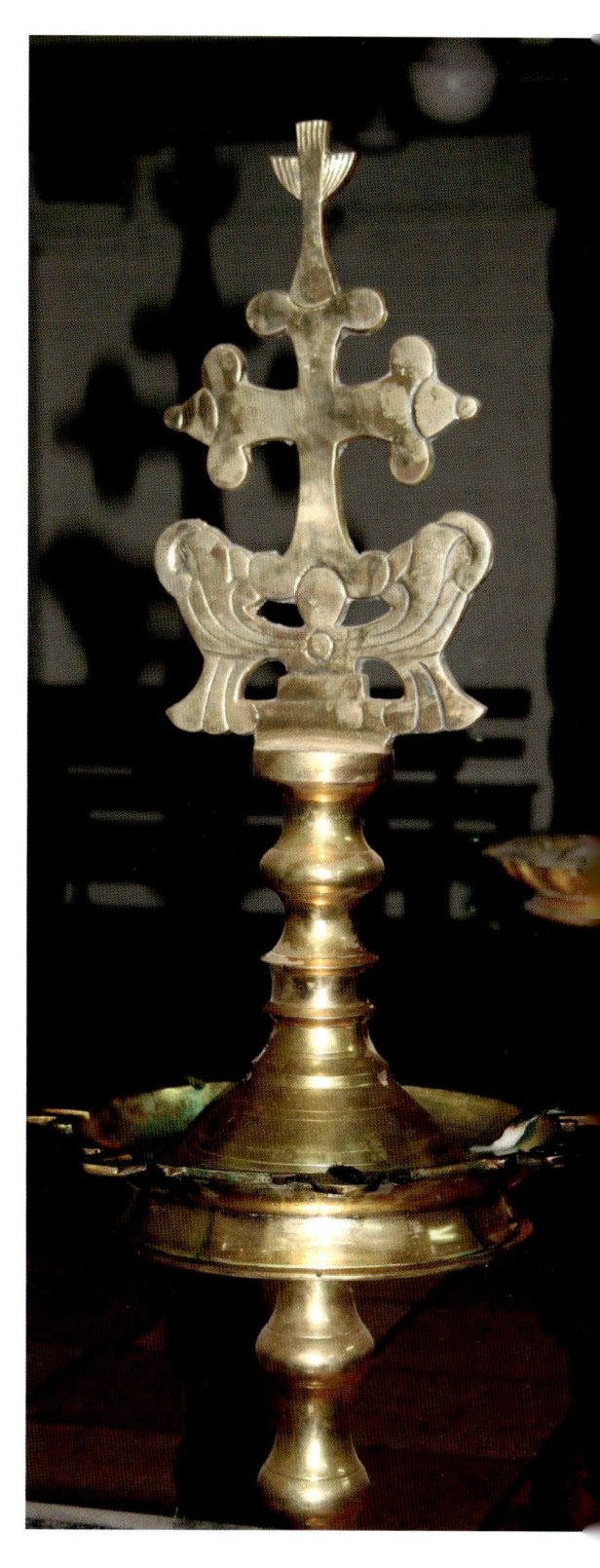

St Thomas travelled round Kerala by boat...

St Thomas mostly travelled round Kerala by boat...

The tradition that locates the Apostle's activity in two places, Kerala on the western and Coromandel on the eastern coast of southern India, corresponds to the historical existence of two communities. However, some calamities have destroyed the eastern community, which at some time (differently specified in the different sources) had to migrate westward and to unite with the one in Kerala. A version of the tradition transmitted by Francisco Roz, the first Latin bishop (residing in Angamaly) of the St Thomas Christians, does not know about the preaching of the Apostle on the Malabar Coast, but holds that all the St Thomas Christians emigrated there from the east. An interesting element of the local traditions is that – at least in Portuguese times – the same stories were told on the western and on the eastern coast, but connected to different localities. At present there is no autochthonous Christian community on the Coromandel Coast. In Kerala almost every village has its local St Thomas tradition, full of miraculous elements. Most of the literature on the question treats the historicity of the Apostle's presence and activities in India, trying to combine the different western and eastern testimonies with elements of local tradition and archaeological findings. The general outcome of these investigations is that the question of the historicity of the tradition is unsolvable by means of the scholarly methods that we have at our disposal.

...and by bullock cart

The strongest argument in favour of this remains in the tradition itself, an unanimous tradition held not only in India, but also in the whole Christian Orient. Here we also face something quite extraordinary, which deserves a different approach. In fact, the very existence of the traditions concerning the Apostle, divergent in their details but unanimous in their core message, and the role of these traditions shaping the self-identity of the community, is a matter of objective fact. Setting aside the question of how true historically the tradition is, we should recognise the St Thomas traditions as constituting an important, if not the most important, factor in the formation of the Nazranies' communal identity.

The tradition of St Thomas preaching and converting in India and apparently converting nobody but members of the higher castes, expresses both the Nazranies' embeddedness in the surrounding majority Hindu society and their separation. It explains why they find themselves integrated into the Indian culture, speaking the same language – Malayalam – as their neighbours. But it also explains why they are separate, professing a different faith, Christianity. It also explains their ambiguous but traditionally well-established position in society. Being Christians, they believe in the absolute truth and the sole saving power of their religion.

When not travelling by boat, as was his wont, St Thomas might well have travelled in bullock carts on the Indian roads, like this one near Mahabilipuram, Tamil Nadu, India (2013).

Nilackal

The tree-clad Sabarimala hillside that was once the site of Nilackal, Kerala, India (2016).

It is perfectly possible that St Thomas and Habban came to Nilackal in the Sabarimala hills if they wanted to travel through the 8,900 foot Kumali Pass through the Western Ghats to Angamoozhy, the main town on the Kerala-Tamil Nadu border to reach the important trading city of Madurai. They would not have travelled alone but only in a group. Some of the journey would have been undertaken by water as well as on foot and by bullock carts on the beaten path. Even though there is no historical evidence of the missionary work of St Thomas in Nilackal, some assumptions of St Thomas' establishment of a church in this place are written on old metal plates and other historical writings.

The route from Nilackal to Madurai was one of three major routes through the Ghats: it was an important trading centre from the sixth c. BC for the export of spices and other items like gold, ivory and silk. Many Jews lived in Nilackal until its total destruction in the 14th century. It was never rebuilt.

The Western ghats rise to 8 - 9,000 feet high, and average 3 - 4,000 feet. Some say that there was no way through and that St Thomas did all his travelling by boat. There are 41 rivers in Kerala which flow from the Western Ghats into the Arabian Sea and the backwaters. Tigers, panthers and elephants are still found in the surrounding forest which was once inhabited by robbers and thugs.

The present church is not built on the site of the old church on the hilltop of Nilackal because it was sacked and abandoned in the 14th century. Nilackal (also known as Chayal) was one of the biggest trade centre in Kerala in spices and timber, having business relations with Romans, Jews and Persians. Its destruction resulted in a massive migration of Syrian Christians from Nilackal to other places, especially to Chengannur, Mallappally, Vaipore, Kanjirappally, Puthuppally and Aruvithura.

A new church was rebuilt on Hindu land in 1984 but as this became in a dilapidated state, yet another church has been built under the joint auspices of all the Christian denominations of Kerala at the site given to it by the Nilakkal Hindu authorities and agreed upon by all concerned. This rebuilt ecumenical church at Nilakkal has historical significance as the first church built and dedicated by all denominations as an example of the unity of all the Christian churches and also of communal harmony as a symbol of St Thomas' heritage.

Nilackal Ecumenical Church, Kerala, India (2016).

The Nilackal Ecumenical granite cross erected in 2011. Nilackal, Kerala, India (2016).

St Thomas' footprint, Malayattoor

St Thomas' footprint on the rock at Malayattoor where he is said to have made the sign of the Cross and blood poured forth from it. Later a golden cross appeared here.

Malayattoor, a meeting place of mountain and river, shot to prominence when according to the legend, it was blessed by the missionary work of St Thomas the apostle who founded the famous seven churches or communities. On his way to Mylapore, he stopped at Malayattoor. Oral tradition says that while travelling through Malayattoor, faced with hostile natives, St Thomas fled to the hilltop where he is said to have remained in prayer and that he left his footprints on one of the rocks. According to this legend, during prayer, he touched a rock, upon which blood poured from it. In deep anguish and agony, St Thomas prayed to the Lord and he made the sign of the cross on the rock. The Virgin Mary appeared to console and strengthen him. He descended from the top of the hill and continued his journey to Mylapore in Tamil Nadu.

The chief festival at Malayattoor is on the first Sunday after Easter. It is believed that St Thomas used to make the Sign of the Cross on the rock, kiss it and pray at Kurisumudi. It is said that a miraculous golden cross appeared at that particular spot. Years later, while out hunting, the local people found a divine light emanating from the hard rock and on examining the source, they found a golden cross. They later discovered the footprint of the saint and when this extraordinary piece of news reached the plains, people began to flock to the hills of Malayattoor.

Portion of a mosaic panel of the Virgin Mary, 10th c., The Benaki Museum, Athens, Greece (2016).

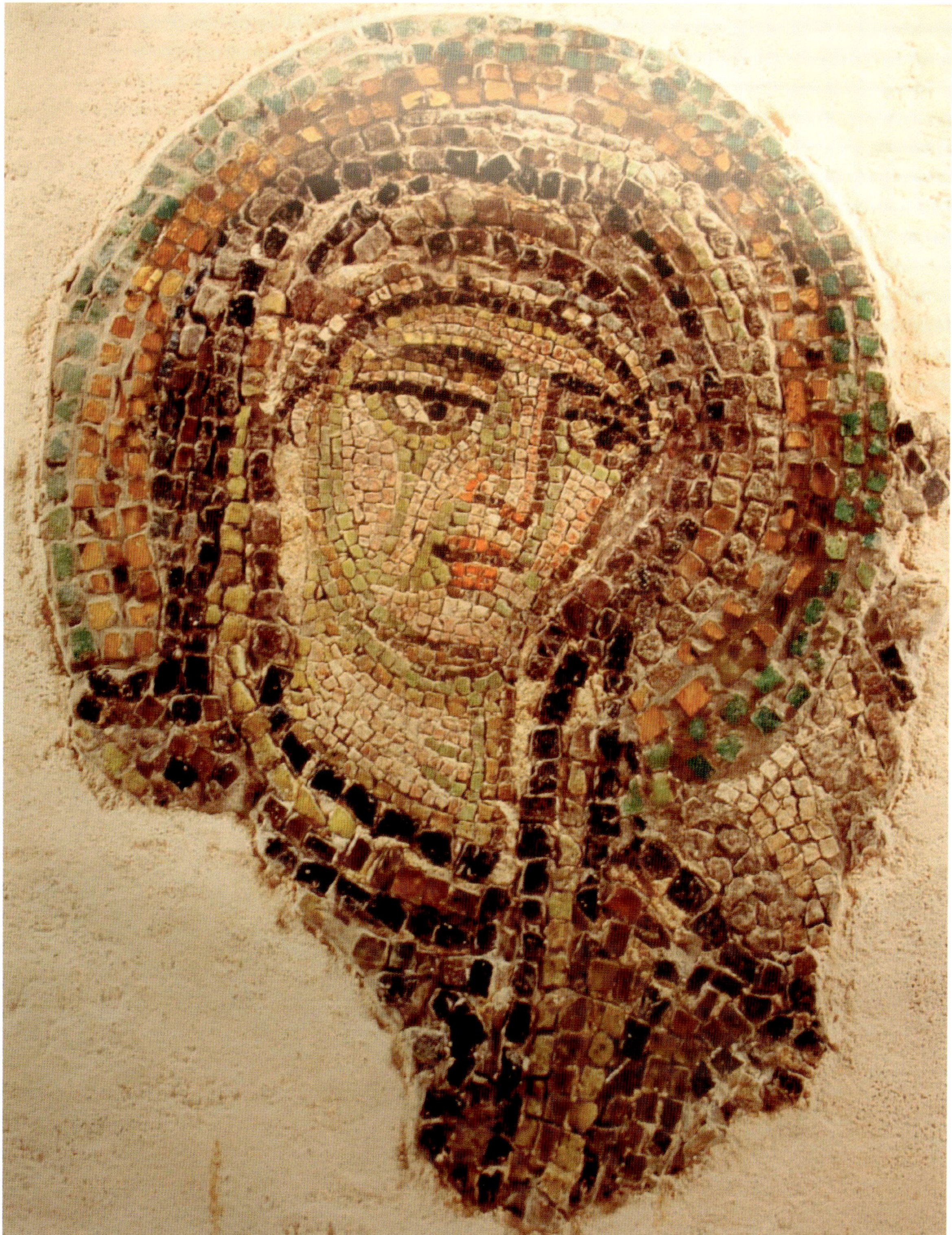

7.
Tamil Nadu:

Madurai
Mahabalipuram

Madras - Chennai
The arrival of the Portuguese
St Thomas's Mount

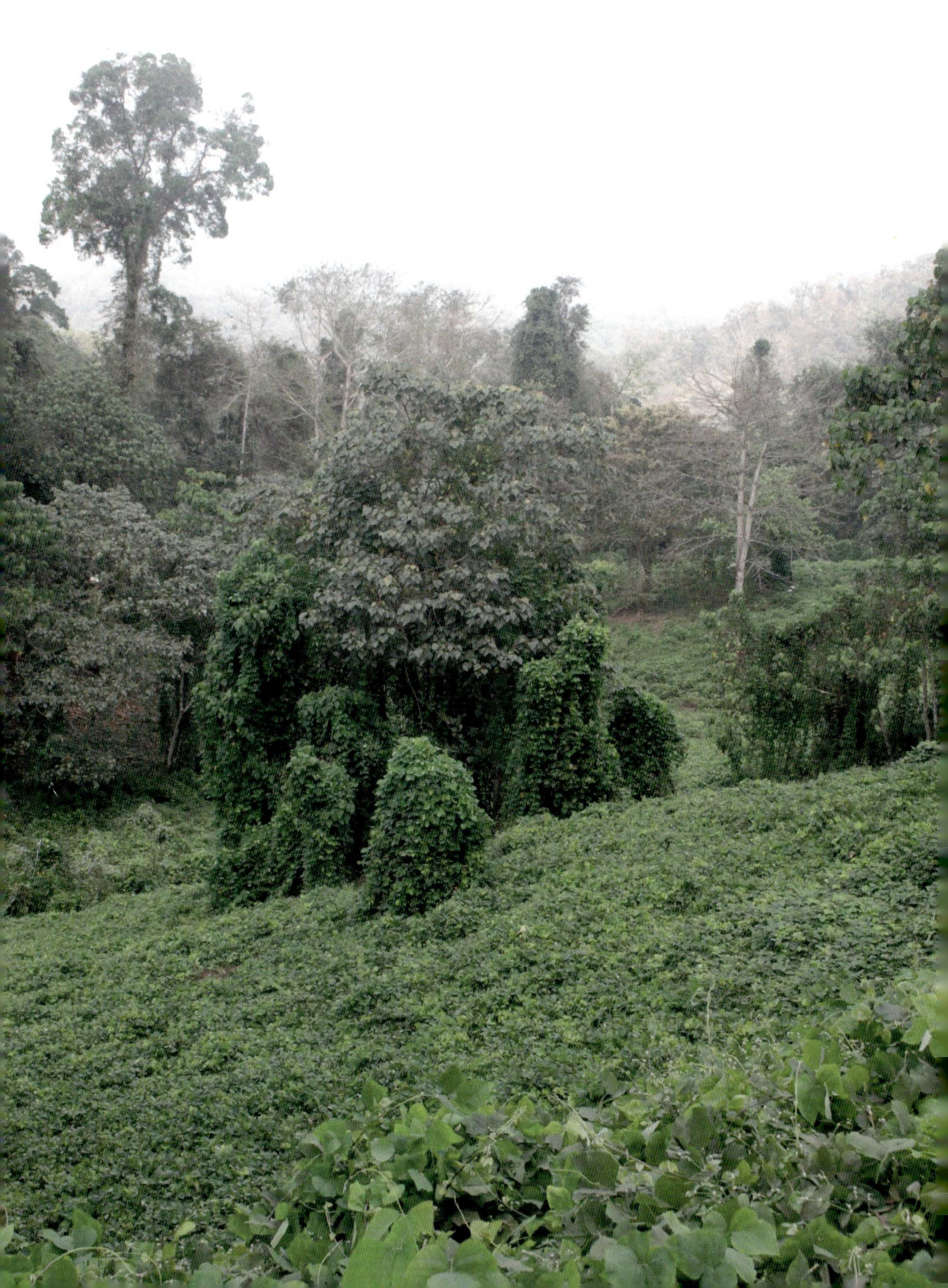

Madurai

Madurai would have had a *tank* but this is from the 14th c. The Gopuram is 16th-17th c. (2013). Gopurams (monumental gateways) did not exist in St Thomas' time, only Hindu cave temples.

Madurai was founded in the 6th century BC and was always a crossroads for trade. It has been a major settlement for two millennia and is one of the oldest continuously inhabited cities in the world. Chinese and Roman traders met here from the third century BC. Three routes led over the Western Ghats from Cochin, Quilon and Trivandrum to Madurai, and from there they moved on to Trichy and Mahabalipuram on the Bay of Bengal.

The Meenakshi Amman Temple on the southern bank of the Vaigai River in the temple city of Madurai, Tamil Nadu, India is dedicated to Parvati, known as Meenakshi, and her consort, Shiva, here named Sundareswarar.

Its skyline is dominated by the 14 colourful gopurams (gateway towers) of Meenakshi Amman Temple. Covered in bright carvings of Hindu gods, the Dravidian-style temple is a major pilgrimage site.

St Thomas and Habban would almost certainly have come to this important city on their way to Mahabalipuram.

Previous page: The beginning of the path through the Western Ghats, Nilakkal, Kerala, India (2016).

Right: Hanuman image, Meenaskshi temple, Madurai (2013).

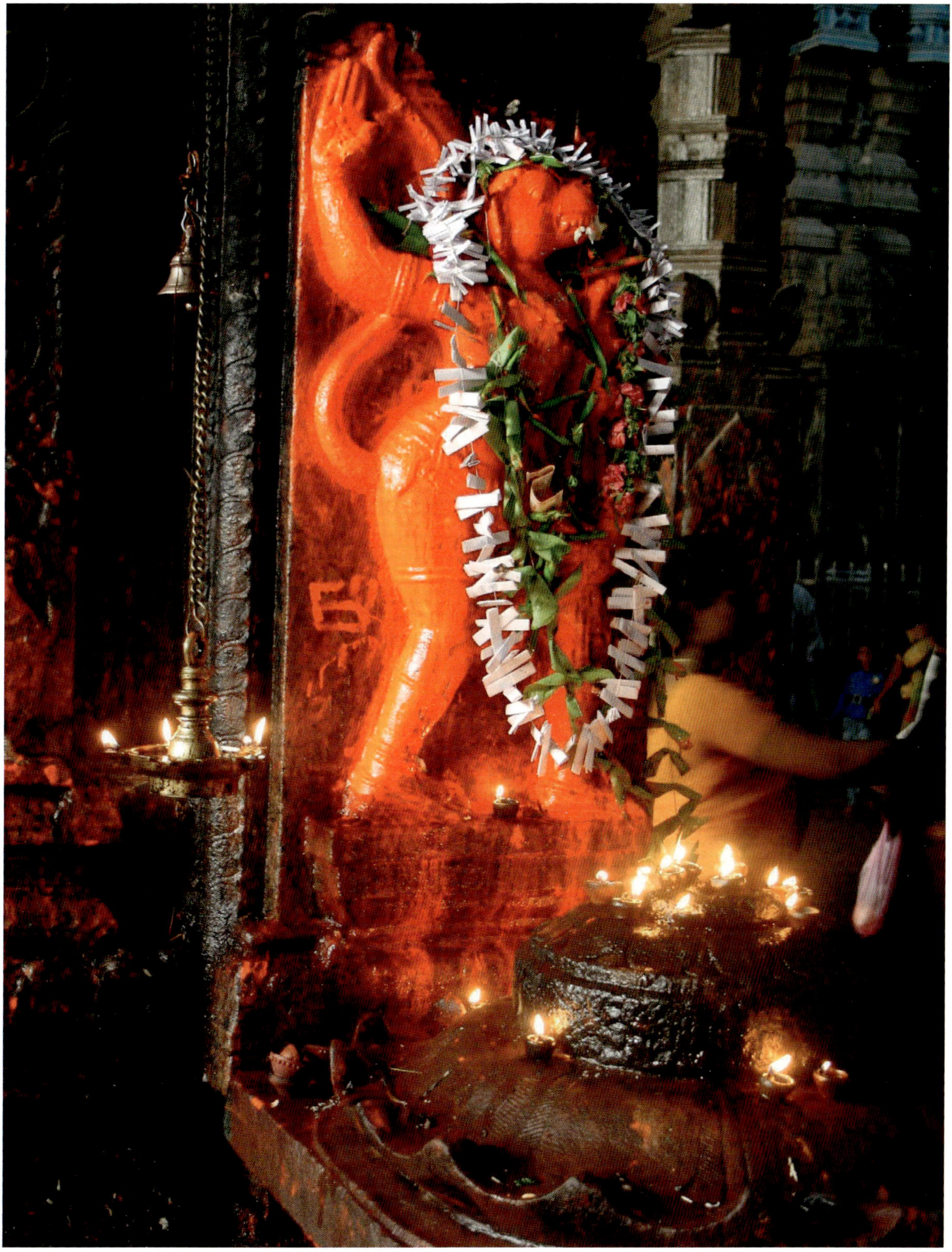

Tanjore

The Brihadeeshwara Chola Temple, early 11th c, Tanjore, Tamil Nadu, India (2013).

Hinduism would have been practised here when St Thomas came to Thanjavur. Trichy is mentioned by Ptolemy in the second c BC. The Chola fortifications date from the second century AD.

The Peruvudaiyar Kovil is a Hindu temple dedicated to Shiva in the city of Thanjavur (Tanjore) in Tamil Nadu. It is an important example of Tamil architecture of the Chola dynasty built by Raja Raja Chola I in AD 1010. It is a luminous example of the heights which the Cholas achieved within Tamil architecture. This temple is one of India's largest and greatest architectural glories. It stands in the middle of fortified walls which were probably added in the sixteenth century. There is one temple tower: 216 feet high (which people call Vimana). It is also one of the tallest towers of its kind in the world.

The Kumbam, Chikharam or Kalasha (the bulbous structure on top of the temple) is carved out of a single stone. The entire structure of the temple is made of granite from near Tiruchirappalli, which is nearly 40 miles west of Tanjore. The single rock carved statue of Nandi (the sacred bull) at entrance of this temple measures about thirteen feet high and sixteen feet long.

Right: The saree-clad goddess Parvati, the consort of Lord Shiva, in a niche in the temple, Tanjore, Tamil Nadu, India (2013).

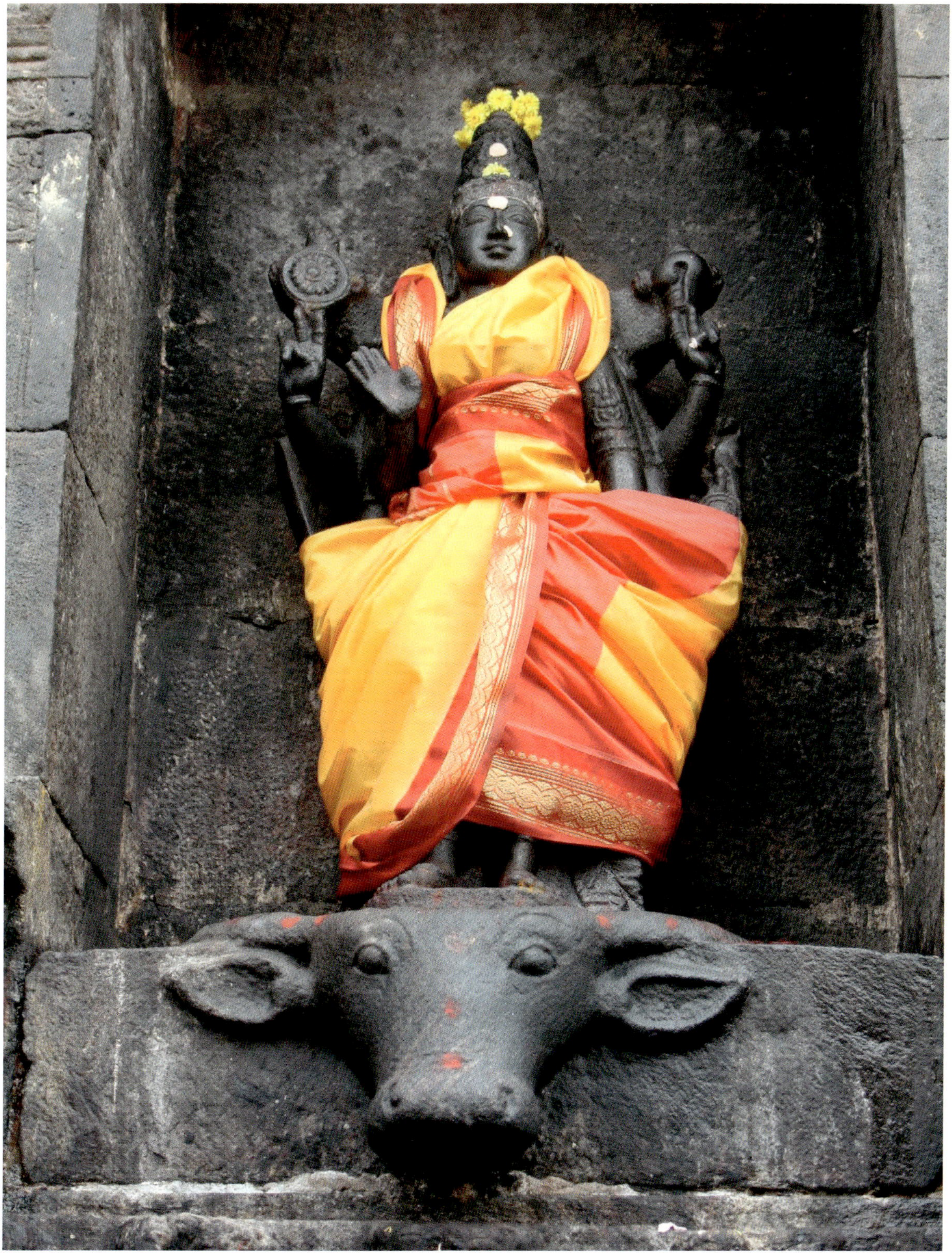

Mahabilipuram

Local fishing boat on the shore of the former port of Mahabilipuram, Tamil Nadu, India (2016).

It is likely that St Thomas reached the bay of Mahabalipuram, a lively and important port on the Bay of Bengal with its sheltered harbour for Roman and Chinese shipping from the 1st century BC.

St Thomas would have found a suitable cave in which to pray and this Shiva cave just north of the old port is a possible contender.

Poduca (Pondicherry), a little further north up the coast, was also used by Chinese boats. It is logically possible that St Thomas went to China. Roman artefacts have been found in Arikamedu, the port of Poduca.

When St Thomas had finished his first round of mission in the Tamil country, he returned by boat to Kerala. St Thomas spent eight years in total in the Tamil country.

Right: Krishna's butterball, a prehistoric stone that would have been here when St Thomas was in Mahabalipuram, Tamil Nadu, India (2014).

Lord Krishna's butterball

Cave temple, Mahabilipuram

Shiva cave temple, north of Mahabilipuram, not far from ancient Calamina, Tamil Nadu, India (2016).

On Roman maps of the 1st century AD, Calamina is shown inland of the Bay of Bengal, about halfway between Mahabilipuram and Mylapore.

"The apostle Thomas after having preached the gospel to the Parthians, Medes, Persians suffered martyrdom at Codamina, a town of India".
Hippolytus, who died a martyr during the reign of the Roman Emperor Sirrus (225-235). This is the first time that the place, Codamina or Calamina, is specified.
E Kenneth, *St Thomas The Apostle of India*.

Pseudo-Sophronius (seventh century AD) indicates the place name 'Calamina' where St Thomas was martyred and buried.

"Thomas was martyred and buried in Calamina, a city of India".
Isidore of Seville (AD 636).

Qalimaya, an approximation of Calamina, is found in a Syriac manuscript of AD 874.
Hambye "*St Thomas*" cited in *History of Christianity in India*.
A M Mundadan.

Granite Shiva lingam. Mahabalipuram, Tamil Nadu, India (2016).

Mylapore was a town of peacocks

Peacock feeding, Ranthambhore National Park, Rajasthan, India (2014).

Mylapore was a town of peacocks.

"The Lord of Kapaleeswara sat watching the people of Mylapore - a place full of flowering coconut palms - taking a ceremonial bath in the sea on the full moon day of the month of Masi".

Tirujnanasambandar, sixth century.
Poompavai Padikam Thevaram.

The Nasrani Christians assigned the peacock as the mount of St Thomas, saying that when the Virgin Mary died, he flew to Jerusalem for her funeral on the back of a peacock! He needed a carrier in the same way as Nandi Bull is the vehicle of the Dravidian Lord Shiva, the Arian Lord Vishnu has the man-eagle Garuda and the Arian Lord Brahma has a swan (or goose), a symbol of knowledge. The four evangelists all have mounts: St Matthew has the winged man, St Mark the winged lion, St Luke the winged bull, and St John the eagle.

No Keralan has ever found any evidence of St Thomas being killed in mistake for a peacock. Peacocks represent the resurrection.

The Portuguese built the church of Santhome on the site of the original Kapaleeshwarar Shiva temple in Mylapore in 1517: it stands on the ruins of a Jain Neminathaswami temple and a Hindu Shiva temple which had a Nataraja shrine attached. The epigraphical data for the existence of the Jain temple on this site is recorded in Jain Inscriptions in Tamil Nadu. The temple was there until 1561 when the Portuguese demolished it completely. Hindus built the present temple out of whatever they could salvage from the ruins of the old temple.

Over the centuries, the elements took their toll on the small church and it was in dire need of repair. In 1893, this structure was demolished and the present church was built in the Gothic style and the tomb of the saint was placed at the heart of the structure. In 1924 a fragmentary 12th century Tamil inscription of eight lines belonging to Vikrama Chola's time was found on a stone in the cathedral: it registers a tax-free gift for burning a lamp before the image of Kuthadumdevar (Nataraja) at night in the temple of Suramudayar. Moreover, when the *urchava murthy* was taken for procession from the existing Kapaleeswarar Temple in the 16th-18th centuries, there was a practice of lowering it reverently three times before the Santhome church.

Flowering coconut palms, Mylapore, Tamil Nadu, India (2016).

Medieval descriptions of Mylapore

Jesus embraces St Thomas, stone marker, Mylapore, Tamil Nadu, India (2016).

"Thomas was from Jerusalem of the tribe of Juda. He taught the Persians, Medes and Indians; because he baptised the daughter of the King of Indians he stabbed him with a spear and he died. Habban the merchant brought his body and laid it in Edessa, the blessed city of our Lord. Others say that he was buried in Mahluph, a city in the land of Indians".

Mar Solomon, a 13th-century Nestorian bishop: *The Book of the Bee*, edited by E A W Budge.

"It is in the province which is styled the greater India, at the gulf between Ceylon and the mainland that the body of Messer St Thomas lies at a certain town having no great population; it is a place not very accessible."

Marco Polo (was said to have visited the burial place of St Thomas in 1293)

"I.......departed from Tauris, a city of Persians, in the year of Lord 1291, and proceeded to India. And I remained in the country of India, wherein stands the church of St Thomas the Apostle, for thirteen months, and in that region baptised in different places about one hundred persons. The companion of my journey was Friar Nicholas of Pistoia, of the order of preachers, who died there, and was buried in the church aforesaid."

John of Monte Corvino, *Cathay and the way thither*, Vol.III.

"His tomb stands on the peninsula Meilan in India, to the right of the altar in the monastery bearing his name."

A Nestorian writer Amr, son of Matthew (1340), A E Medlycott, *India and the Apostle Thomas*.

St Thomas with his gospel, blessing the people, Mylapore, Tamil Nadu, India (2016).

"There is a journey of ten days to another realm which is called Mobar, and this is very great, and hath in it many cities and towns. And in this realm is laid the body of the Blessed Thomas the Apostle. His church is filled with idols, and beside it are some fifteen houses of Nestorians; that is to say, Christians, but vile and pestilent heretics."

Blessed Odoric (1325) after discussing Malabar, which he calls Minibar.

"The third province of India is called Malabar, and the Church of St Thomas, which he built with his own hands, is there besides another which he built by the agency of workmen. He reports the saint ordering the trunk of a tree that had been cut down on the island: Go and tarry for us at the haven of the city of Mirapolis; which, as Yule observed, is a Hellenised form of the name Mylapore. The Jews, Muslims, and even some of the Christians, regarded the Latins as the worst of idolaters, because they use statues and images in their churches".

John de Marignolli (1349),
A E Medlycott: *India and the Apostle Thomas.*

"Proceeding onwards the said Nicolo arrived at a maritime city, which is named Malepur (should be Malpuria), situated in the second gulf beyond the Indus (the Bay of Bengal). Here the body of St Thomas lies honourably buried in a large and beautiful church: it is worshipped by heretics, who are called Nestorians, and inhabit this city to the number of thousand. These Nestorians are scattered over all India, as the Jew among us".

Nicolo de' Conti (1425-1430):
R H Major's *India in the fifth century.*

"The houses as well of saint Thomas the apostle have commenced to be occupied by some Christians who are looking after the repairs; they are situated at a distance from our aforesaid Christians of about twenty-five days, and stand in a city on the sea named Meliapor, in the province of Silan, which is one of the provinces of India".

Nestorian Bishops (1504),
A E Medlycott: *India and the Apostle Thomas.*

Little Mount

The cross in the cave of Little Mount, Chennai, India (2016).

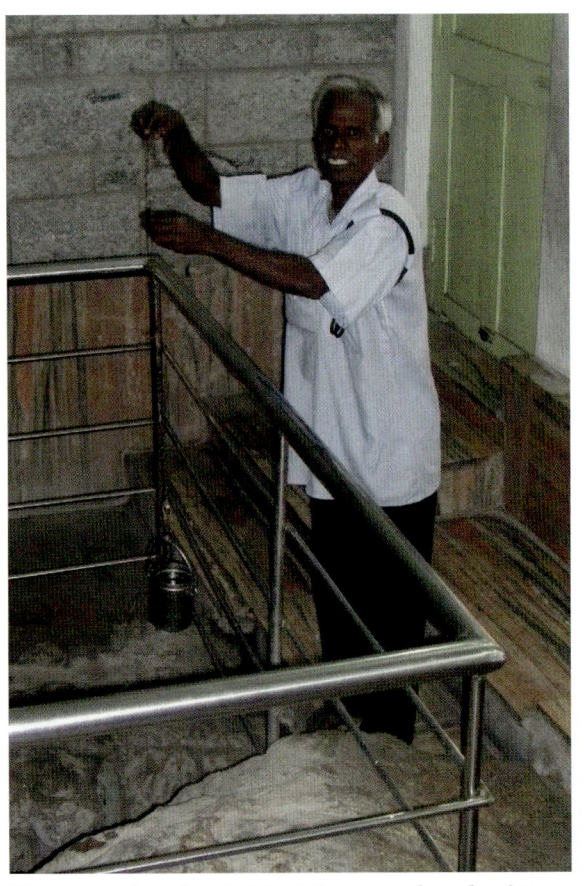

The natural spring behind the new church of Our Lady of Good Health, Chennai, India (2016).

Little Mount, made up of the Charnockite rock formations just south of the city centre, is believed to be the place where St Thomas was in hiding when he was martyred on top of the mount. He is said to have sought refuge from persecution in the Little Mount Caves when he was speared to death while praying before a stone cross here.

Inside, next to a small, natural window in the rock, are impressions of what are believed to be St Thomas' handprints, created when he tried to make his escape through this tiny opening.

Tradition has it that this was created when St Thomas struck the rock, so that the crowds who came to hear him preach could quench their thirst. The spring is believed to have been in existence from the time of St Thomas and many devotees carry this water home with them.

There was no claim for martyrdom for several centuries. Mylapore is correct as the probable location, but the site where Santhomai now stands was polluted by Gnostics when the Portuguese arrived in 1498.

The ancient town of Calamina where St Thomas was said to have been martyred was south of Mylapore and a little inland in the 1st c. AD.

It is accepted that St Thomas was first in Soqotra, then Taxila, then Kerala and then Mylapore. Neither Sri Lanka nor China are confirmed although they would both have been possible thanks to the sea routes.

A Catholic devotee praying before a statue of St Thomas in the cave where he is said to have been speared to death, Little Mount, Chennai, India (2016).

St Thomas's Mount

"*By St Thomas were the Chinese and the Ethiopians converted to the Truth*" and in an Anthem: "*The Hindus, the Chinese, the Persians, and all the people of the Isles of the Sea, they who dwell in Syria and Armenia, in Javan and Romania, call Thomas to remembrance, and adore Thy Name, O Thou our Redeemer!*"

The Chaldaean breviary of the Syro-Malabar Catholic Church in its office of St Thomas.

The Mylapore Cross is considered to be the oldest in India. Based on the type of script used, most of these crosses are attributed to between the 6th and 8th centuries. Only the second cross of Kottayam, which has a Syriac inscription, is dated to the 10th century. This Cross been venerated by all St Thomas Christians from ancient times. It has inscriptions in Pahlavi (Middle Persian) and Syriac, which indicate that it dates to before the 8th century.

During excavation at St Thomas Mount in 1547, the Vicar of Mylapore discovered a bleeding cross with old Pahlavi inscriptions. It had spots that looked like bloodstains which, it was claimed, reappeared after being rubbed away. This cross is built into the wall behind the altar of the church on the Mount dedicated to the Madonna of the Mount. The tradition about this cross is that it was chiselled from a rock by the apostle himself. It is said that it used to bleed periodically. The first publicly noticed bleeding was after the arrival of the Portuguese on 15 December 1558, and the last in 1704.

The Mar Thoma cross above the altar discovered by the Portuguese in the ruins of the church on St Thomas's Mount in AD 1547 and a piece of bone of the Apostle, recently given to the Catholic St Thomas's Mount shrine here by St John Paul II, Chennai, India (2016).

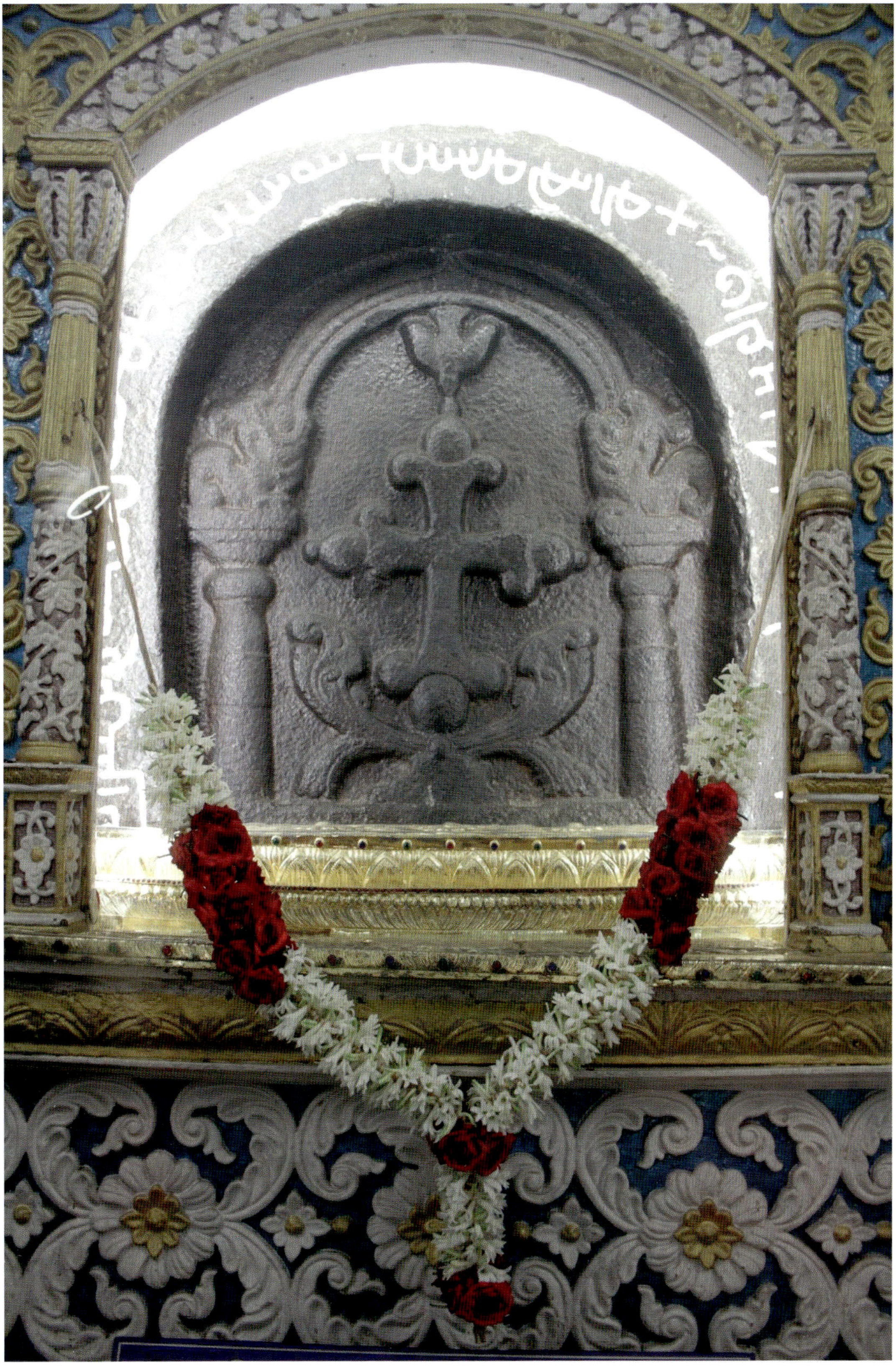

Santhome

Ancient writers used the designation "India" for all countries south and east of the Roman Empire's frontiers. India included Ethiopia, Arabia Felix, Edessa in Syria (in the Latin version of the Syriac Diatessaron), Arachosia and Gandhara (Afghanistan and Pakistan), and many countries up to the China Sea.

St Thomas performed miracles which made the local King Mahadeva offer him a place near the seashore where the old church of Mylapore now stands. His body was brought to Mylapore and buried in AD 73 at a spot which was forgotten for many centuries.

Armenian Christians merchants discovered St Thomas' grave in the sixth century and a church was built on the site, a village now called Mylapore, in Chennai. Traders called this village 'Betumah' or 'Town of Thomas'.

Marco Polo's indication of the position of the Shrine of St Thomas is the first geographical identification of it, save one. At the same time as his homeward voyage, another Italian, John of Monte Corvino spent thirteen months on the Malabar coast on his way to China, and in a letter from there in 1292-1293 he tells of burying the companion of his travels, Friar Nicholas of Pistoia, in the church of St Thomas.

Odoric, some thirty years later, found beside the church "some 15 houses of Manicheans," but the Church itself filled with idols. Conti, in the following century, speaks of the church in which St Thomas lay buried, as large and beautiful, and says there were 1,000 Nestorians in the city.

Nestorian bishops in 1504 write:
"The houses as well of Saint Thomas the apostle have commenced to be occupied by some Christians who are looking after the repairs; they are situated at a distance from our aforesaid Christians of about twenty five days, and stand in a city on the sea named Meliapor, in the province of Silan, which is one of the provinces of India".

A E Medlycott,
India and Apostle Thomas.

If Mylapore had been known as the burial place of St Thomas it would have been a great hub of Christianity, in fact nothing was here when the Portuguese arrived in Mylapore in 1517, they were surprised to find a shrine there, but the shrine itself was almost in ruins. The Portuguese rebuilt the church in 1523.

The papal seal over this whole story was stamped in 1956 when Pope Pius XII gave it recognition as a Minor Basilica, all the four major ones being outside India. The Basilica Cathedral of Santhome is one of only three basilicas or cathedrals built over the tomb of one of Jesus' apostles. The other two are the Basilica of St Peter, built over the tomb of St Peter in Rome, and the Cathedral of Santiago de Compostela, built over the tomb of St James in Spain.

Santhome, Mylapore, Tamil Nadu, India (2016).

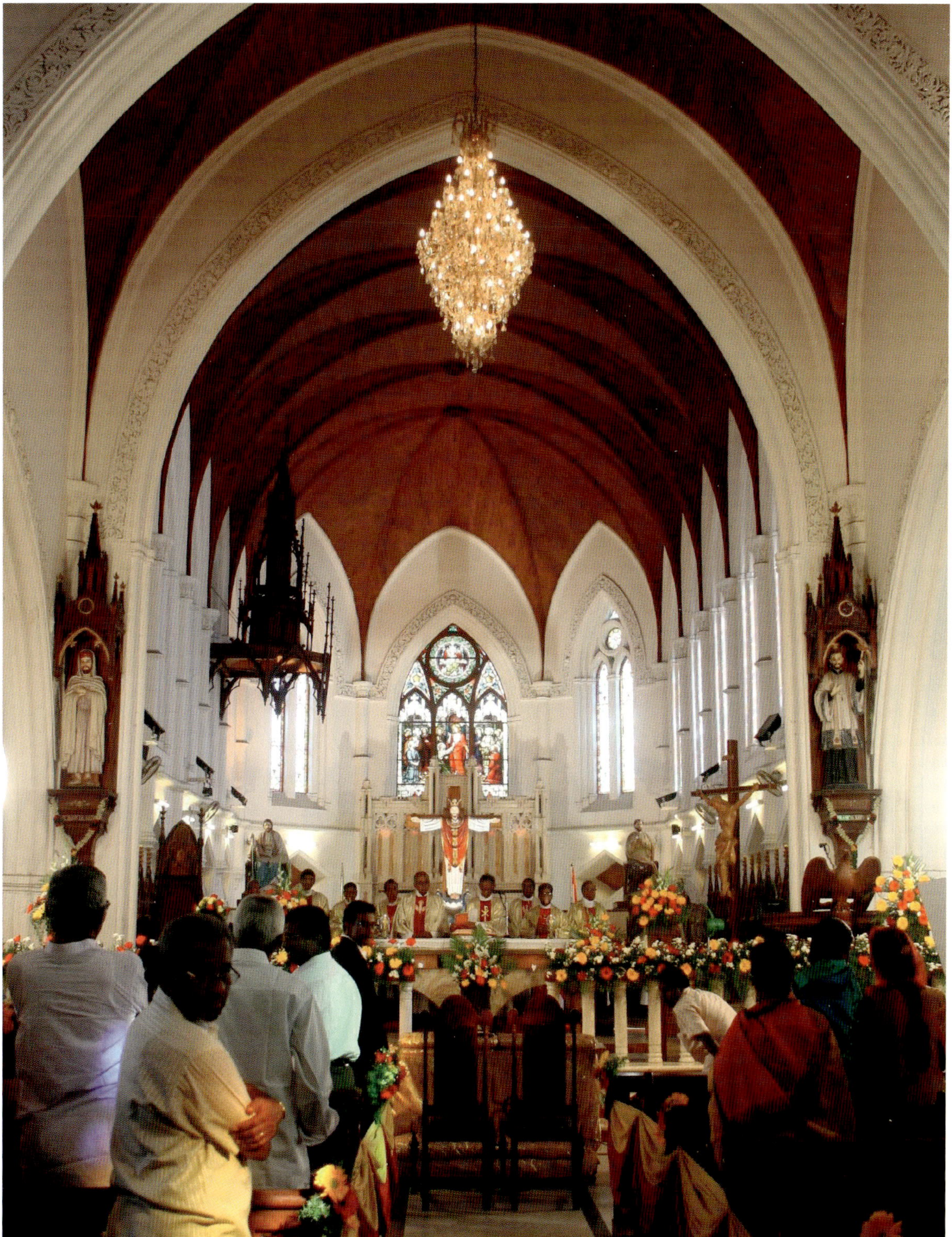

St Thomas of India

Front cover and above: modern icon based on the prototype of Christ Pantocrator; Istanbul, 13th c. AD.

This icon was created as a gift to the people of the Madhya - Kerala Diocese of the Church of South India (CSI) as a means to let them know of the concerns and prayers of the Diocese of Oregon for them as they recover from the devastation of the December 2004 tsunami. A cross, similar to an ancient sixth century AD. cross – believed to be the one carved by Thomas - is reproduced on the back of this icon. A dedication "carta" is also affixed to the back of the icon. St Thomas is the patron saint of India, Sri Lanka and Pakistan, architects, builders, carpenters, geometricians, stonemasons, surveyors, theologians, blind people and people in doubt.

St Thomas is shown here as he might have looked after spending several years in India. He is shown as a man in the prime of his life; energetic and a great builder of churches throughout the region. St Thomas was known as an architect and church builder, as well as an Apostle.

The icon is configured as a within a 16 x 16 square. These are two of the most powerful symbols in architecture. Placing the circle in the square also produces the third very important architectural "icon" the bracket, often found in church buildings supporting roofs and vaulted ceilings.

The four brackets surrounding the circle of the icon are filled with scrollwork derived from carved marble decoration found in the Taj Mahal in India. Included within the scrollwork are logos representing Trinity Episcopal Cathedral, Oregon and the Church of South India, Kerala.

There is no reliable historical fact concerning St Thomas' date of birth; he was undoubtedly Jewish and his martyrdom is recorded as having occurred in AD 72 at what was said to be an advanced age. Thomas was with Jesus, whose life and ministry ended in about AD 30 so at the time of Thomas' ministry with Jesus, it may be concluded that Thomas must have been an adult, perhaps similar in age to Jesus.

Historical references purport to show that Thomas was in India for a total of some 20 years. Working in the Byzantine tradition, iconographers are obliged to seek prototype images within the Canons of the Eastern Orthodox Church. Those of St Thomas that are extant show him as a very young man; none show him in or after his later years in India.

St Thomas's main body form is taken from a 14th-c. icon of Christ Pantocrator (a full-frontal Byzantine presentation), copied from a 13th-c. mosaic in Hagia Sophia, Istanbul, Turkey. The saint is dressed in non-clerical garments typical of the Byzantine era. Thomas carries an open scroll, that of a philosopher, on which it is customary to write portions of Scripture. In this instance the words are the response that St Thomas gave to Christ's challenge: "My Lord and My God". He is no longer the "Doubting Thomas" but the believer. The saint's halo is of pure gold, as is the background of the larger circle. Surrounding the halo are twelve red garnets representing the twelve Apostles and a red fire opal, in the flame of the Holy Spirit above St Thomas' head, symbolises the blood of martyrdom.

St Thomas was slain by a spear or a lance and his remains lie in Ortona, Italy, having been taken there (after several other resting places) in 1258. Some of his remains are also in the Cathedral of Mylapore, India.

Marco Polo's account

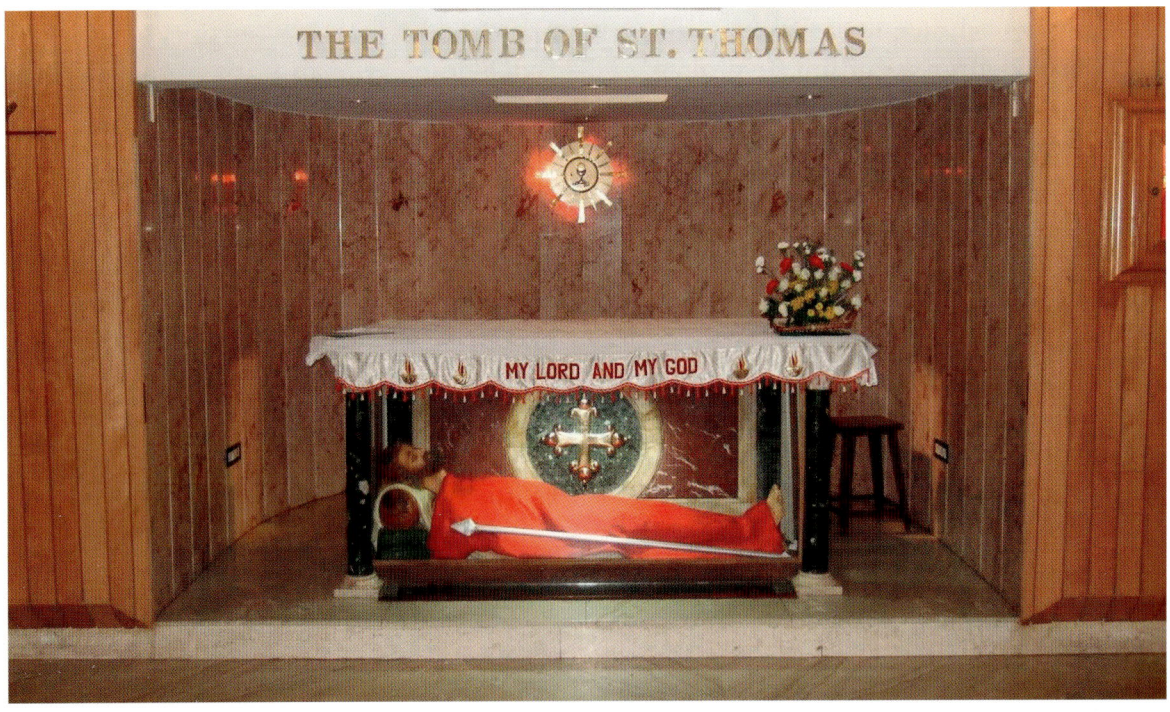

Tomb of St Thomas, the Catholic Santhome Cathedral, Mylapore, Chennai, India (2016).

Discoursing of the Place Where Lieth the Body of St Thomas the Apostle; and of the Miracles Thereof:
The Body of Messer St Thomas the Apostle lies in this province of Malabar at a certain little town having no great population. 'Tis a place where few traders go, because there is very little merchandize to be got there, and it is a place not very accessible. Both Christians and Saracens, however, greatly frequent it in pilgrimage. For the Saracens also do hold the Saint in great reverence, and say that he was one of their own Saracens and a great prophet, giving him the title of Avarian, which is as much as to say "Holy Man." The Christians who go thither in pilgrimage take of the earth from the place where the Saint was killed, and give a portion thereof to any one who is sick of a quartan or a tertian fever; and by the power of God and of St Thomas the sick man is incontinently cured. The earth, I should tell you, is red. A very fine miracle occurred there in the year of Christ, 1288, as I will now relate.

A certain Baron of that country, having great store of a certain kind of corn that is called rice, had filled up with it all the houses that belonged to the church, and stood round about it. The Christian people in charge of the church were much distressed by his having thus stuffed their houses with his rice; the pilgrims too had nowhere to lay their heads; and they often begged the pagan Baron to remove his grain, but he would do nothing of the kind. So one night the Saint himself appeared with a fork in hand, which he set at the Baron's throat, saying: "If thou void not my houses, that my pilgrims may have room, thou shalt die an evil death," and therewithal the Saint pressed him so hard with the fork that he thought himself a dead man. And when morning came he caused all the houses to be voided of his rice, and told everybody what had befallen him at the Saint's hands. So the Christians were greatly rejoiced at this grand miracle, and rendered thanks to God and to the blessed St Thomas. Other great miracles do often come to pass there, such as the healing of those who are sick or deformed, or the like, especially such as be Christians. (The Christians who have charge of the church have a great number of the Indian Nut trees, whereby they get their living; and they pay to one of those brother Kings six groats for each tree every month.)

Now, I will tell you the manner in which the Christian brethren who keep the church relate the story of the Saint's death. They tell that the Saint was in the wood outside his hermitage saying his prayers; being of the lineage of those called Govi that I told you of, having gone with his bow and arrows to shoot peafowl, not seeing the Saint, let fly an arrow at one of the peacocks; and this arrow struck the holy man in the right side, insomuch that he died of the wound, sweetly addressing himself to his Creator. Before he came to that place where he thus died he had been in Nubia, where he converted much people to the faith of Jesus Christ.

The children that are born here are black enough, but the blacker they be the more they are thought of; wherefore from the day of their birth their parents do rub them every week with oil of sesame, so that they become as black as devils. Moreover, they make their gods black and their devils white, and the images of their saints they do paint black all over.

They have such faith in the ox, and hold it for a thing so holy, that when they go to the wars they take of the hair of the wild-ox, whereof I have elsewhere spoken, and wear it tied to the necks of their horses; or, if serving on foot, they hang this hair to their shields, or attach it to their own hair. And so this hair bears a high price, since without it nobody goes to the wars in any good heart. For they believe that any one who has it shall come scatheless out of battle.

Marco Polo,
1254 - 1324,
The Travels of Marco Polo.

Marco Polo, the Venetian traveller and author of *The Description of the World*, popularly known as *Il Milione*, is reputed to have visited South India in 1288 and 1292. The first date has been rejected as he was in China at the time, but the second date is accepted by many historians. He is believed to have stopped in Ceylon (Sri Lanka) and Quilon (Kollam) on the western Malabar coast of India, where he met Syrian Christians and recorded their legends of St Thomas and his miraculous tomb on the Coromandel coast.

The arrival of the Portuguese

The Portuguese nobleman Vasco da Gama (1469-1524) sailed from Lisbon in 1497 on a mission to reach India and open a sea route from Europe to the East. After sailing down the western coast of Africa and rounding the Cape of Good Hope, his expedition made numerous stops in Africa before reaching the trading post of Calicut, India, in May 1498. By the time Vasco da Gama returned from his first voyage to India in 1499, he had spent more than two years away from home, including 300 days at sea, and had travelled some 24,000 miles. Da Gama received a hero's welcome back in Portugal, and was sent on a second expedition to India in 1502, during which he brutally clashed with Muslim traders in the region. Two decades later, da Gama again returned to India, this time as Portuguese viceroy; he died there. Though the local Hindu population of Calicut initially welcomed the arrival of the Portuguese sailors (who mistook them for Thomas Christians), tensions quickly flared after da Gama offered their ruler a collection of relatively cheap goods as an arrival gift. This conflict, along with hostility from Muslim traders, led Da Gama to leave without concluding a treaty and he returned to Portugal.

The St Thomas Christians were greatly affected by the arrival of the Portuguese in 1498 because they attempted to bring the community under the auspices of Latin Rite Catholicism, resulting in permanent rifts in the community.

Under the influence of St Francis Xavier, the Church started to divide in 1653 and the Nasranis denounced the Catholic Church by taking the *Oath of the Wooden Cross* and declared independence. In 1663 Bishop Chandi abandoned the Nasranis and joined the Catholic Church, taking many Nasranis with him.

All the churches were built between 1500 and 1800 after the Portuguese invasion of 1498, with a 10 foot by 10 foot sanctuary, the same as the proportion of temples. The Jesuits were working here and favoured the Baroque style which was accepted as the standard structure.

From the 19th century, thanks to the British, Protestantism spread here and many Nasranis became Protestant.

Right: The coast of Goa, India (2014).

The Coast of Goa

8.
Sri Lanka
China

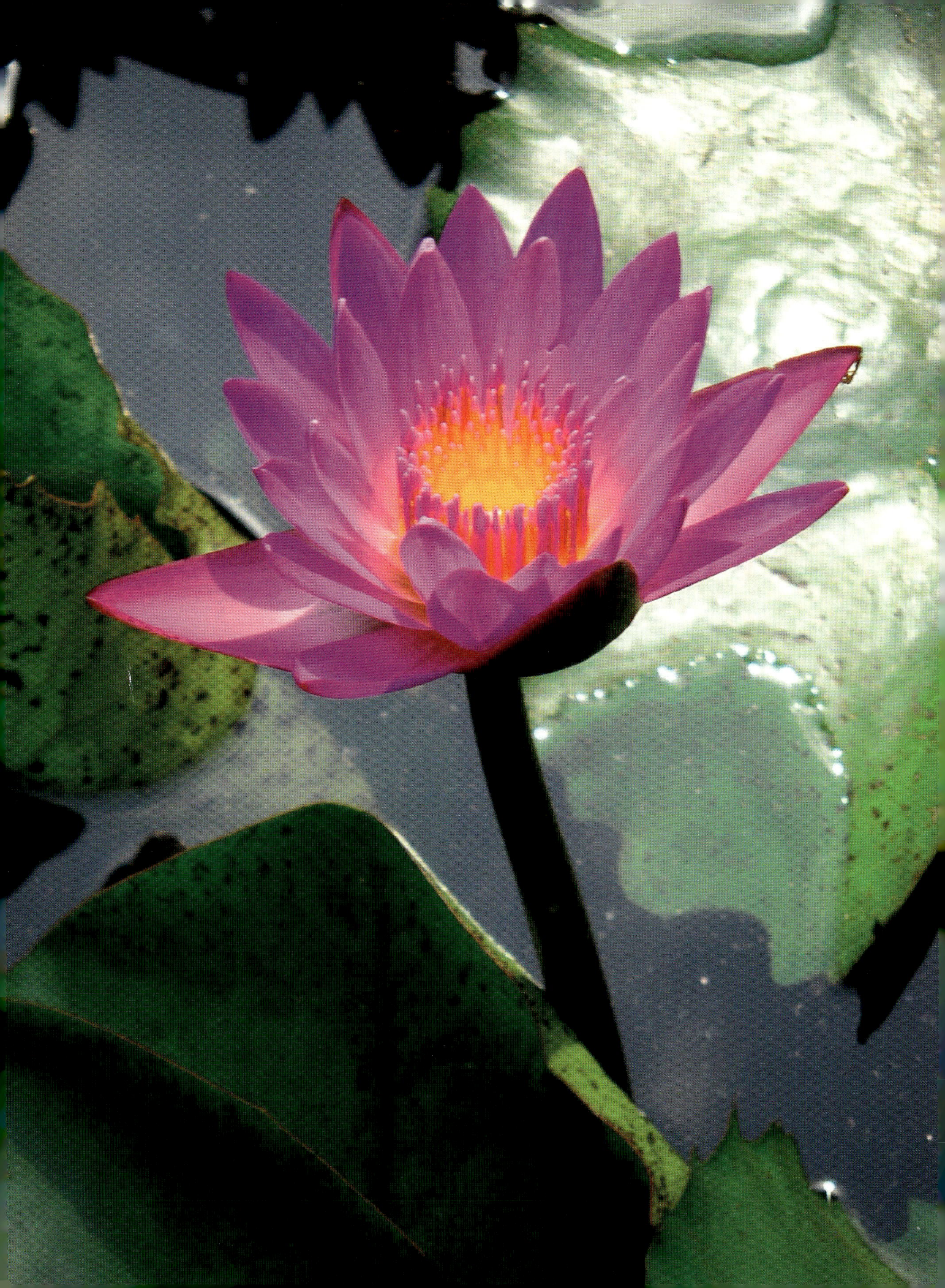

Sri Lanka

The painted feet of the Buddha, Dambulla, Sri Lanka (2013).

Buddhism reached Sri Lanka in the third century BC during the reign of Devanampiya Tissa of Anuradhapura when a sapling of the Bodhi Tree in Sarnath (India) was brought to Sri Lanka and the first monasteries and Buddhist monuments were established. The Pali Canon, having been preserved as an oral tradition, was first committed to writing in Sri Lanka around 30 BC. During the rule of the Greco-Bactrian King Menander I, Mahadharmaraksita, a Yoni monk, led 30,000 Buddhist monks from "the Greek city of Alasandra" (north of modern Kabul, Afghanistan) to Sri Lanka for the dedication of the Ruwanwelisaya in Anuradhapura, indicating that Greco-Buddhism contributed to early Sri Lankan Buddhism.

Joao de Barros, the Portuguese historian, in his book, *"Asia de Joao Barros, dos fectos que od Portuguese fizeram no descobrimento & conquista dos mares & teras do Oriente"* published after 1563, relates: "a king of the island of Ceilam, called Primal, went in a ship to the coast of Muscat, to join other kings, who were going to

adore the Lord, at Bethlehem, and that he was the third." According to de Barros, the Tamil king Primal (Perumal) was one of the Magi who went to Bethlehem, to worship the newborn infant Jesus. It is difficult to dismiss the fact that an early king of Jaffna was one of those who adored the infant Jesus; also that Christianity was in existence in Lanka since the very beginning of the Christian era. There is a tradition that this Peria Perumal came to south India and was baptised by St Thomas the Apostle as Gaspar. This is described by Fr Motha Vaz: "Peria Perumal, the King of Jaffna (Ceylon) journeyed to India to meet the Apostle. As soon as he saw St Thomas, he requested him: 'O Apostle of the Redeemer of the world! I am one of the Magi Kings who at the sight of the star in the East, followed it and visited the Holy Infant Messiah at Bethlehem. Therefore, please explain to me His life and teachings and baptise me. The saint, accepting the request and having been instructed on the life and teachings of the Saviour, baptised him as Gaspar."
St Thomas 'started for the country which is now of the Tamils'. At the time of the Apostle, all the three kingdoms (of the Chera, Chola and Pandia) were the country of the Dravidians.

When we take into consideration the spread of Christianity in the coastal region of Kerala, and the existence of an ancient Syrian Church, even today, it is very difficult to dismiss the possibility from all these sources, that it is not simply the imagination of the Early Church Fathers that St Thomas the Apostle evangelised Sri Lanka.

The south-west coast of Sri Lanka, Galle (2013).

St Thomas and Sri Lanka

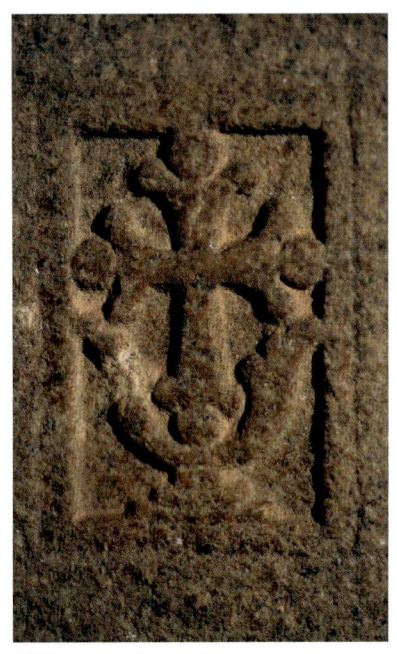

This carved granite cross was discovered during excavations in Anuradhapura in 1912.

The island of Lanka, Taprobane, Ceylon, now known as Sri Lanka became a unitary state only under British colonial administration in 1832. Prior to this, and throughout its known history, the island was made up of a number of independent but related kingdoms. Local skirmishes, primarily related to land acquisition as well as possession of Buddhist sites, changed boundaries and resulted in the migration of kings and courts across the island.

While it is the stuff of folklore, there is no evidence that St Thomas crossed to the island of Lanka via the small outcrops of land dotted across the Palk Strait. There does appear to be some literary and archaeological evidence that Syrian Rite Christians were present amongst these small kingdoms between the 2nd and 8th centuries. Conventional wisdom ascribes these earliest presences to Persian trading routes, rather than being directly from the communities of St Thomas on the Malabar coast.

In the Kingdom of Anuradhapura (north central Sri Lanka) there is a particular example of a Nestorian cross carved in sunk relief upon a granite stone within the royal palace grounds. This example is now commonly held to be indicative of the presence of a Nestorian Christian community here in the sixth century, although, when discovered in 1912, the cross was originally assumed to be a 'Portuguese' cross.

In the annals of the Kingdom of Kotte (now a suburb of Colombo) and famed for its trade in cinnamon, cloves and peppers, there is recorded evidence of 'high Christian officers' being presented to Court. Given that the kingdom's heyday was in the 15th century but declined into the sixteenth, and that the Portuguese arrived in the kingdom in 1505, it cannot be assured to which Christian tradition such officers belonged. Keralan commentators repeatedly refer to traders taking Christianity to Lanka and this is perfectly comprehensible. Certainly to this day trading communities in Sri Lankan port towns represent ethnically and religiously diverse traditions, with a mingling of Malabari, Malay and Chinese influences as well as Arab.

The Revd Prebendary Dr Brian Leathard,
Rector, the Parish of Chelsea.

Right: the great stupa, Anuradhapura, Sri Lanka (2013).

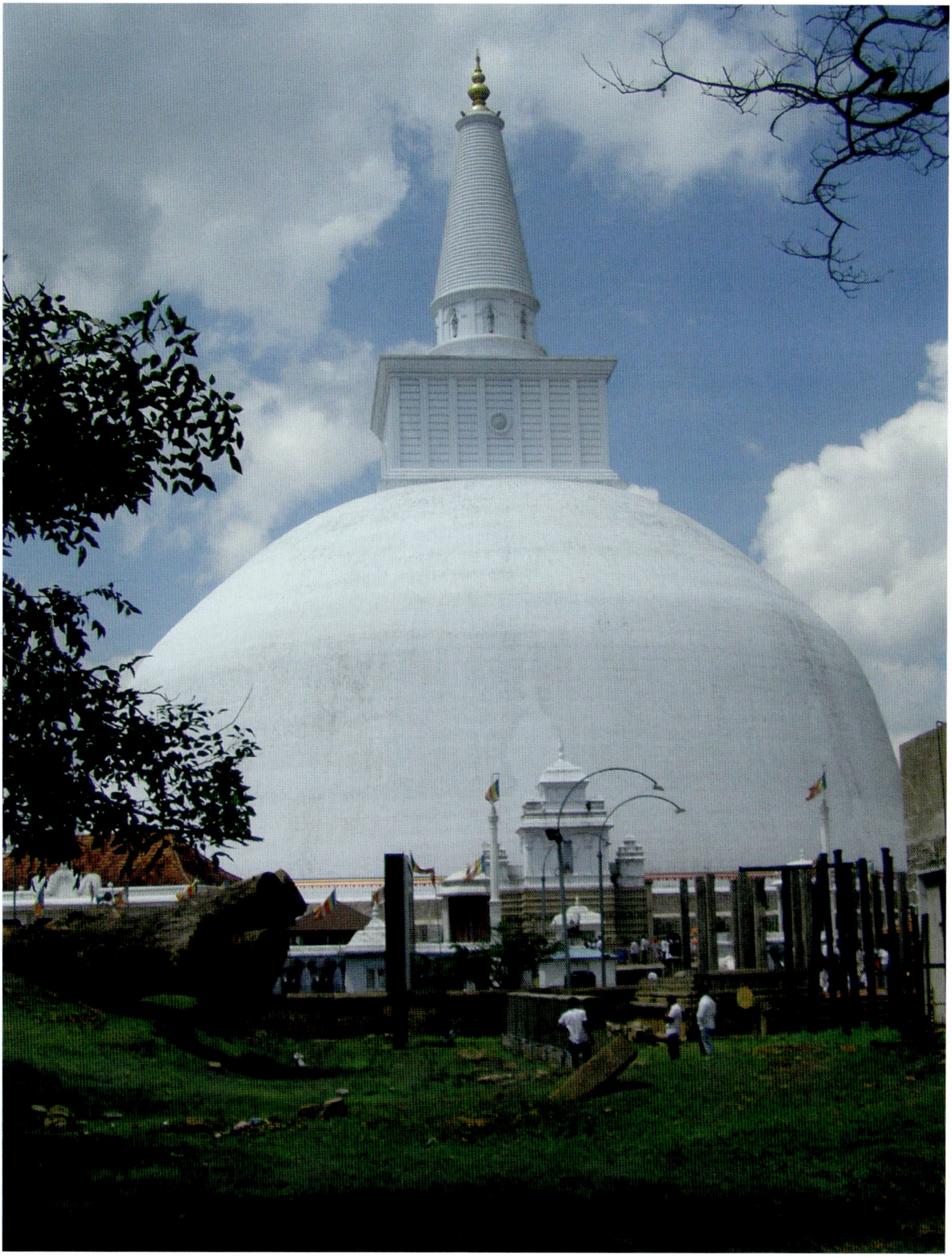

By sea to China

Chinese boats sailed regularly from the Kerala and Malabar coasts to Malacca, China and Japan.

The Chinese had been sailing through the Indian Ocean since the second century BC, travelling to Mahabalipuram in India. This was followed by many recorded maritime travellers following the same route to India, including Faxian, Zhiyan and Tanwujie. Vessels could leave southern India in late December, arriving in the China Sea in April or May with an arrival in Canton for the summer. The return voyage would depart in the autumn and cross the Bay of Bengal in January.

St Thomas preached first in India's Chola Empire. In the course of this work he was in touch with local ruling houses and performed many miracles. Various Eastern Churches claim that St Thomas personally brought Christianity to Malacca and to have gone as far afield as China and Japan in AD 64 and 70 respectively, but that he came back and stayed in the Chola Kingdom for another year.

It would have been perfectly possible for St Thomas to have done so because of the trade routes, but was there time?

Chang'an in China had an ancient Christian presence held by the Church of the East (probably Nestorian or Chaldean) which existed from the first century onwards.

The Chinese made the first move to pierce the land barrier separating them from the West. In 138 BC the Han Emperor Wu Ti dispatched an envoy to Bactra to seek allies against the Hsiung-nu (Mongolian nomads). Although the envoy failed to secure an alliance, the information he brought back amounted to the Chinese discovery of the West. Intrigued above all by his envoy's report indicating great interest in Chinese silks and his description of the magnificent Western horses, Wu Ti resolved to open trade relations with the West. His armies pushed across the Pamir Mountains to a point close to Alexandria Eschate (Khojend), founded by Alexander the Great as the northern limit of his empire.

Shortly after 100 BC, silk began arriving in the West, traded by the Parthians. Wealthy private merchants carried on this trade, organized into caravans that required large outlays of capital. When the Chinese soon moved back across the Pamirs, the Kushans of India became middlemen, selling the silk to the Parthians and later to Western merchants coming by sea to India.

Pure silk gauze sari with gold thread, Benares, India (2013).

9.
Martyrdom:

Relics
Tombs of St Thomas

Lancea com q
fi ñto S. Thom

The Martyrdom of St Thomas

After the outpouring of the Holy Spirit on the day of Pentecost in the Upper Room in Zion, the apostles dispersed everywhere to preach the Gospel, and Thomas went to India. He worked there as a slave at one of the friends of the king, whose name was Lukios, who brought him to the king who inquired about his profession. Thomas said: "I am builder, carpenter and a physician. He preached in his master's palace, and Lukios' wife believed and all his household.

The king asked him about his achievements, and he said: "The palaces that I built were the souls that have become the temples of the King of Glory; the carpentry that I did was the Gospel that removes the thorns of sin; and the medicines I practised are the Holy Mysteries which heal the poison of the evil one. The king became angry and tortured him, and bound him among four poles, cut off his skin and rubbed his wounds with salt and lime. The apostle Thomas endured the pains. Lukios' wife saw him suffering, and she fell from the window and died. Lukios came to him and said: "If you raise my wife from the dead, I will believe in your God." Thomas went to the room where the dead body was, and said: "Arsabona (Arsonia), rise up in the Name of the Lord Jesus Christ." She rose instantly and bowed to the Saint. When her husband saw that, he believed and many more with him from the people of the city, and Thomas baptised them.

Once the sea drove a huge tree to the shore that no one could lift up. St Thomas asked the king for permission to lift it up and to use its wood in building a church. He got the permission, he made the sign of the cross, and he raised it and later he built the church, to which he ordained a bishop and priests. St Thomas left and went to a city called "Kantoura" (Kontaria), where he found an old man weeping bitterly because the king killed his six children. The Saint prayed over them, and the Lord raised them up. The idol priests were angry, and wanted to stone him. The first raised a stone to throw it at him, and his hand was paralysed. The Saint prayed over his hand, he was healed instantly, and all the idol priests believed in the Lord Christ.

Then St Thomas went to the city of "Parkenas" and other cities, where he preached in the Name of Jesus Christ. The king heard about him, and he put him in prison. When he found out that he was teaching the prisoners the way of God, he tortured him, and at last he cut his head off, and he received the crown of martyrdom. He was buried in "Melibar", then his body was relocated to El-Raha.

The Martyrdom of St Thomas the Apostle. The Coptic Synaxarium, (The Coptic Orthodox Calendar) 26 Pachans (The 26th Day of the Blessed Month of Bashans).

The flagpole on Santhome Basilica, Mylapore, Chennai, Tamil Nadu, India (2016).

The log carried by St Thomas from the seashore to build a church in Mylapore (2016).

Previous page: The tip of the lance that killed St Thomas, Santhome, Mylapore, Tamil Nadu, India.

St Thomas and the King's wife

Thomas went to the city of Kenas, and to the city of Makedonya, and he preached to the men therein in the Name of the Lord Jesus Christ. And when the king and governors heard about them, they seized him, and shut him up in prison.

Now the king had a wife, and she and many of the people who were with her came unto the saint secretly, in prison; and he taught them the way of God, and many believed on his words.

And the king was exceedingly angry because of his wife, but he could not kill the saint among his people, and therefore he had him taken outside the city; and he commanded four of his soldiers to spear him with their spears, and they speared him until he delivered up his soul.

And the king's son stood by looking on at them. And when the men of the city knew (this), they came to deliver Thomas from the hands of the soldiers, and they found that he had delivered up his soul; then they swathed him for burial and laid him in one of the royal tombs.

Then a Satan leaped upon the king's son, and he fell into an epileptic fit. And (the servants of the king) came to the body of St Thomas, the apostle, to take away a little piece of his grave clothes, to hang over the body of the king's son.

And when they opened the door of the tomb, they could not find the body of the saint therein, for God had translated it; and they took some of the dust from his tomb in faith, and they hung it up over the king's son, and he recovered immediately.

And St Thomas the apostle appeared unto many of the men of that city, and made them to know that he was alive, and that our Lord Jesus Christ had received him, and he commanded them to be strong in the True Faith, in the Name of the Father and the Son and the Holy Ghost.

The Coptic Synaxarium,
(Coptic Orthodox Calendar).

A Dravidian wife, Tamil Nadu, India (2014).

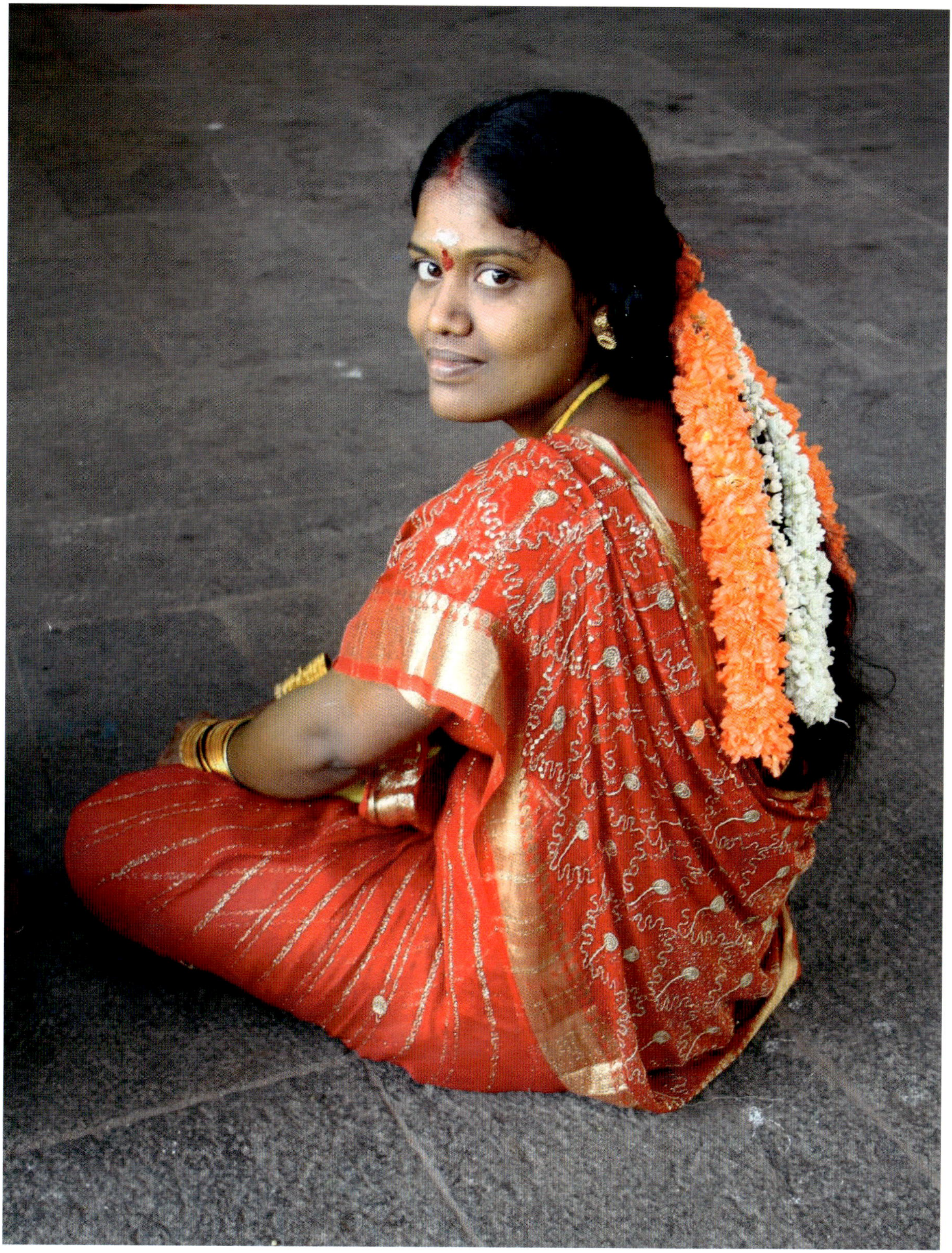

The Acts of Thomas

In the Acts of Thomas, the original key text to identify St Thomas with India (which all other India references follow), historians agree that the term India refers to Parthia (Persia) and Gandhara. The city of Andropolis named in the Acts, where Judas Thomas and Habban landed in India, has been identified as Sandaruk (one of the ancient Alexandrias) in Baluchistan.

According to tradition, St Thomas was killed in AD 72. Nasrani churches from Kerala in South India, claim that St Thomas was martyred at Mylapore near Chennai in India and his body was interred there. St Ephraim the Syrian (c. 306–373) alone states that the Apostle was martyred in India, and that his relics were then taken to Edessa. This is the earliest known record of his martyrdom.

In AD 232, the greater portion of relics of the Apostle Thomas are said to have been sent by an Indian king and brought from India to the city of Edessa in Mesopotamia, on which occasion his Syriac Acts were written. The Indian king is named as "Mazdai" in Syriac sources, "Misdeos" and "Misdeus" in Greek and Latin sources, respectively, which has been connected to the "Bazdeo" on the Kushan coinage of Vasudeva, the transition between "M" and "B" being a current one in Classical sources for Indian names.

There are six tombs for St Thomas in South India. Two are in Santhome Cathedral at Mylapore, built by replacing the Kapaleeshwarar Temple; a third on an island south-west of Cochin, a fourth in a Syrian church at Tiruvancode in Travancore, a fifth in a Shiva temple at Malayattoor in Travancore, and a sixth at Kalayamputhur, west of Madurai near the Palani Hills.

Later in the 16th century, the Portuguese in India are said to have created a myth that St Thomas was killed in Chennai by stoning and lance thrust by local priests, based on the incorrect interpretation of inscriptions found on the Pahlavi Cross discovered at St Thomas Mount in 1547. No Mar Thoma Christian believes this.

Later decipherments of the inscriptions by experts proved this to be false. Since at least the 16th century, the St Thomas Mount has been a common site revered by Hindus, Muslims and Christians. The records of Barbosa from the early 16th century inform us that the tomb was then maintained by a Muslim who kept a lamp burning there.

A few relics of St Thomas are kept in the museum beside the Basilica.

St Thomas the Apostle, modern statue, the Basilica of Santhome, Mylapore, Tamil Nadu, India (2016).

Deus Meus

ST THOMAS

The bones of St Thomas

The "Acts of Judas Thomas" state that the bones of the Apostle were removed from his grave at Mylapore during the lifetime of the king who sentenced him to death. This tradition says that the translation took place in the very Apostolic age itself: "Now it came to pass after a long time that one of the children of Misdaeus (Mahadeva) the king was smitten by a devil, and no man could cure him, for the devil was exceeding fierce. And Misdaeus the king took thought and said: I will go and open the sepulchre, and take a bone of the apostle of God and hang it upon my son and he shall be healed. But while Misdaeus thought upon this, the apostle Thomas appeared to him and said unto him: Thou believedst not on a living man, and wilt thou believe on the dead? Yet fear not, for my Lord Jesus Christ hath compassion on thee and pitieth thee of his goodness.

"And he went and opened the sepulchre, but found not the apostle there, for one of the brethren had stolen him away and taken him unto Mesopotamia; but from that place where the bones of the apostle had lain Misdaeus took dust and put it about his son's neck, saying: I believe on thee, Jesu Christ, now that he hath left me which troubleth men and opposeth them lest they should see thee. And when he had hung it upon his son, the lad became whole. "Misdaeus the king therefore was also gathered among the brethren, and bowed his head under the hands of Siphor the priest; and Siphor said unto the brethren: Pray ye for Misdaeus the king, that he may obtain mercy of Jesus Christ, and that he may no more remember evil against him. They all therefore, with one accord rejoicing, made prayer for him; and the Lord that loveth men, the King of Kings and Lord of Lords, granted Misdaeus also to have hope in him; and he was gathered with the multitude of them that had believed in Christ."

Bardesanes of Edessa,
The Acts of Thomas, c. 201.
13th Act. No. 170.

The best known of these documents are the "sayings" called *The Gospel of Thomas,* a non-canonical work which some scholars believe may actually predate the writing of the Biblical gospels themselves. The opening line claims it is the work of "Didymos Judas Thomas" - who has been identified with St Thomas. This work was discovered in a Coptic translation in 1945 at the Egyptian village of Nag Hammadi, near the site of the monastery of Chenoboskion. Once the Coptic text was published, scholars recognised that an earlier Greek translation had been published from fragments of papyrus found at Oxyrhynchus (Egypt) in the 1890s.

Modern Russian icon of St Thomas; Novgorod, Russia.

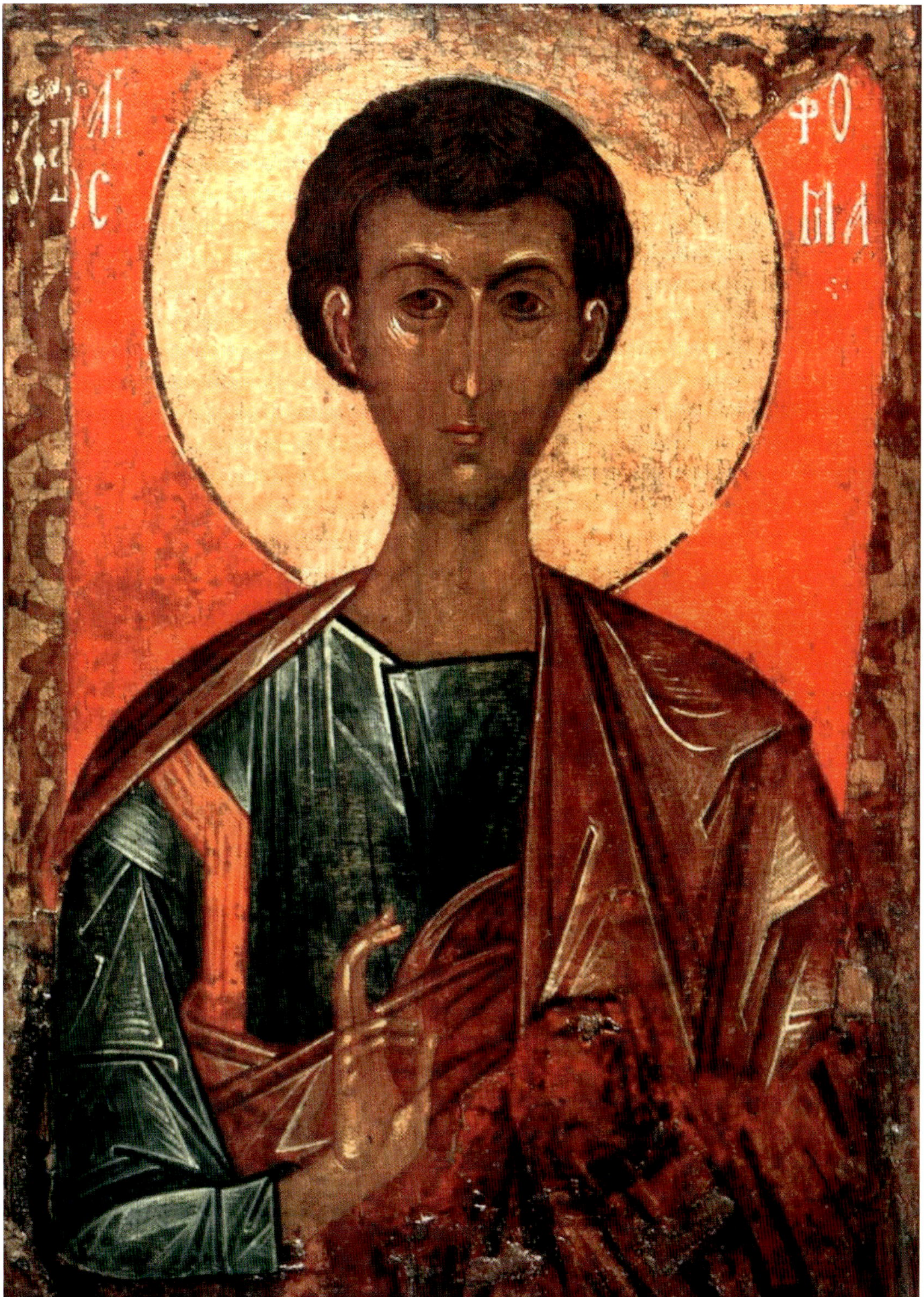
ФОМА

Edessa

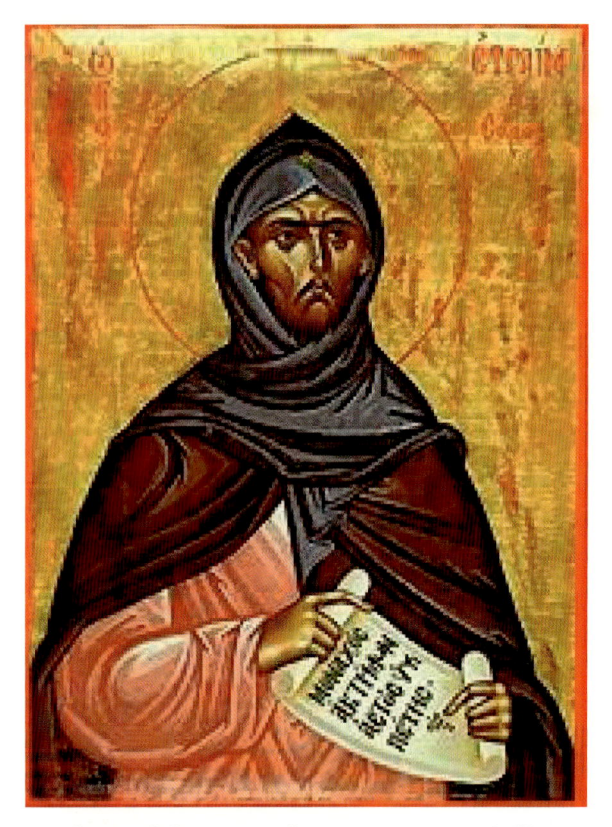

"Relics of the Apostle were so specially venerated in the very city in which Ephraim resided, the city which, largely owing to his influence, became the general centre of Syrian literature".

The fourth century martyrium erected over St Thomas' burial place stood until it was destroyed by a flood in AD 210; the saint's remains were sent there from India in AD 72.

A long public tradition in Edessa honouring Thomas as the "Apostle of India" resulted in several surviving hymns, that are attributed to St Ephraim, copied in codices of the eighth and ninth centuries. References in the hymns preserve the tradition that Thomas's bones were brought from India to Edessa by a merchant, and that the relics worked miracles both in India and Edessa. A pontiff assigned his feast day and a king and a queen erected his shrine. The Thomas traditions became embodied in Syriac liturgy, thus they were universally credited by the Christian community there.

In the 42nd of his "*Carmina Nisibina*" St Ephraim (c. 306 - 373) writes that the Apostle was put to death in India, and that his remains were subsequently buried in Edessa, brought there by an unnamed merchant. A Syrian ecclesiastical calendar of an early date confirms the above and gives the merchant a name. St Ephrem surely had the translation of the relics in mind when he wrote in one of his hymns: "Whence is thy origin, O! Thomas that so illustrious thou shouldst become. A merchant has conveyed thy bones, a (priest) pontiff has made a celebration for thee; and a king had erected a shrine (for thee)".

Rufus, the Church historian who lived in Edessa and wrote the *Chronicles of Edessa* contended that in AD 394 the relics of St Thomas were transferred to Edessa.

The fifth century *Martyrologium Hieronymianum* assigns the 3rd of July as the day of the translation of the body of St Thomas, who suffered in India, to Edessa.

The Citadel, Edessa, Turkey.
Photograph: Nicholas Talbot-Rice (2013).

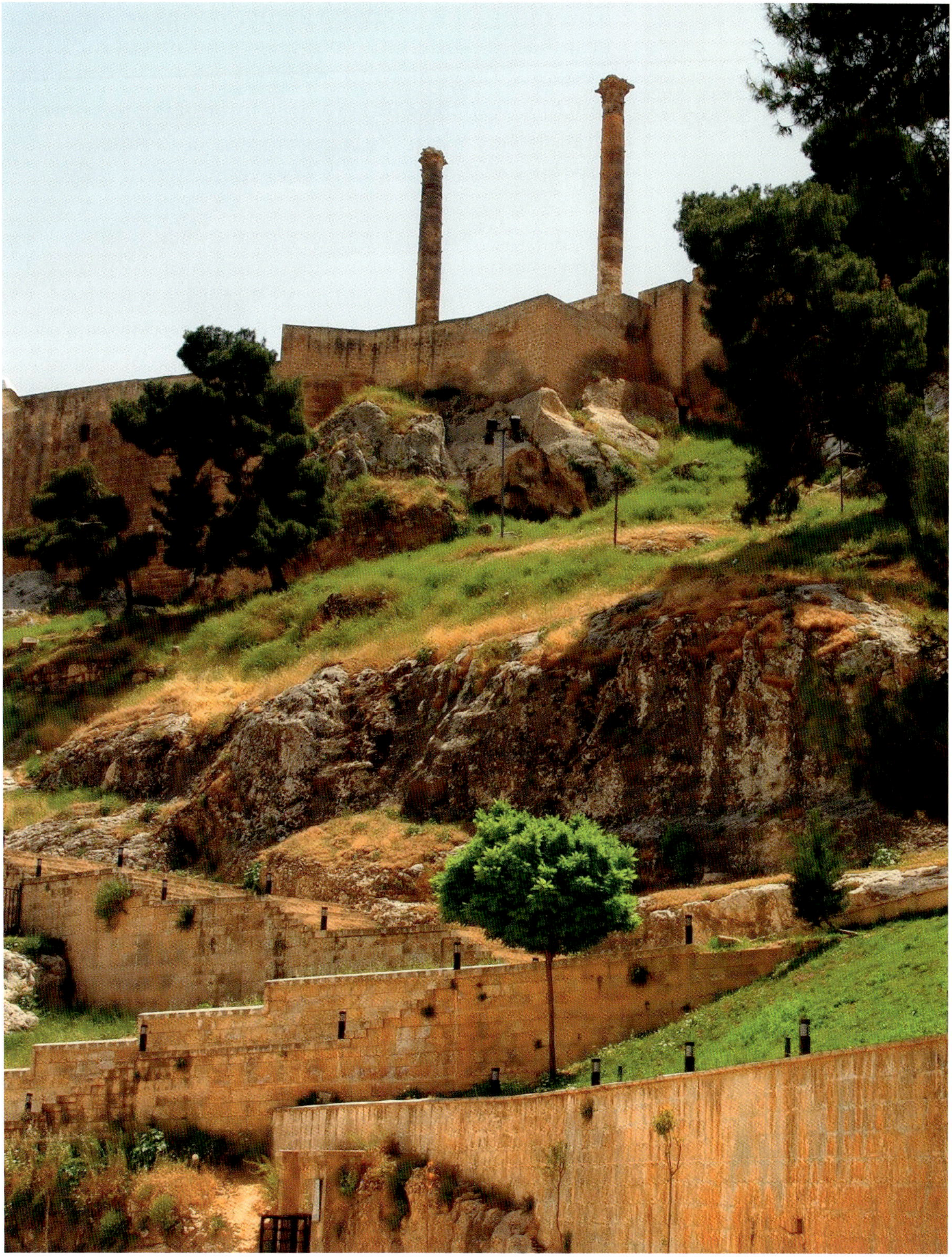

The relics of St Thomas

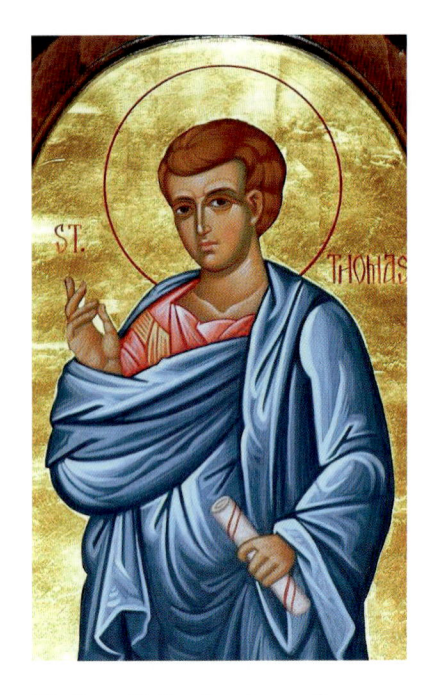

Modern Orthodox icon of St Thomas.

"The merchant Kahbin, and the inhabitants of the entirely Christian town that possessed a splendid church, having matured the plan to enrich both of them with an invaluable treasure, seized the body of St Thomas in 230. The faithful soon started to venerate the body of the saint; and the chronicle of Edessa relates the translation of the Apostle's relics to a big church dedicated to him on 22nd August 394 (in the time of Bishop Cyrus).

The importance of Edessa diminished after 609 as a result of the different foreign occupations of the Persians, the Arabs and the Byzantines. The town was entirely destroyed in 1146. It is interesting to know that already when the relics were kept in Edessa, portions of the relics were also venerated in Italy.

Professor George Menachery recounts how this happened: in AD 394 on the occasion of the removal of the relics from the old church at Edessa to the newly built Basilica of St Thomas, some portions of the relics were secured on behalf of three principal churches in Italy known as the Cathedral of Nola, the Cathedral of Brescia, and the Cathedral of Milan, during the times of their respective bishops, Paulinus, Gaudentius and Ambrose.

After the destruction of Edessa by the Muslims in 1144, as the whole country was liable to be overrun by the rising power of Islam, Abba Marcos states that in order to save the venerated body of the Apostle, the European crusaders and the natives carried the relics to the island of Chios. The Byzantine and Syrian Churches indicated 6th October 1146 as the date of this translation.

At Chios, the worship of the saint developed very quickly. The existence of a church dedicated to St Thomas is proved historically, as well as the body of the saint being placed in a silver casket presented by Anatoles Stratelates in 753 while at Edessa. The chronicles attest to numerous miracles and healings around the relics of the apostle."

Abba Marcos,
History of the relics of St Thomas the Apostle."

According to tradition, in 232 AD, the greater portion of the relics of St Thomas are said to have been sent by an Indian king from Mylapore and brought to the city of Edessa, in Mesopotamia, on which occasion his Syriac Acts were written. The Indian king is named as "Mazdai" in Syriac sources, "Misdeos" and "Misdeus" in Greek and Latin sources respectively, which has been connected to the "Bazdeo" on the Kushan coinage of Vasudeva I, the transition between "M" and "B" being current in Classical sources for Indian names.

In the fourth century, the magnificent martyrium erected over St Thomas' burial place brought many pilgrims to Edessa. In 441, the *Magister militum per Orientem,* Anatolius donated a silver coffin to hold the relics. As these relics had been so specially treasured in that city from an early period, and as St Ephraim had lived there for another ten years until his death in the summer of 373, it seems strange that in the numerous published works of prolific writers, direct evidence about the Apostle is missing from St Ephraim's hymns in the very city in which he lived, the city which, largely owing to his influence, became the centre of Syriac literature.

In 1144, Edessa was conquered by the Zengids and the shrine destroyed. It was not until the middle of the 19th century that evidence of the whereabouts of St Thomas's remains were forthcoming.

The bell tower of the former Basilica of St Thomas, now the Jama Masjid, Edessa, Turkey. Photograph: Nicholas Talbot-Rice (2007).

Sardis

Ruins of a fourth century church at the south-eastern corner of the Temple of Artemis, Sardis, Turkey.

Sardis was one of the "Seven Churches" of the Book of Revelation. (However, this is not strictly correct, as congregations, not the actual buildings, were meant by "churches" at that time.) Sardis became the western terminus of the Royal Road from Susa and as such it is likely that St Thomas' body would have passed through the city on its way to the port of Ephesus, from where it would have been taken by boat to the Greek island of Chios.

Sardis had a series of Lydian tombs dating from the seventh century BC and later, a gymnasium and a synagogue. The Temple of Artemis in the Pactolos Valley was one of the seven largest ancient temples in Asia Minor with eight columns on its short side and twenty along the long side. It was believed that an altar dedicated to Artemis and Zeus had existed there as early as the fifth century BC. It was begun about a generation after the conquest of Alexander in 300 BC and the enormous scale was clearly meant to rival the three great Ionian Temples at Ephesus, Samos and Didyma. Further construction took place in the second century BC and again in the second century AD.

Ephesus

During the Classical Greek era, Ephesus was one of the twelve cities of the Ionian League. The city flourished after it came under the control of the Roman Republic in 129 BC. When Augustus became emperor in 27 BC, he made Ephesus the capital of Proconsular Asia (which covered western Asia Minor) instead of Pergamum. Thanks in part to its port, Ephesus then entered an era of prosperity, becoming both the seat of the governor and a major centre of commerce. According to Strabo, it was second in size and importance only to Rome.

The Temple of Artemis (completed around 550 BC) was one of the Seven Wonders of the Ancient World. In AD 268, it was destroyed or damaged in a raid by the Goths. Constantine the Great rebuilt much of the city and erected new public baths near the port. The town was partially destroyed by an earthquake in AD 614. The city's importance as a commercial centre declined as the harbour slowly silted up.

Ephesus is one of the seven churches that are mentioned in the Book of Revelation.

The marble-paved main street of Ephesus with its monuments and temples, down which the body of St Thomas would have been carried on its way from Sardis to the great port of Ephesus, from where it would have sailed for the Greek island of Chios.

Chios

Mosaic floor, the Basilica of St Isidore, Chios, Greece (2016).

The early Christian basilica of St Isidore (an officer in the Roman navy who was martyred in AD 251) was built on the remains of an earlier Roman structure. According to tradition, the small fifth-century church was rebuilt in the second half of the seventh century, during the reign of Constantine IV Pogonatos, "the Bearded", who was Byzantine Emperor from AD 668 to 685. In the course of its long history, it has undergone several repairs, probably during the Frankish occupation, in the late Byzantine period and in modern times. Five architectural phases can be discerned in the building, which was ruined by the earthquake of 1881.

Today the remains are partly covered by a later, small church with a low cement roof. In the basilica are ancient mosaic floors decorated with geometric patterns. The church has a subterranean vaulted crypt where the relics of St Isidore and St Myrope (also martyred in Chios during the third century) were once kept.

The veneration of St Isidore, patron saint of Chios, spread throughout the Mediterranean and he became a protector of sailors. In 1125 his remains were brought from Chios to the Venetian Basilica of St Mark, and hidden in the palace of the Doge; it was re-discovered in the early 14th century in a small chapel containing the sarcophagus. His skull was discovered in Chios, encased in a silver and jewelled reliquary, and was sent to Venice in 1627.

This church was the one to which the body of St Thomas was brought from Edessa by Byzantine and Latin Christians in 1146 and from where it was taken to Ortona in Italy in 1258 in the same way as the Venetians took the body of St Isidore to Venice.

Processional cross, 10th c.: the Byzantine Museum, Athens, Greece (2012).

The robbery of the relics from Chios

The Lion of St Mark above the window of the Doge's Palace, Venice, Italy (2009).

During the war between the republics of Venice and Genoa in the mid 13th century, Venice destroyed several Greek islands recently conquered by Genoa, one of which was the island of Chios. At the time, Chios was thought to be the place where St Thomas, after his martyrdom in India, had been buried.

Ortona's three galleys (warships) reached the island of Chios in 1258, led by Admiral Leone Acciaiuoli, an admiral of the Prince of Taranto in southern Italy.

Giambattista de Lectis, a 16th-century physician and writer of Ortona, reports that after the looting, Admiral Leone went to pray in the main church of the island of Chios and was drawn to a chapel adorned and resplendent with lights.

An elderly priest, Father Angi Falconiero, the guardian of the church, through an interpreter, informed him that the venerated body of St Thomas the Apostle was in the oratory. Admiral Leone fell into deep prayer. At that moment a light hand twice invited him to come closer. Admiral Leone reached out and took a bone from the largest hole of the tombstone, on which were carved the Greek letters XP and a halo depicting a bishop (from the waist up). Here was confirmation of what the old priest had said: that you are indeed in the presence of the Apostle's body.

Admiral Leone returned to the galley and planned the theft for the following night, along with fellow sailor Ruggiero Grogno. They lifted the heavy gravestone and saw the relics beneath it; they wrapped them in snow-white cloths, laid them in a wooden box and brought them aboard the galley, together with the chalcedony gravestone (which had also come from Edessa) and took Father Falconiero with them to Bari as a prisoner. They skirted the Greek islands, stopping briefly in Nauplion (a Venetian possession in the Peloponnese) to take on provisions, and reached the coast of the Adriatic without trouble.

Greek Orthodox monk, Patmos, Greece (2013).

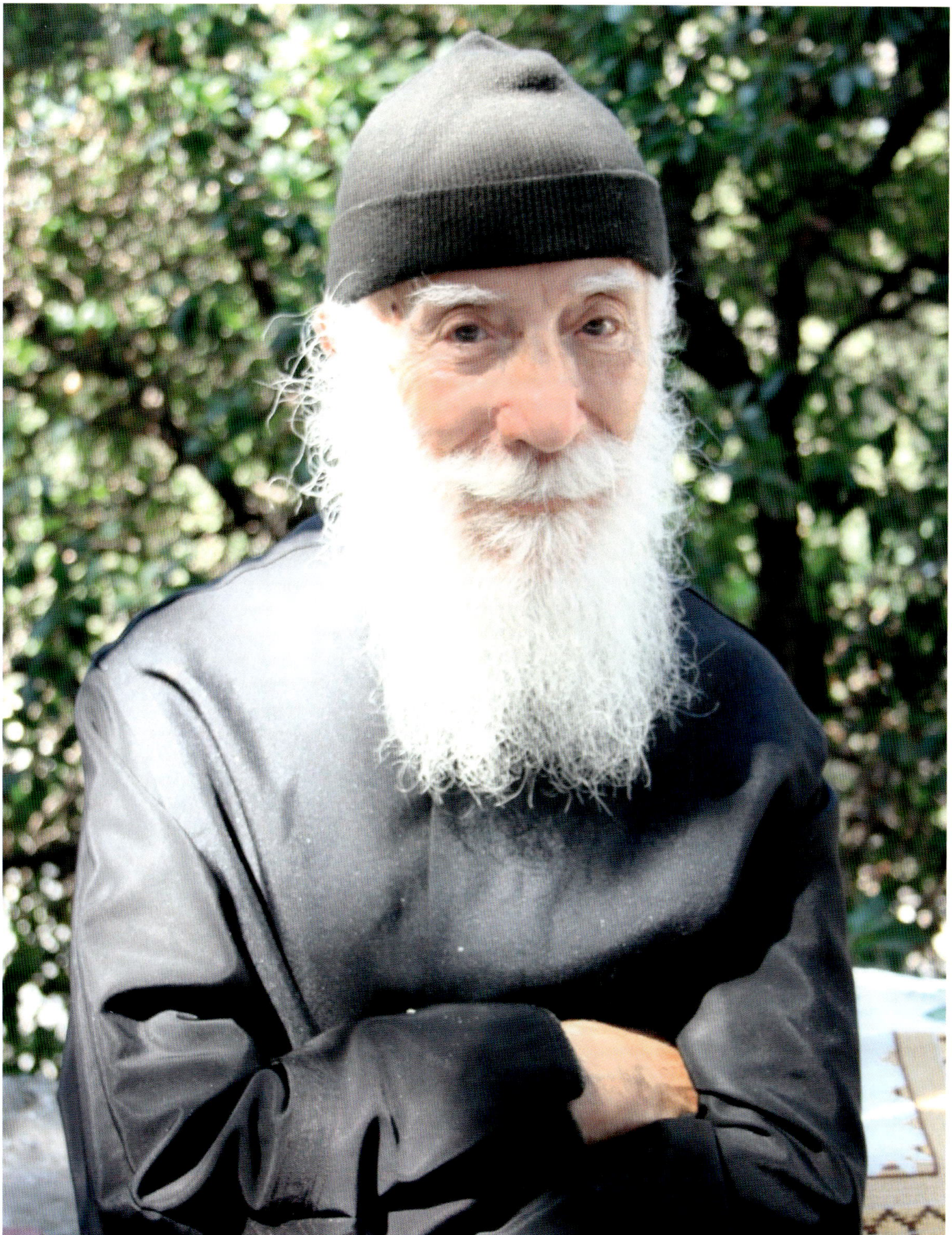

The Basilica of St Thomas, Ortona

Above: Modern oil painting showing St Thomas's body leaving Chios with shipowner Admiral Leone Acciaiuoli's three galleons in 1258 (2016).

Below: The greeting accorded the arrival of the remains of St Thomas in Ortona on September 6th 1258; both in the chapel of St Thomas in the Basilica of St Thomas, Ortona, the Abruzzi, Italy (2016).

Left: The Holy Door of the Basilica of St Thomas, Ortona, the Abruzzi, Italy, restored after the Nazi bombing of 1944. Some of the door's medieval carvings were saved (2016).

Ortona

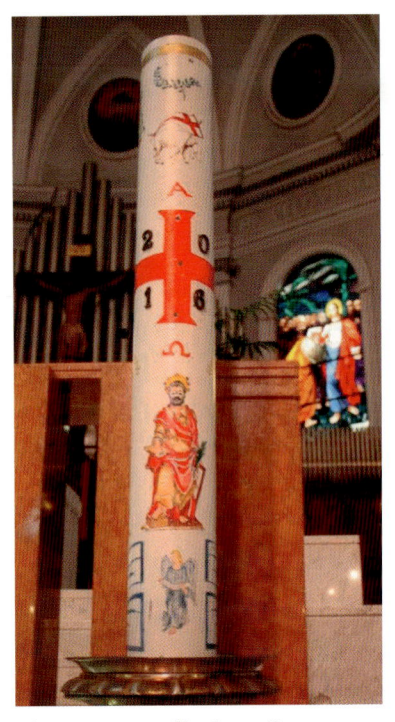

The 2016 candle (2016).

A Bronze Age settlement was discovered near the Aragonese castle; Greek colonisers established an acropolis above the two ports and the later Roman town followed this first settlement. Sections of paved roads and urban walls, as well as some archaeological findings remain from this period. Ortona was part of the Byzantine Empire for several centuries, before it was annexed by the Lombard Kingdom. In 803 the Franks incorporated Ortona into the county of Chieti.

In 1447, Venetian ships destroyed the port of Ortona; consequently the King of Sicily commissioned the construction of a castle to dominate the renovated port. In 1582 the town was acquired by Margaret of Parma, daughter of Emperor Charles V as part of her dowry as Duchess of Parma. In 1584 she built a great mansion (the Palazzo Farnese), but it was never completed due to her death. After the establishment of the Kingdom of Italy in 1860, Ortona became one of the first sea resorts on the Adriatic.

St Thomas was buried in Mylapore and his remains were later brought to Edessa, the centre of Syriac Christianity in Mesopotamia where the silver casket was presented by Anatoles Stratelates in 753.

The genuineness of the relics is testified by this chalcedony slab which covered the Apostle's relics in both Edessa and Chios. It is in fact a plaque used to cover a tomb made of lower-quality material, a practice used in early Christian times. It has an inscription and a bas-relief similar to those in the Syrian Mesopotamian area of Edessa. The inscriptions are in Greek unicals and are dated from the third to the fifth centuries and mention *"Thomas osios"*. Careful study found some traced signs over the words, which change the meaning to that of "the real Thomas". The bas-relief depicts a religious figure with a halo in the act of imparting, with his right hand, the blessing (according to the rites of the Eastern Church and indicating the first two letters, XP in Greek, of the word Christ). The word *osios* is a translation of the Syriac word *mar* (Lord), attributed in the ancient world, but also to the present day, to a saint or a bishop. In his left hand he holds an object that could be a sword, which is a clear reference to the martyrdom of St Thomas. The lower part of the stone has two holes of different sizes, such as those found in various tombs of the early centuries of Christianity, used in order to introduce balms or make libations on the grave of the deceased.

At the time of the scientific study of 1984, the skull was in a silver bust with the rest of the bones in a bronze urn. The bones were extracted, identified and measured. Most of the arm bones were missing, along with most of the ribs. The skull, spine, and legs were largely intact, allowing estimates of the height. The skeleton belonged to a man of light build, about five foot three inches tall, aged between 50 and 70, with arthritis in the spine and fingers, a benign tumour on the front of the skull, and a fracture of the cheekbone which occurred either just before or just after death. After the study, the bones were interred in a new casket and placed under the altar in the crypt of the basilica.

The same team studied a supposed arm bone of St Thomas that had been in the possession of the cathedral in Bari (some 200 miles further down the Adriatic coast) since 1102. This was identified as a bone of the upper arm, and of such a size as to be from an individual about the same height as the Ortona skeleton. How this bone came into the possession of Bari Cathedral is a mystery: the relics of St Thomas were supposed to be still in Edessa in 1102, although it is possible that an arm was removed by the Crusaders when they took the city in 1099.

The tomb of St Thomas beneath the High Altar, the Basilica of St Thomas, Ortona, the Abruzzi, Italy (2016).

Postscript

The tomb and final resting place of the skeleton of St Thomas the Apostle is in the little town of Ortona in the Abruzzi, Italy, under the main altar in the church dedicated to the Virgin Mary, which later became a Basilica and took the name of St Thomas.

Illustrious pilgrims paid visits to the tomb of the apostle, among them St Bridget of Sweden in the 14th century. From 1479 onwards, numerous papal indulgences were granted to the pilgrims who visited the body of St Thomas: by Pope Sixtus IV in 1479, by Pope Gregory XIII in 1575, by Pope Clement VIII in 1596, by Pope Benedict XIV in 1742, and by Pope Pius XII in 1949.

Ortona is an under-visited destination for the final resting place of so important an Apostle. Perhaps this is due to the destruction caused by the fierce fighting between the Nazis and the 1st Canadian Infantry Division during the Italian Campaign in 1944. The Germans established the defensive Gustav Line at Ortona (extending towards Cassino on the opposite coast of Italy). Ortona offered the Allies a supply port on the Adriatic but it was fiercely defended by the Germans. The ferocity of the Battle of Ortona led it to be known as the "Little Stalingrad".

The town, perched on its high ravine and formally protected by its ruined Aragonese castle, is dilapidated, with no good hotels, a few bars and only one decent restaurant. The two ports below the fort are no longer filled with the multitude of shipping that in classical and medieval times plied the Adriatic to the Dalmatian coast and beyond.

Ortona is served by a small branch railway line from Pesaro, with no taxis at the dead-end railway station and an infrequent bus service to the top!

Nevertheless, on the first Sunday in May every year, 30-40,000 pilgrims visit the tomb of St Thomas and believe that their sins will be washed away.

I was thrilled to have the entire basilica to myself for hours on end over two days, with the exception of Mass on Friday morning, when I joined six faithful parishioners.

Looking into the face of St Thomas was an emotional moment: his final resting place and my journey's end following in his footsteps.

Serena Fass,
October 2016.

Desecrated by the Turks in 1566, the relics are now kept in an urn of gilded copper made in 1612 by Tommaso Alessandrini from Ortona.

The third c. Armenian-Mesopotamian chalcedony slab from Edessa, Turkey, showing a portrait of St Thomas as a Syrian bishop; the Basilica of St Thomas, Ortona, the Abruzzi, Italy (2016).

10.
Authors
Sources
Maps
Timeline

Aid to the Church in Need

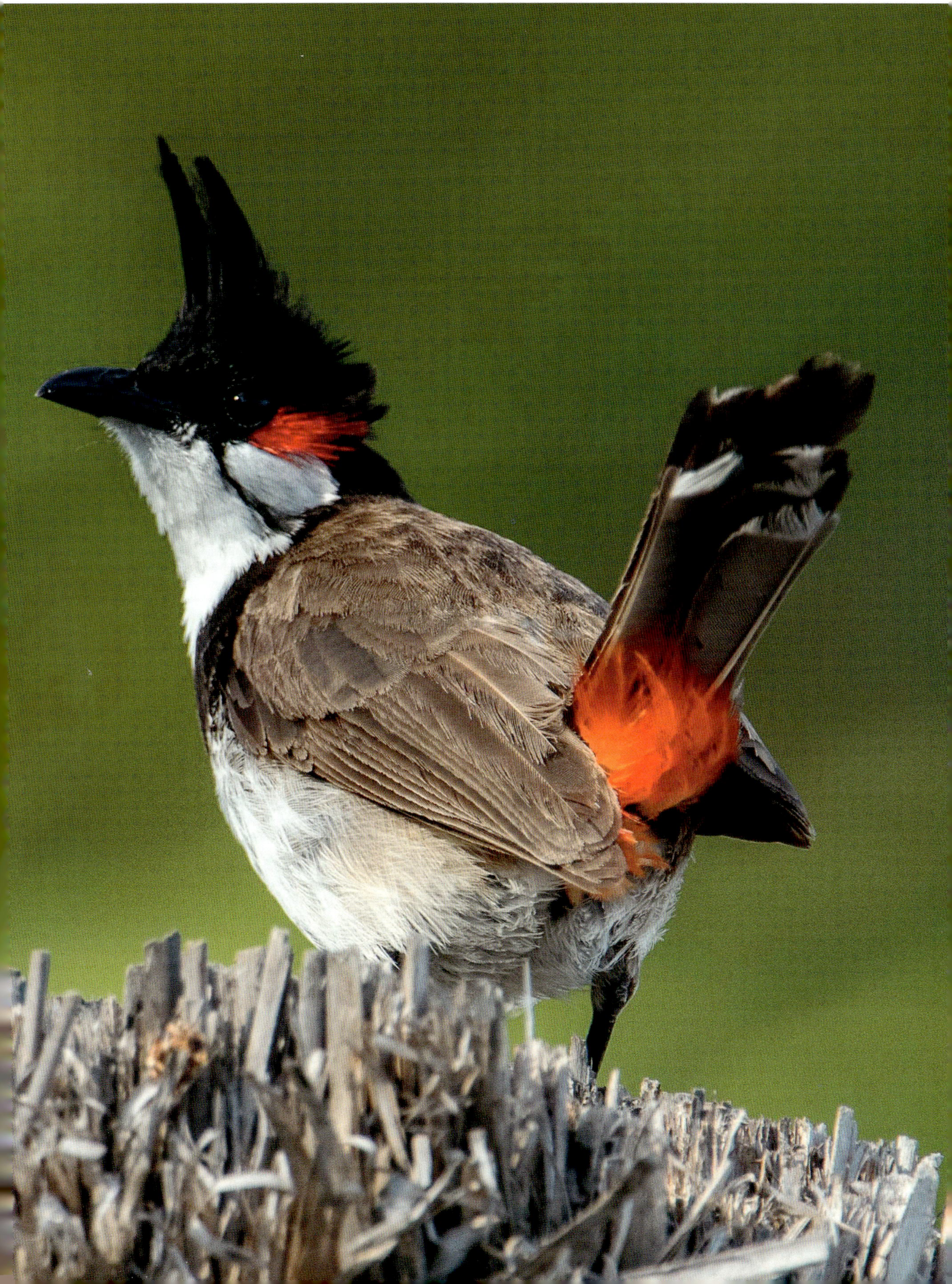

Sources

Syriac Christians in their full regalia at a consecration ceremony of new bishops, Kerala, South India.

Alopen, Bishop: *The Sutra of Jesus the Messiah,* (638).
Axworthy, Michael: *Iran, Empire of the Mind*, Penguin 2007.
Bhaskaram, Vijayan P: *The Legacy of St Thomas*, St Paul's, Bombay (India) 2012.
Bissell, Tom: *Apostle*, Faber & Faber 2016.
Brown, Bishop Leslie: *The Indian Christians of St Thomas*, Cambridge University Press 1956, updated 1982.
Byron, Robert: *The Road to Oxiana*, Penguin 1992.
Chackalayil, Abraham Itticheria: Nilackel *Silver Jubilee souvenir* (India) 2012.
Cherrian, PJ & Menon J: *Unearthing Pattanam*, National Museum Delhi 2014.
Frankopan, Dr Peter: *The Silk Roads*, Bloomsbury 2015.
Giritharan, V N: *Nallur Rajdhani* (India).
Katz, Nathan: *Who are the Jews of India?* 2000.
di Martino, Remo: *Viaggiando con l'Appostolo Tommaso*, Carsa (Italy) 2004.
Mehr, Farhang: *The Zoroastrian Tradition*, Mazda Publishers Inc 2005.
Meyer, Marvin: *The Gospel of Thomas: the hidden sayings of Jesus*, HarperCollins 1992.
Meyer, Marvin: *the Gospel of Thomas* HarperSanFrancisco 1992.
Moule, A C: Christians in China before the year 1550, Macmillan 1930.
Mudaliyar C: *Ancient Jaffna* (India).
Muthiah, S: *Madras Discovered*, Affiliated East-West Press, Chenai (India) 2013.
Podipara, Placid J: *The Thomas Christians*, Darton Longman & Todd, London.
Rasanayagam, Keung, Lee Shiu: *The Cross and The Lotus*.
Roux, Georges: *Ancient Iraq,* George Allen & Unwin 1964.
Russell, Gerard: *Heirs to Forgotten Kingdoms*, Simon & Schuster 1988.
Segal, J B: *A History of the Jews of Cochin* 1993.
Thomas, Dr Maledath Kurian: *The way of St Thomas*, MOC publications India) 2012
Yule, Col H: *Cathay and the Way Thither*.
Wiesewhofer, Josef: *Ancient Persia*, I.B. Tauris, 2001.
Seraphim, Abba: *A pilgrimage to Malabar*, British Orthodox Press London, 2010
Vaz, Fr Motha: *Peria Perumal, the King of Jaffna* (Ceylon).

Authors

Abba Marcos, India 2012
Abba Seraphim el Suriani, Metropolitan of Glastonbury 2015
The Anglican collect for St Thomas' day, 3rd July.
Bardesanes of Edessa: *The Acts of Thomas*, No 170, 13th Act. c. 201
Benedict XVI, Pope: pronouncement 2012
Coptic Synaxarium, (Coptic Orthodox Calendar).
Elia, Dr Giancarlo, 2015
Eudoxus of Cyzicus, c. 130 BC
Eusebius of Caesarea: *Church History V.10* 263 - 339
Herodotus: *The Histories, IV: 44* 484 - 425 BC
Hildesheim, John of: 1364–1375
John of Monte Corvino, John of: a letter in 1292-1293
Joseph Jr. Ken,"*Jijika no Kuni, Nihon*" "*Japan: The Nation of the Cross*"
Kapur, Vijay, Essay on Hinduism, New Delhi, 2010.
Nehru, Pandit Jawaharlal, 1889 - 1964
Pliny the Elder: Historia Naturae VI:26 and XII 23 - 79
Polo, Marco: *The Travels of Marco Polo* 1254 - 1324
Prasad, Dr Rajendra 1884 - 1963
Ptolemy: *Periplus* and *Modura Regia Pandyan* c.100 – c. 170
Schneider, Pierre, France 21st c.
Singh, Giani Zail, President of India (1982 – 1987)
St Addai, 1st c.
St Ambrose of Milan, 337 - 397
St Bede the Venerable, 672 - 735
St Ephraim the Syrian, c. 306 - 373
St Gaudentius, Bishop of Brescia c. 427
St Gregory of Nazianzus, 330 - 389,
St Gregory of Tours, 538 - 594
St Jerome: *Scti Hieron Epistolae, LIX, ad Marcetla,* 347 - 420
St John Chrysostom: Excerpt from the Homily on St Thomas Sunday 347-407
St John of Damascus 676 - 749
St John's Gospel 1st c.
St Luke's Gospel 1st c.
St Paulinus of Nola 354 - 431
Strabo: Book II: 5.12. 64/63 BC – c. 24 AD
The Acts of Judas Thomas, c.154
William of Malmesbury, 1080 - 1143
Wright, John L F 2015

Previous page: Red-vented bulbul. These songbirds are indigenous to the Indian Sub-Continent. Photograph: Jim Wheeler.

PONTUS
CASPIA
SEA
GREEKS
Wine
Laodicea
Diospolis
Brass
Copper
Iron
Euphrates
Chara
Spasi
NABATAEANS
Arsinoe
Cloth
Petra
MALICHAS
Apologus
Mussel
Harbour
(MyosHormos)
White
Village
PERSIA
SEA
LYBIA
ARABIA
ARABIAN GULF
Berenice
CARNAITES
BERBERS
Wine
Grain
Frankin
Ptolemais of the Hunt
ELEAZU
CHARIBAEL
Sabat
Meroe
Adulis
CHOLAEBUS
SABAITES
ZOSCALES
Muza
Saphar
Axumiles (Axum)
Coloe
HOMERITES
OCELIS
Eudaemon A
AETHIOPIA
Ivory
Avalites
Mosyllum
Malao
Mundus
BERBERS
Spices
CYENEUM
Cinnamon
Slaves
AFRICA
AZANIA
Sarapion

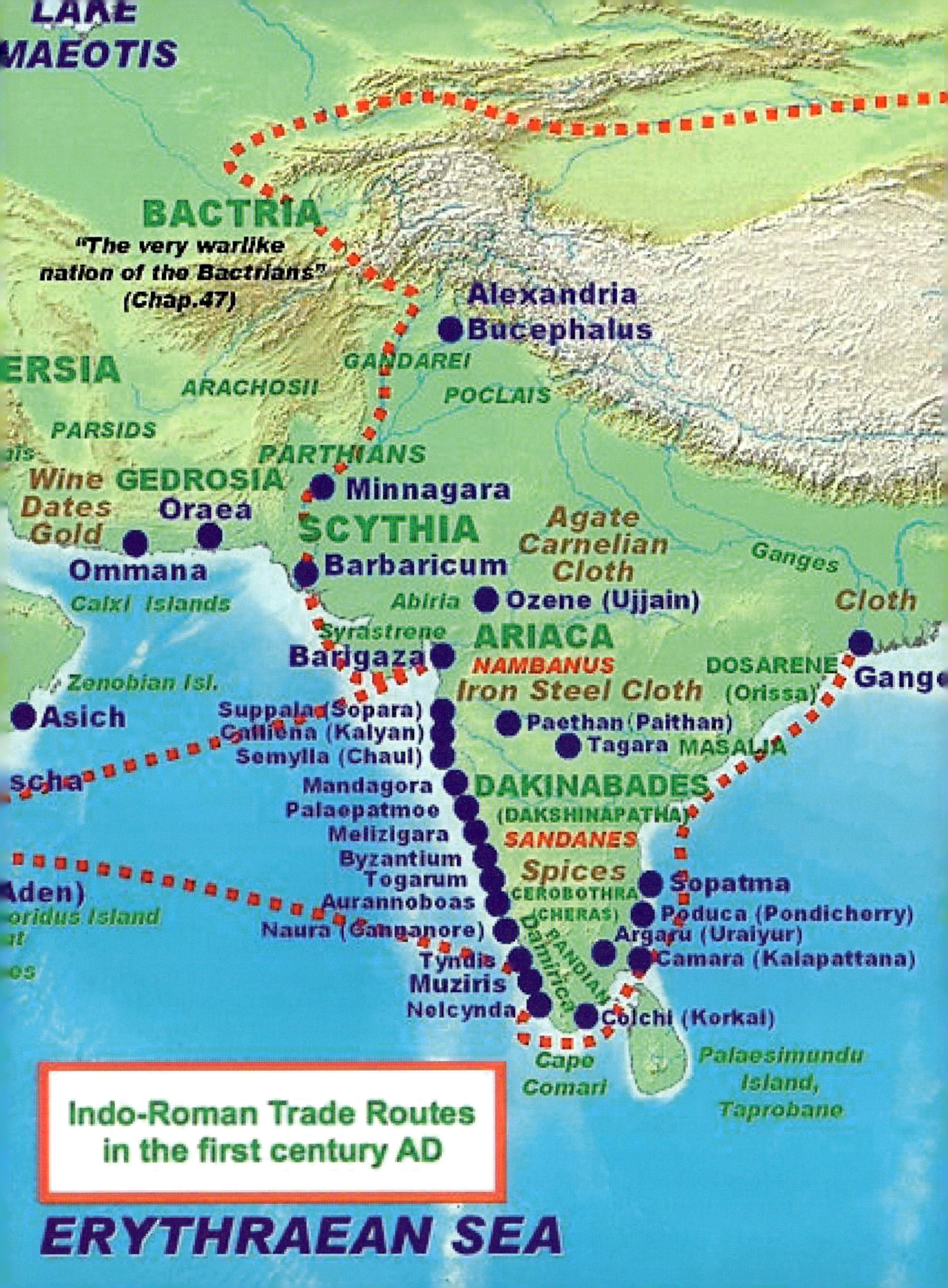

Indo-Roman Trade Routes in the first century AD

Chronology

From 1000 BC: Roads existed through the Western Ghats.

961 BC: The first Jewish settlers arrive in Kerala from Babylon.

From the 6th c BC- 300 AD: Madurai traded with Rome & Chinese Empires.

400 BC–400 AD: The three kingdoms of the non-Arian Chola & Pandyan empires, traded with Rome.

3rd c BC: Buddhism arrived in Tamil Nadu & Kerala.

c.270 BC- c.710 AD: The early Chear Empire.

247 BC - 224 AD The Parthian Empire.

2nd c. BC: Trichy mentioned by Ptolemy: Cochin was a trading port since at least Roman times, also trading with China.

118 or 116 BC: The Indian Ocean was first sailed from the Mediterranean by Eudoxus of Cyzicus (a Greek).

By 50 BC: there was a marked increase in the number of Greek and Roman ships sailing from the Red Sea to the Indian Ocean.

50 BC- 300s AD: Kushan Empire: King Kanishka 78 BC–AD 100.

AD 21-c. 47: Parthian King Gondophares I reigned from his capital at Taxila (now Pakistan).

c. 30: The Crucifixion, Resurrection and Ascension of Jesus.

c. 30: St Thomas leaves for Parthia via Edessa & the Tur Abdin (Turkey) and Mosul, Hatra & Babylon (Iraq).

c. 42: St Thomas together with Habban reach the court of King Gondophares in Taxila.

47: The Hippalus wind was discovered which led to the direct voyage from the Red Sea ports to the S-W coast of India in 40 days.

c. 48: Death of the Virgin Mary in Jerusalem; St Thomas returns briefly to Jerusalem.

52: St Thomas lands in Muziris, and converts and baptises eight communities in Kerala, (India) beginning in Muziris.

59: St Thomas reaches Tamil Nadu (India).

64: St Thomas returns to Tamil Nadu from China.

72: Martyrdom of St Thomas in Mylapore (India).

154 - 223: Bardesanes of Edessa writes the Acts of Judas Thomas in Edessa.

201: St Thomas' basilica in Edessa is destroyed by a flood.

232: The greater portion of St Thomas' relics are returned to Edessa (Turkey).

263 - 339: Eusebius of Caesarea writes about St Thomas' body being brought to Edessa.

From c. the 4th century AD: the arrival of the Aryans in South India.

c. 306 - 373: St Ephraim the Syrian writes about St Thomas.

324: Kana Thomas and 72 Christian families from Persia arrive in Muziris. From then onwards St Thomas Christians were known as Syrian Christians.

352: The St Thomas Christians became subjects of the Patriarch of Antioch at the Council of Nicea.

c. 384: Egeria (the Franco-Spanish nun) saw the tomb of St Thomas in Edessa.

441: The Magister militum per Orientem Anatolius donated a silver coffin to the basilica to host St Thomas' relics.

451: The Council of Chalcedon: Nestorianism rejected.

486: The Catholicos with his seat at Seleucia Ctesiphon began to be called the Patriarch of the East (Babylon) and the Church officially accepted the Nestorian faith.

522: Cosmas Indicopleustes (called the Alexandrian) visited Kerala.

530: Armenian Christians arrived from Persia.

587: Black Jews settled in Kerala. (White Jews came much later with the Dutch.)

822: Two Nestorian bishops, Mar Sabor and Mar Proth arrived in Quilon.

825: Two more Nestorian bishops, Shappur and Arthrod, arrived in Quilon and a great convention was held in at the behest of King Kulashekhara.

1144: Edessa conquered by the Zengids and the shrine of St Thomas was destroyed. His remains were saved and taken to the island of Chios.

1258: The remains of St Thomas reached their final resting place in Ortona, Italy.

1288 & 1292: Marco Polo visited the Nestorian chapel in Mylapore.

1341: The harbour of Cranganore became silted up and the town lost its significance as a port.

1498: The arrival of the Portuguese on the Malabar coast.

1500: Vasco da Gama reached Cochin.

1523: The tomb of St Thomas in Mylapore is rediscovered by the Portuguese, who built a church on the ruins of the Kaleshwara Temple.

1542: The arrival of St Francis Xavier in Goa and reaching Cochin in 1544.

1565: The Jewish settlement in Cranganore is finally abandoned.

1566: The Kapaleswar temple in Kanchipuram was destroyed by the Portuguese.

1605: The arrival of the Dutch on the spice route with their headquarters in Batavia, Indonesia.

1610: Bishop Chandi (of the Thomas Christians) joins the Catholic Church.

1612: The arrival of the British in Gujarat and in 1640 in Madras.

1652: The Oath of the Coonan where the Thomas Christians maintain their ancient rites and traditions.

1672: The French (Catholics) established themselves at Pondicherry.

1757: The Battle of Plassy, suppremacy of the East India Company.

1857: The Indian Mutiny; India comes under the British Crown.

1947: India attains her Independence.

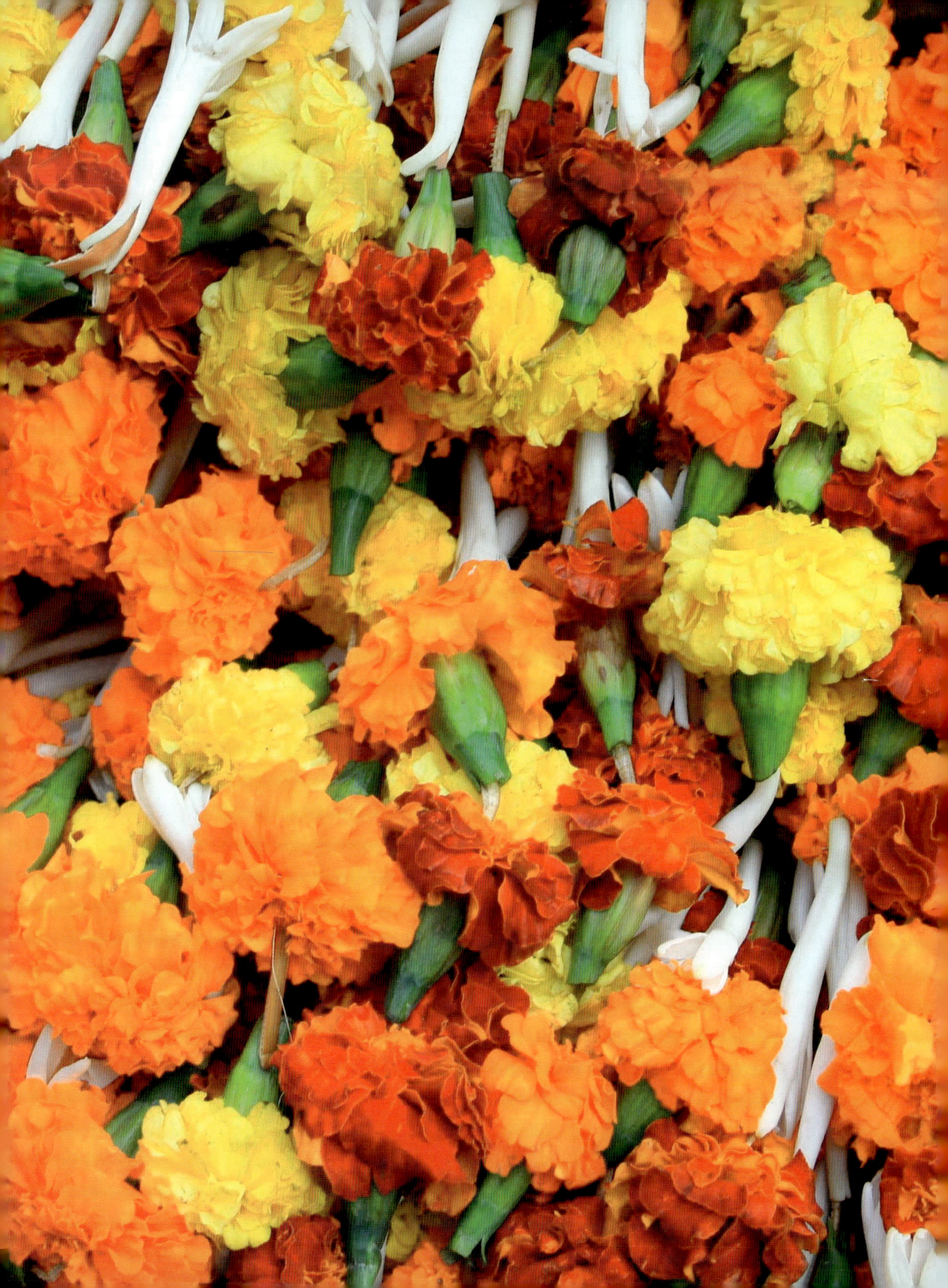

Aid to the Church in Need
Prayer • Information • Action

Aid to the Church in Need is a registered charity in England and Wales (1097984) and in Scotland (SC040748)

Since discussing the plight of Christians in their ancient homelands, I have become more and more concerned about their future, and of the many churches and monasteries where I have been privileged to worship with them from Iran to Egypt.

The monastery of St Thomas which I visited in Mosul, Iraq, has been ransacked, as have the ancient churches of Maalula and Seidneya in Syria: all three provided such a link with the past and I fear the ancient church in the house of Ananias in Damascus will go the same way. Lebanon is not immune, Egyptian Copts suffer frequently, Jordanian Christians may well find themselves under threat, as indeed may Turkish Christians especially those of the Syriac churches in the Tur Abdin.

Aid to the Church in Need does an outstanding job in making us all aware of their plight and in raising funds, building tented camps and houses, medical centres and feeding them, truly being the voice and the hands of Jesus in their distress. They have spent some £5 million to house and care for the exiles and to build a number of schools for thousands of refugee children.

I am making a contribution to *ACN* from the sale of this book. If any readers would like to do so too, however large or small your donation, please write to:

Aid to the Church in Need, 12-14 Benhill Avenue, Sutton, Surrey SM1 4DA
Tel: 020 8642 8668 or go online at https://acnuk.org/shop/ or www.acnuk.org/donate to receive regular information and updates.

ACN stock this book and can also send you the other two books in my trilogy: *The Cross, Meditations and Images*, with a foreword by HRH The Prince of Wales and *The Magi, their journey and their contemporaries,* with a foreword by HM King Simeon of Bulgaria.

Donations from these books go to *ACN* specifically to help the suffering Christians in Syria and Iraq, especially those returning to Mosul from the Nineveh Plains.

Morning garlands, the flower market, Calcutta, India (2016).